Listening

Music
Movement
Mind

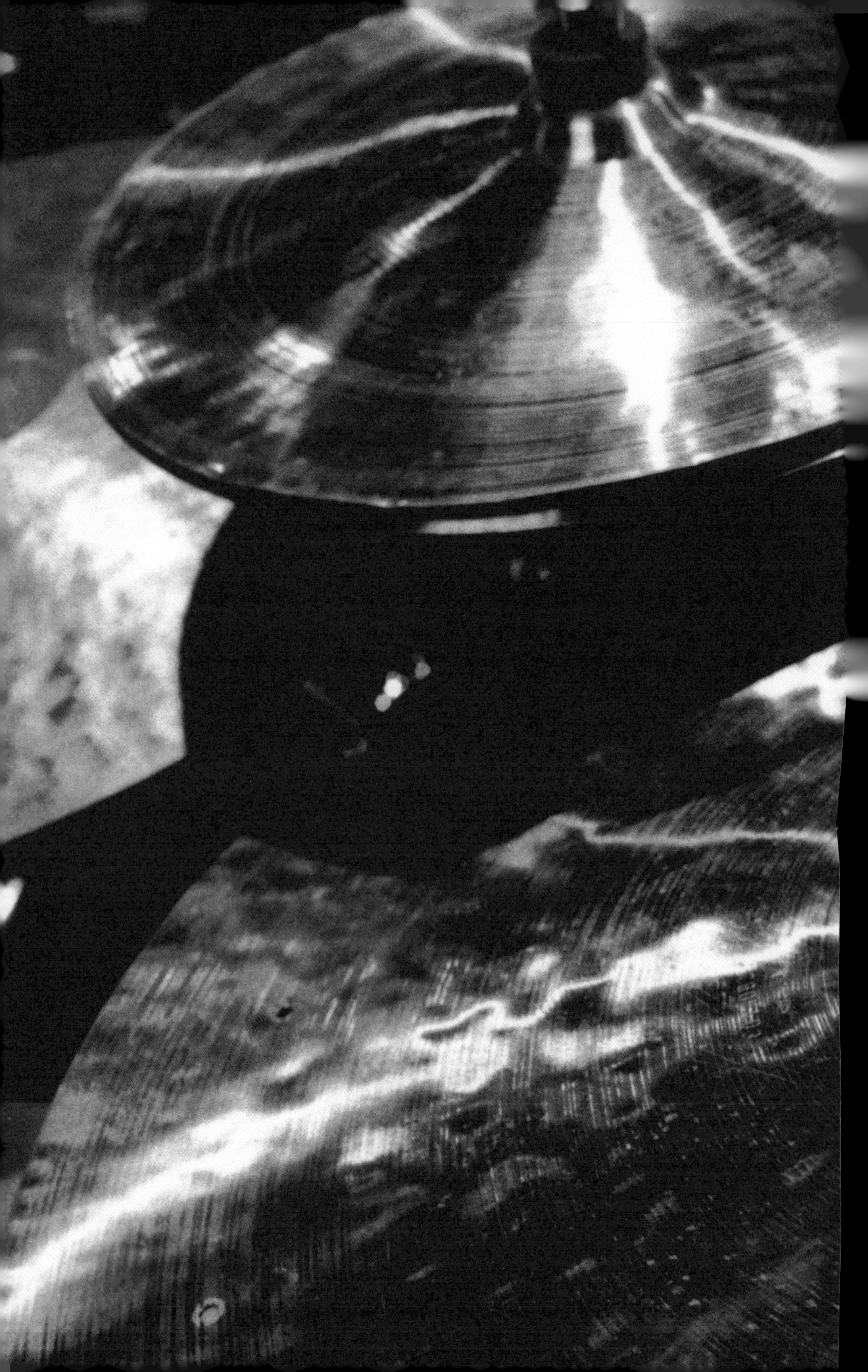

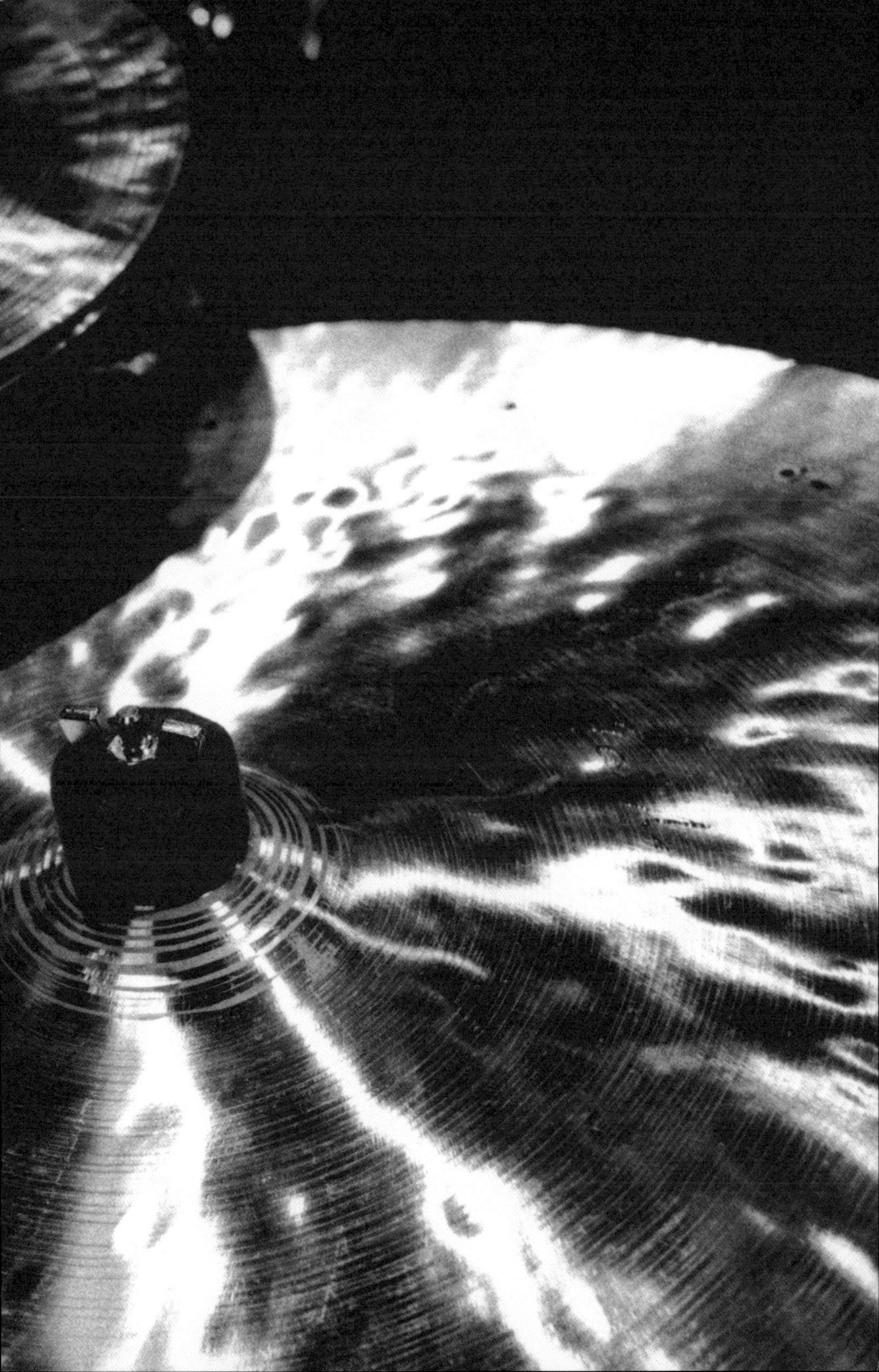

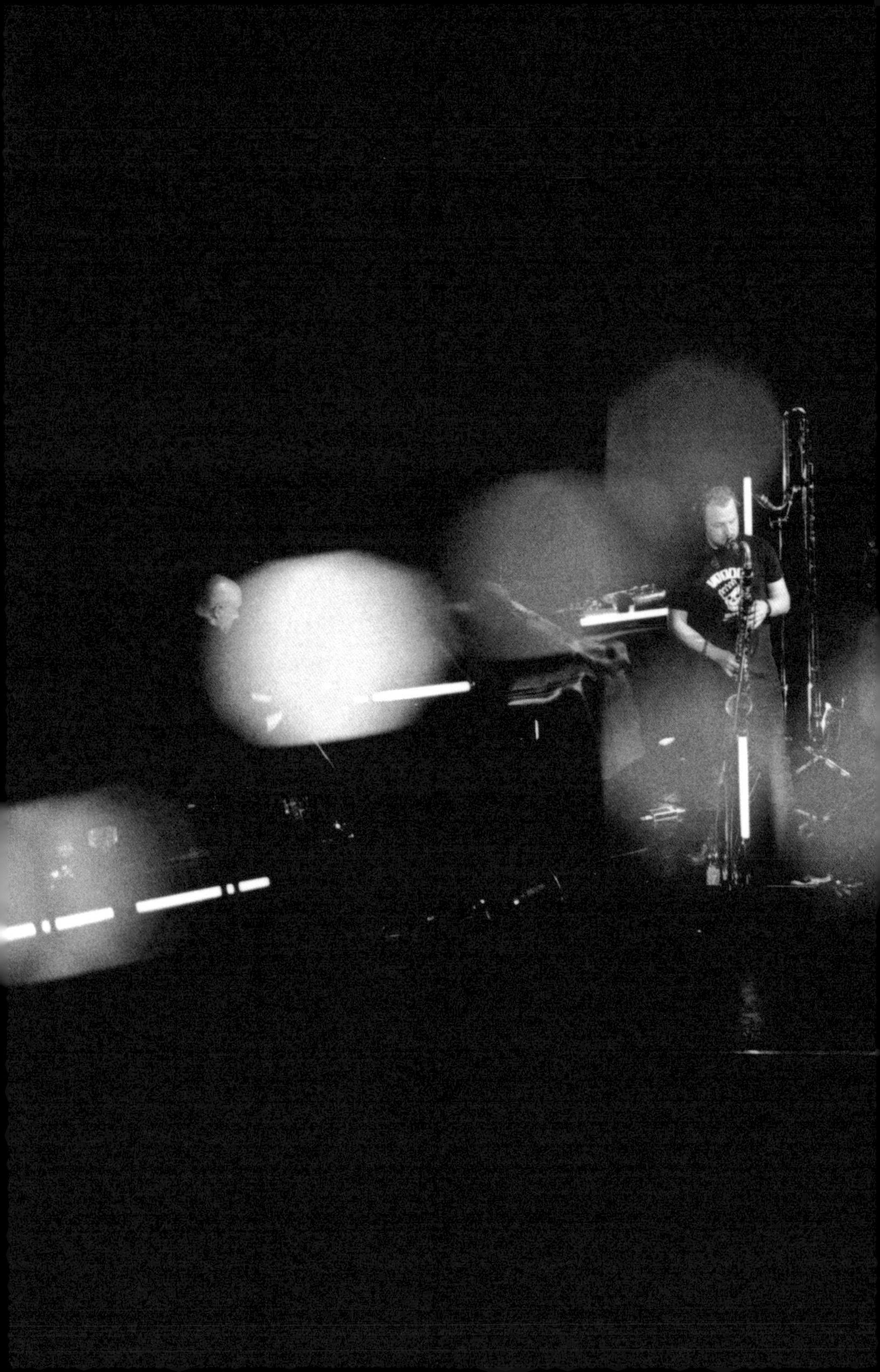

For Aina, Ilva and Mika

Nik Bärtsch

Listening

Music
Movement
Mind

A Useless Guide for Everything

In collaboration
with Andrea Pfisterer

Lars Müller Publishers

Bio-Poetic Phenomena

Music Movement Mind Charts

Preface

This book wants to listen to you – to your thoughts and comments and your attentive silence. Children require balance in learning how to walk and they are remarkably precise observers. Working on those two qualities, balance and attentiveness, is a lifelong endeavor. Attentive listening is the most important skill of a musician. As we show in this book, it is an attitude, an interactive quality, a partner-oriented strategy of action.

Music moves us, but we also move music – with our body and mind. A sound is produced by a complex connection of physical and mental processes. The shape of the sound is the immediate feedback in the listener's ear. In the sound we hear the intention behind the sound. A sound is a note, a word, a resonance of action. This book explores such phenomena.

The challenge for a creative and community-oriented person is to find clarity and coherence in the roaring diversity of our noisy world and its infinite opportunities. Focusing on a few essential interests fosters the ability to act. In-depth learning means to choose a few things. This choice has nothing to do with an absolute truth but it does guarantee the fruitful pursuit of one's own creative path.

In contact with the world we need presence and resonance. This need is amplified in the performing arts. In music, dance, theater, sports, martial arts, circus arts, fashion, film and even in teaching, we feel the powerful immediacy of interactive presence. More often than not, body knowledge is more fruitful in these cases than reflection. Body knowledge can and needs to be trained. This is where the fruitful and promising combination of music and the martial arts comes in.

The relationship between composing and improvising is especially interesting. They are both not only relevant, but evolutionary, creative and playful strategies of survival in music. Creative actions draw energy from the tension between compositional precision and improvisation. How can we outfox ourselves and transcend our knowledge? In playing live music we face the same spiritual challenges as in Zen meditation with its curious philosophy of constantly reinventing yourself by making yourself disappear.

Creativity is a quality of life itself – "life" as a mystic and cosmic phenomenon. Art is a part of life and is nourished by its energy and manifestations. Conversely, biology is often inspired by art as we can see in the beautiful example of Llyrìa in this book (pp. 148, 206). The name of a novel inspired a maritime scientist's name for a deep-sea creature which in turn inspired a musician to give the name to an album. They are all connected by a chain of inspiration, not only a poetic chain, but a chain of action. In this book, we also show other chains of inspiration that connect scientists, species and artists.

This book traces the history of ideas and current work of the ritual groove music, which is more a perspective and a magnifying glass than a style or a pointer for discovery. The book is a testimony of practical aesthetics and poetics and unites several insights, exercises and texts. Already published texts are placed in a wider context and related to practical training methods, visualizations, systematic reflections and short stories about striking insights and poetic experiences. The book shows the light and heavy sides of creativity and their interaction.

I deeply appreciate Igor Stravinsky's craft, creativity, humor and intellect. He said about the challenge of talking about music as a musician: "Sometimes I feel like those old men Gulliver met on the trip to Laputa: They renounced language and tried to communicate with objects. A composer is always in this position because he has no verbal control over his music. The only real comment on a piece of music is another piece of music."

Nevertheless, words and concepts do give us a great deal of inspiration and information. Our sense perception and language are inseparably connected and influence each other. We overlook many aspects of this relationship because of their simplicity and familiarity. We do not notice them because they are lying right in front of our eyes – or ears. This insight makes me think again and again about the basic facts of life and art: balance, communication, community, dramaturgy. And it raises all sorts of seemingly unnecessary, trivial or funny questions. I have shared some of them here with you, and at least some of my answers.

Nothing can be learned, nothing can be created without partners. This book is the result of countless relationships and collective processes. The contributions of my mentors, my band mates, my students and my wife, Andrea Pfisterer, are inestimable. Since Andrea and I met, we have talked almost every day about culture, science, politics, education, partnership and love. The book was created in collaboration with her; it is the result of our partnership, of mutual inspiration between a scientist and a musician, of two movement people.

Thank you for listening.

Nik Bärtsch, March 2021

How Can You Hear a Silent Movement?

Listen!

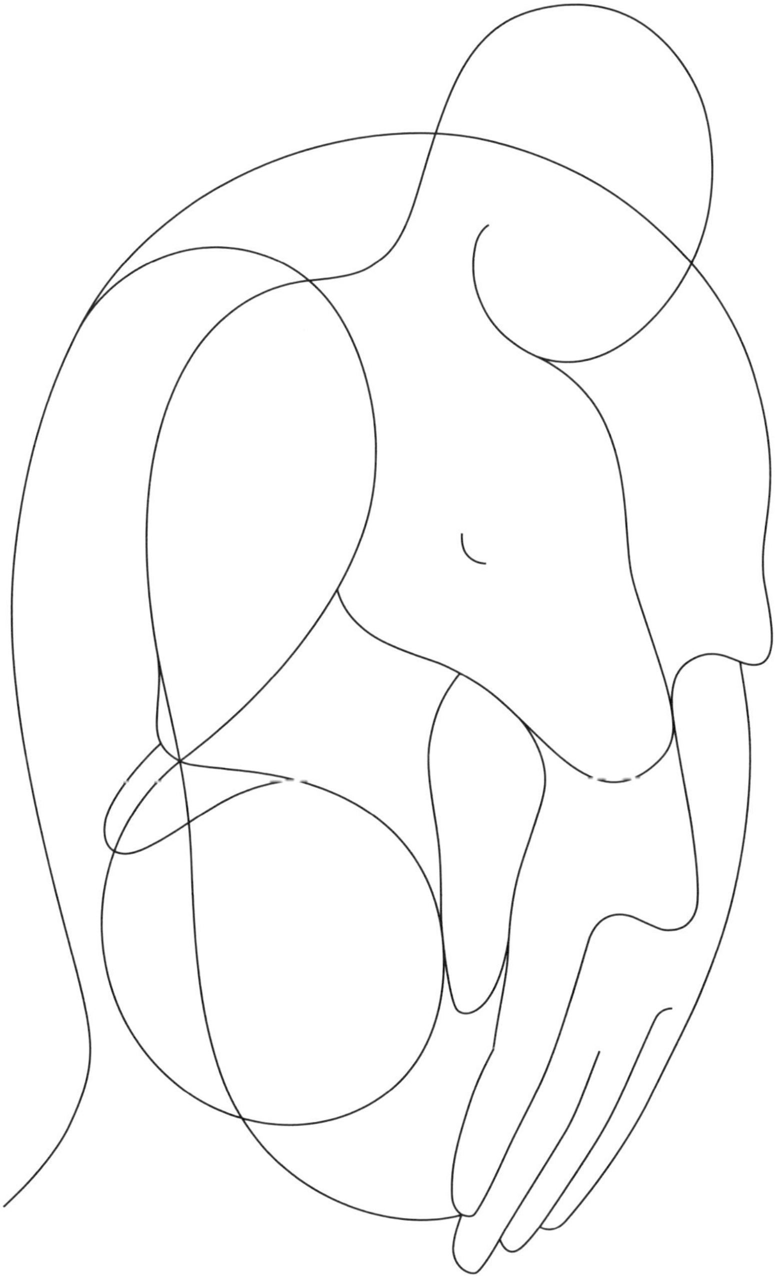

Digital drawing by Yves Netzhammer from the series *Gravitational Assertions*

Quite often we hear our aikido sensei Lewis Bernaldo de Quiros in seminars say: "Listen to your partner!"

Why "listen"? And not rather "watch" or "feel"? What is the advantage of this listening attitude for an aikidoka? Why is it a mind-opening approach in a partner situation?

It is first of all obvious that this is meant primarily metaphorically and not literally. It means that all our senses should be set to the listening mode. Rarely do we really close our eyes and try to "catch the noise" of the movement of the opponent, to be *awase* like the blind samurai Zatoichi in fiction. But what does "Listen!" actually mean in that metaphorical sense for our awareness?

Lewis Bernaldo de Quiros, 6th Dan aikido teacher in *hanmi* position: a mentally and physically balanced posture, which enables connecting and listening to the attacker.

To understand this better, we should note that language has several pairs of terms to describe the difference between a receiving and an active form of perception: see – watch, hear – listen, feel – sense. We differentiate between an open, active and focused presence and a passive, receiving one. In our case we need to specify what advantage active "listening" has compared to "watching" or "sensing."

The most important consequence is as simple as it is effective: when you listen, you cannot talk. Watching and sensing usually start our inner commentator, like a reflex. Listening needs a silent mind and mouth. In a metaphorical sense, your whole presence is in the listening mode, not analyzing, not talking to someone else or to yourself in your head. There is silence on the mat because of pure presence and full neutral engagement with the partner. Like in Zen meditation the noises of the world and of your inner monkey mind are diffuse, distracting and therefore irrelevant for the total presence in the here and now of a martial art situation.

Listening in partner situations is usually also an active start or support of a true dialogue without preconception, without signaling that you do or want something. You can invite someone to an action without attacking, just by connecting. In a physical sense this means you are just there, present, actively receptive. While a glance can already be offensive, true listening evokes pure respectful presence.

The initial listening moment is followed by a sequence, which we can describe as a musical process: the silent mind is open to the whole hearing horizon. The focal point of the moment of attack feeds the right rhythm of the movement as a merging answer. Our capacity to intuitively merge form and flow, stability and flexibility, space and movement, self and togetherness is nourished more by our musical than our visual capacity. Musical in the sense of a feeling for tempo, rhythm, dynamics and timing as a sequence, called "a phrase" in music. Our visual perception is usually slower and requires more complex processing in the brain. This is the reason, for example, the 100 m sprint is started by a pistol shot and not by a visual sign like a flag. But at the same time, tempo, rhythm, dynamics and timing can apply just as much to visual sense as to musical sense.

This leads us to an interesting comparison with an old martial art poem, which points out how we should sharpen our mental capacity in combination with our physical capacity. There are two lines in there about seeing and hearing:

"I have no eyes – the lightning flash will be my eyes;
I have no ears – the five senses are my ears."

So listening as a metaphorical help to connect all senses to create a sixth sense seems to be an old topic.

Our ears cannot be closed by a reflex, like our eyes. In that sense, listening is more instantaneous and intuitive than watching and therefore valuable as direct spontaneous interaction. So the listening attitude seems to offer a wonderfully paradoxical mix of conscious *and* intuitive connection in a situation.

Sensei Morihiro Saito evading multiple attackers and turning one of them against the rest

Think of a movement as a sound

But the metaphorical teaching-directive "listen!" means more than catching the right moment and timing for a sudden interaction and answer to an attack out of nothing. It also means to listen to the movement itself and the awase as a sound sequence, previously called "a phrase" in music. We can understand this easily when we turn our attention to the weapons work, where we actually hear the result of the movements.

Lewis often emphasizes the relevance of our wooden weapons as "percussive weapons." It means we usually hit and do not "cut." The sound of the two weapons hitting each other reveals directly how the movements and the awase are done. Like in music when a movement of a skilled player is executed naturally, based on training and knowledge of every detail of it, the resulting sound is natural: clear, round and with a core, not hard and garish or dull. Hit a drum or gong and you can experience this yourself. So the timing, rhythm, tempo, swing, rebound and spin of a movement are essential for its precision, power and responsiveness. The "clack!" shows us the energy and intention behind the hit.

Although we only hear the result of the movement, we can think of it as a whole "visual" sound sequence: "sssssSSS clack!" like in a comic strip. Starting point, flow, hitting point and relaxation. Skilled singers start a musical phrase of a breath length without a noticeable inhalation and partition the breath over the whole phrase. It comes out of nothing and goes to nothing. Just like a movement in martial arts: starting without signaling and happening as a natural, simple and effective phrase – a "silent movement."

The founder of aikido, O sensei Morihei Ueshiba, executing a technique with one of his tremendous *kiais*

Onomatopoetic teaching and *kiai* as kinetic sound energy

So that is maybe the reason why Lewis in teaching also often intuitively uses onomatopoetic sounds to describe and explain a movement. "k, k, k," "uuuuuuu gong" can help to understand a movement physically and directly and not by language logic.

This is now even meant literally: hear your movement!

On the other hand we should anyway train the effectiveness and directed power of a movement with a strong *kiai.* "Ki-ai" is written with the same kanjis as "ai-ki." So it should help us to bring body energy and mental presence into focused flow by "acoustic" breathing from our center. We hear a kinetic and directed sound as a natural result of inner rhythm in response to an attack, a *sounding togetherness*. The subsequent *Zanshin* is a result of this: a powerful silence, in which the flash moment of interaction resonates and reflects in space and attention.

Now we have a beautiful paradox: we should move invisibly, that means silently, but also with a natural intense *kiai* sound which makes the birds fall from the trees.

Or as a new Zen *koan:* How can you HEAR a silent movement and SEE the *kiai?*

Asterix in Spain by Albert Uderzo and René Goscinny, 1969, movement lines and sounds

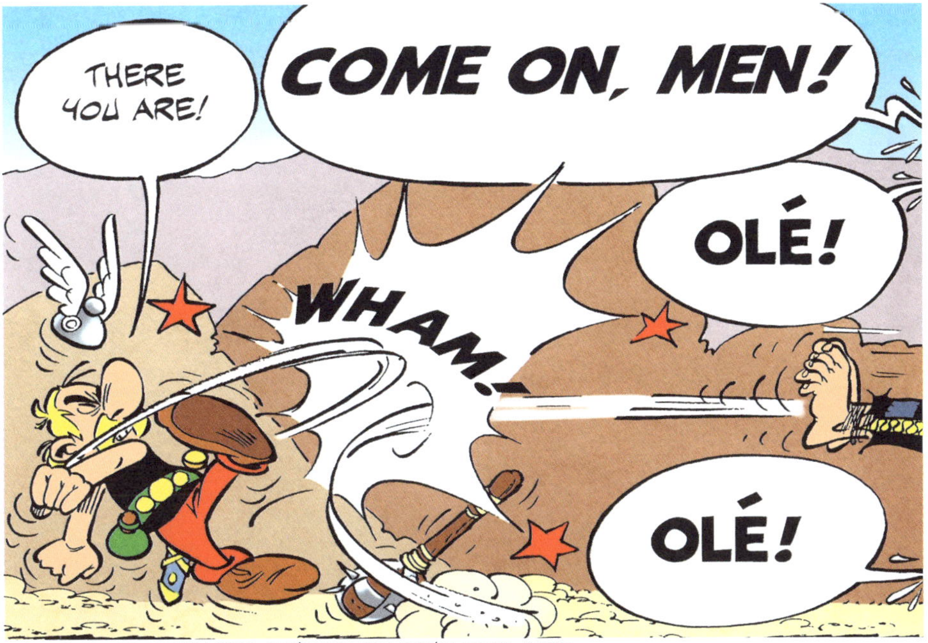

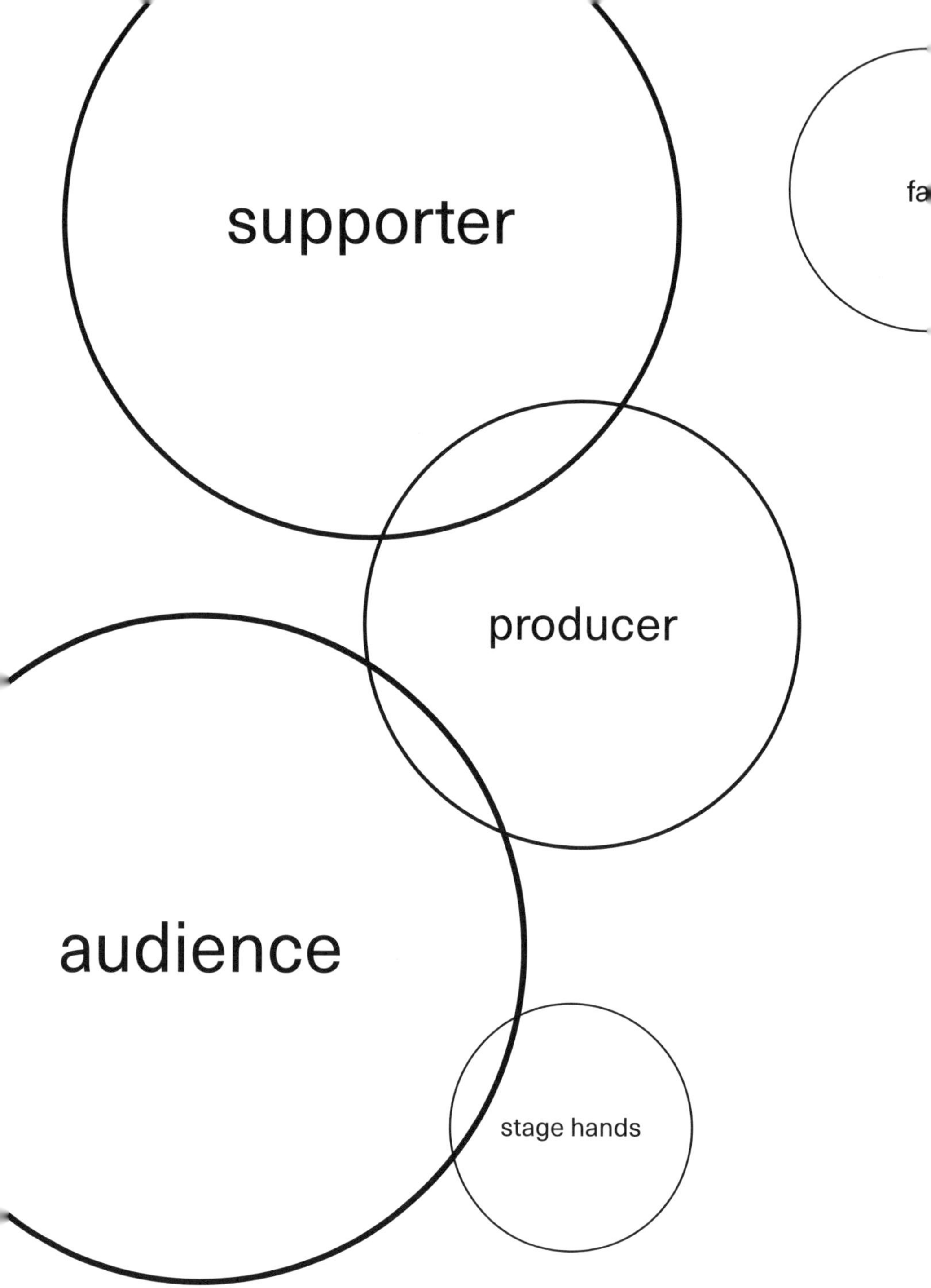

Functions to Enable Live Performances

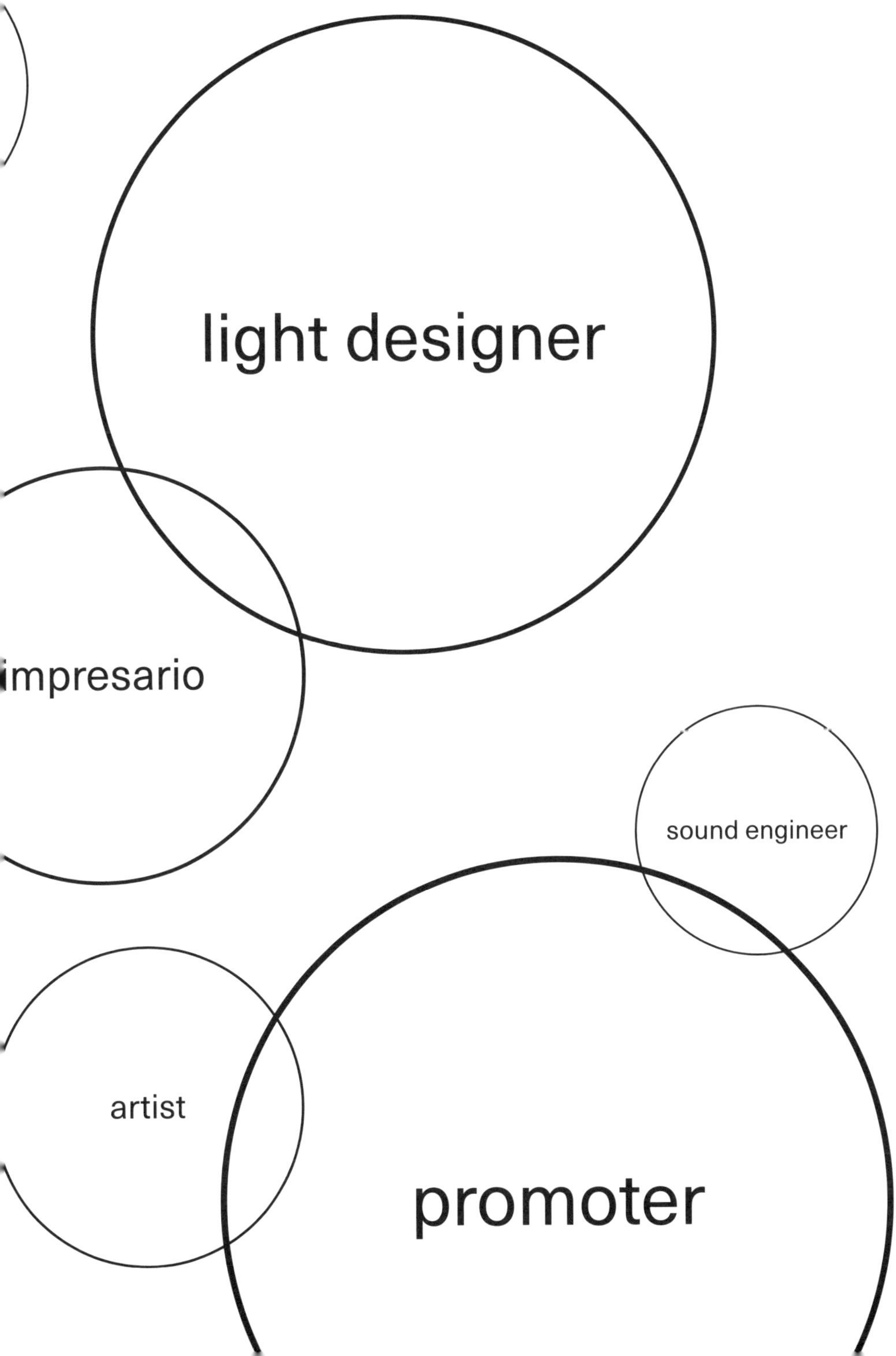
light designer
impresario
sound engineer
artist
promoter

“I have no ears.
The five senses
are my ears.”

Samurai poem

The *Ligne Claire* as Inspiration

Tintin in Bucharest

I have a crystal-clear memory of finding the Tintin comic book *Red Rackham's Treasure* on my bed when I woke up on my 8th birthday on August 3, 1979 in an old, sophisticated hotel in Bucharest, Romania. I was with my family on a crazy summer holiday trip through communist Romania, also experiencing fantastic folk and Roma music, finally ending up in Sfântu Gheorghe, a small, charming village without cars in the Danube Delta at the Black Sea. Freaky fact for Swiss tourists: the only "luxury" goods one could get there were Chinese chocolate and Chinese pocket knives.

But back to Bucharest: the comic book birthday was carefully prepared by my mother who was a bit worried about my growing interest in mainstream comics, especially the weekly issues of Donald Duck and Mickey Mouse – understandably so, since she usually read ancient Greek myths to me as bedtime stories. So she had gone to her favorite bookstore to ask if there was something like a serious, quality comic book. The style of drawing and the structure of the story were important to her as an interior designer and lover of the arts. Her artistic sensibility was cultivated while studying at the legendary Kunstgewerbeschule Zürich, run by the influential Bauhaus teacher Johannes Itten[1] until 1954

Tintin in Tibet by Hergé, 1958, is an example of clarity and balance in each line, sign, figure, picture, panel, strip, lending the entire page clear action and dramaturgy.

and later by his followers. She absorbed the spirit of this seminal education, like my biological father and graphic designer Roland Bärtsch, my stepfather and architect Enrico Somaini and my later mentor, the fashion designer Christa de Carouge.

But back to Tintin: I was fascinated and inspired by this adventurous, humorous and delightfully funny universe from the very first encounter. After reading *Red Rackham's Treasure*, the second volume of the story about the hunt for the treasure of Captain Haddock's ancestors, I couldn't wait for the prequel and the rest of the volumes in that series. While diving into this magical world, I also became interested in its background and making of. My discovery of the so-called *ligne claire* school (French for "clear line"), created and pioneered by Belgian comic author Hergé, was a serious and sustainable childhood inspiration. The designation was coined by Dutch comic artist Joost Swarte in 1977, a sophisticated cartoonist and designer himself. This school inspired unique artists like him or Yves Chaland, my favorite figure of the next generation. The style uses clear lines all of the same width, clear colors, a clear narrative structure with clear characters and clearly balanced pictures and text. "Clear" is another word for simple. But the result is anything but a simple-minded children's story. The clearness in each line, figure, picture, panel, strip, page, double page, chapter and finally in the dramaturgy of the whole album creates a coherent AND complex world. The recognizable style, characters, roles, rules and rituals foster a richness of running gags, variations and surprises.

Reductive strategies of this kind are used in many fields. Composer Morton Feldman, himself a modern radical reductionist and close friend of avant-garde icon John Cage, quotes French writer Stendhal, who had a sign on his desk which read:

1 Itten also founded the Rietberg Museum for non-European art, especially East Asian art, and was its first director.

"To be clear at all costs."

Hergé's style is clear at all costs. At what costs? To create a coherent, consistent comic cosmos, Hergé had to unconditionally love it, focus on it and believe in it; he had to ignore a lot of alluring offers and interests – on a daily basis. He lived in and for his cosmos, remaining true and modest to create space and energy for essentials. This is comparable to Stravinsky's dictum of freedom arising from self-imposed restriction.

One-Night Stand with an Idea

Morton Feldman describes this in his Darmstadt lecture of 1984, speaking in his typically nonchalant and striking fashion: "I have ideas that I throw away in two minutes that the poorest one in this room would give me at least ten thousand Marks for. And the reason I do that is because I don't want to be influenced with my own thought. That might divert me from the focus of that moment. But I don't think that that moment is essentially a kind of a one-night stand with an idea. I wouldn't say that it's a short-term commitment. I just have to be focused and doing my best at that particular moment because it's a very serious operation. There are a lot of questions to ask, and some of the most important questions are: your attitude as a composer. Schoenberg once wrote in a letter that some days he gets up in the morning, and he can't even do a simple little exercise. Composing is so difficult. To write something lousy is so difficult. And a lot of the difficulty is not so much whether your idea is right or wrong. It doesn't make a difference what the idea is. Chekhov once said that even a lie leads to salvation. Anything – it doesn't make any difference what you do: Number one, you have to believe in it; Number two, you have to be absolutely focused on it."[2]

2 Morton Feldman, *Essays*, ed. Walter Zimmermann (Kerpen: Beginner Press, 1985), pp. 186–87.

As mentioned above, Igor Stravinsky made a precise point about the "costs" or the challenge of freedom and focus in his *Poetics of Music*, initially given as a series of lectures at Harvard University in 1939: "As for myself, I experience a sort of terror when, at the moment of setting to work and finding myself before the infinitude of possibilities that present themselves, I have the feeling that everything is permissible to me. If everything is permissible to me, the best and the worst, if nothing offers me any resistance, then any effort is inconceivable, and I cannot use anything as a basis, and consequently every undertaking becomes futile. [...] So here we are,

The opening sequence of *La comète de Carthage* by Yves Chaland, 1986, renews the tradition of the *ligne claire*. The influence of the legendary woodcut *The Great Wave off Kanagawa* by Japanese artist Hokusai is unmistakable.

whether we like it or not, in the realm of necessity. And yet which of us has ever heard talk of art as other than a realm of freedom? This sort of heresy is uniformly wide-spread because it is imagined that art is outside the bounds of ordinary activity. Well, in art as in everything else, one can build only upon a resisting foundation: whatever constantly gives way to pressure, constantly renders movement impossible. My freedom thus consists in my moving about within the narrow frame that I have assigned myself for each one of my undertakings."[3]

The Walking Universe

The creative mind clearly sees the explosive potential and multi-meaning of a matter and thus also its own focus both realistically and modestly. Believe in focus, be clear at all costs. In so doing, you outwit yourself, you have an uncanny sense of security and you feel a miraculous resonance with the world.

When asked, in a 1982 interview with French comic writer Benoît Peeters, about the great resonance of Tintin, Hergé answered, "I also ask myself sometimes, but I have no answer for it. There are obviously reasons for that success, because it has already lasted a long time and is even growing. It must be something like a spark that leaps over. But which spark? For example, I get a lot of mail from India. Just yesterday there were two letters from Kolkata in the office. So what is there in common between a boy from Kolkata and me? I ask myself over and over again without finding an answer to it."[4]

Receiving a response to my own music while giving concerts and workshops – also in Kolkata – I have comparable enriching experiences with music that sparks a reaction. Do these sparks land on individual, cultural or universal orbits?

3 Igor Stravinsky, *Poetics of Music in the Form of Six Lessons* (Cambridge: Harvard University Press, 1947), pp. 63–65.
4 Benoît Peeters, *Hergé – Ein Leben für die Comics* (Hamburg: Carlsen Verlag, 1983), pp. 29–30.

The uncanny intensity of guidance through dedication, clearness and focus is strong and fragile at the same time. We are never safe. This is my interpretation of Zen philosophy. Giving mental and physical direction and not truth, not a doctrine of salvation. To focus carefully on and consistently believe in your cosmos enables you to deal charmingly and creatively with the infinite challenges of art and life. The avant-garde crowbar that violently forces new developments can stay in the toolbox. Evolution happens naturally.

Although the style and composition of the *ligne claire* were technically influenced by the Japanese heroes of color woodcuts, Hokusai and Hiroshige, Hergé himself was drawn relatively late but all the more powerfully to Zen and Taoism: "Recently I read a sentence which impressed me very much: 'It takes a whole universe for only one person to walk.' You see, here we have the relation between the things, between the individual particles and the entirety to which they belong."[5]

To be clear at all costs: Forget the one-night stand with an idea, it took a whole universe to make Tintin walk!

5 Peeters, *Hergé,* p. 29.

> I bought this print by comic author Ted Benoit when I was a teenager and its balance of clarity, humor and artlessness has been an inspiration ever since; it is what I am constantly looking for in my own ritual groove music. Benoit's gallery Champaka writes about this picture: "This is in fact one of the very rare drawings done in homage to Tintin by Ted Benoit, who himself was the artist most solicited to do pieces dedicated to the world of Hergé or Jacobs. 'The joy of this type of image,' confides the author of *Vers la ligne claire,* 'is the total freedom it brings, because this general idea, drawn from your own imagination, will doubtless be more elegant than a direct response to the original source. What interested me that day was to convey the sense of space and volume of the studio where I lived at the time. Practically empty and totally white, as when I had visited it a year earlier. And given that what motivates me is to draw the void (in this case, the vast expanse of carpet that comes between the observer and the corridor) the impression of space was made all the stronger by positioning a striking detail in the corridor. And what could be more striking, anywhere, than a carved Arumbaya fetish figure? No doubt, someone has already written an exegesis on it, but suffice it to say that "L'oreille cassée" strikes me as an extended nightmare, and the carved fetish as a particularly vivid expression of the unconscious.'"

CHAMPAKA
BOOK

“Humans think because they have hands.”

Anaxagoras, pre-Socratic Greek philosopher (499–428 BC)

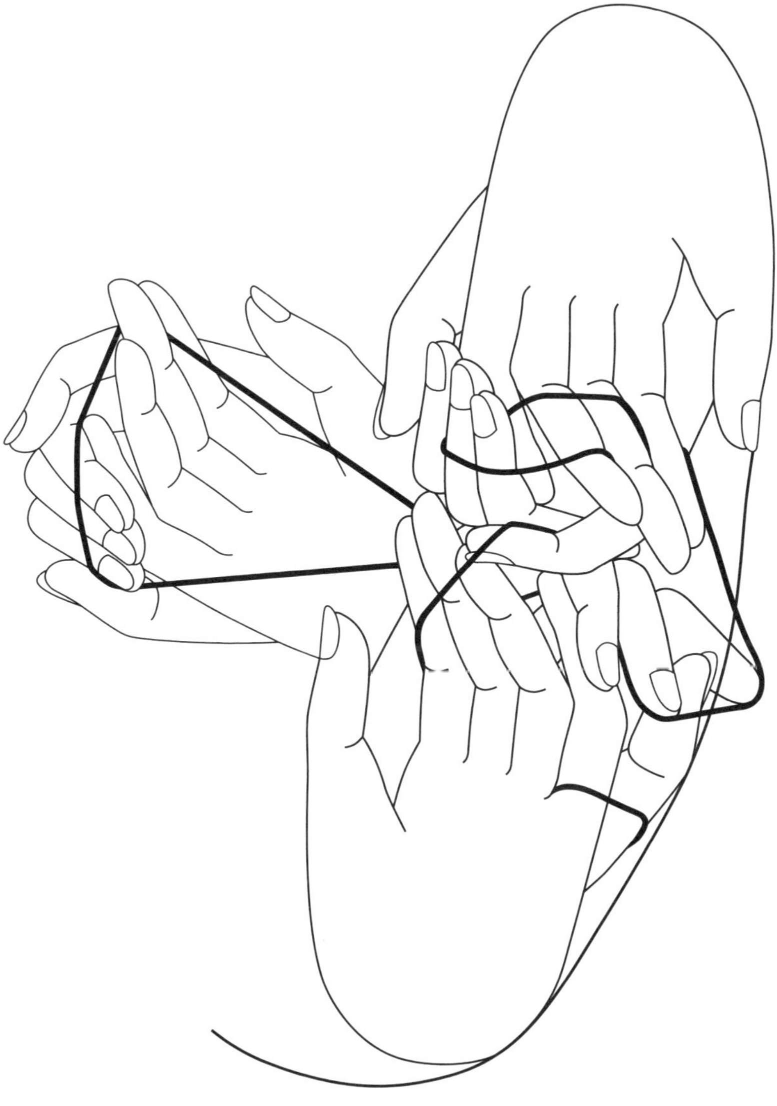

Digital drawing by Yves Netzhammer from the series *Concave Thoughts*

“If I had to live my life again, I would have made a rule to read some poetry and listen to some music at least once every week; for perhaps the parts of my brain now atrophied would thus have been kept active through use. The loss of these tastes is a loss of happiness, and may possibly be injurious to the intellect, and more probably to the moral character, by enfeebling the emotional part of our nature.”

Charles Darwin (1809–1882), geologist and biologist

Bio-Poetic Phenomena

These texts about the poetic potential of phenomena in biology were inspired by existing applications in our own creative work. They show the affinity between musical group processes in improvisation and organism play, on the one hand, and mimicry, swarm behavior, habitats, group communication, on the other. Creative research applies not only to the fine arts, to our music, for instance, but also to science such as deep-sea research: knowledge is extended in both cases.

New discoveries in art or science are often "silent" in the beginning. They need a name, a metaphor, a linguistic context for us to take adequate note of them.

Great Apes
Cooperation and Empathy Are Older Than Philosophical Ethics

Bio-Poetic Phenomenon

Humans, gorillas, orangutans, chimpanzees and bonobos belong to the same scientific family of Great Apes or Hominidae. The latter two species are our closest living relatives. The consequences of this fact and the potential to learn more about ourselves has motivated the research of such leading primatologists as Jane Goodall or Frans de Waal.

In his books, de Waal explores how cooperation, competition, egoism, empathy and emotions correlate, revealing elementary and essential behaviors of togetherness in relationships and groups. His respectful, smart, funny and fresh view of evolutionary biology and primate behavior shows us how old and deeply rooted are the many needs and capacities of humans in the context of a group. Strategic principles such as fairness, cooperation, competition, alliance building, social adaptation, but also feelings like jealousy, violence, revenge, reconciliation, fun, humor, emotions – even an awareness of life and death and a faculty for learning – are all deeply rooted in age-old processes of evolution. Illuminating insights can be gleaned from the evolutionary and natural sciences and not only from psychology and philosophy.

Empathy, cooperation and a rich emotional life have long been fundamental conditions of our survival and development as mammals and still are at least as important as competition and egoism.

A band is a non-verbal organism, a horde of apes that often acts faster than thinking or talking and, in fact, has to when on stage. A live concert is subject to jungle conditions, the band needs to be fast, focused and present, needs to rely almost blindly, as it were, on deeply rooted cooperative skills. Diplomas, explanations and safety nets do not count on stage – only the thinking body, which was developed long before the reflections of Socrates, Kant and Foucault. Our intuitive knowledge is a true and valuable source of attentiveness.

Coral Reefs Megalopolis

Bio-Poetic Phenomenon

Coral reefs are a fascinating ecosystem composed of up to one million different species. Besides their inherent value as biological world wonders, they are of paramount importance for humankind. They serve as a natural coastal protection, a source of food and a pharmaceutical resource. They also form an integral part of the world climate. Today, reefs are under extreme threat from environmental pollution, overfishing, harmful fishing methods, uncontrolled mass tourism and global warming.

They have often been compared to big cities; here are just a few parallels: Population density in cities and reefs is much higher than in the surrounding areas. Service industries and a well-functioning infrastructure are particularly important. In both cities and reefs there are dentists, sewage treatment plants and rubbish collection; not everyone can do the same thing; there is specialization and there are many different jobs; innovative products are in high demand, often at the expense of traditional or less innovative products.

In coral reefs the pygmy seahorse (Hippocampus bargibanti, only 2 cm in size) imitates the coral that it lives on. It is so successful at hiding that it was not found until its home was being studied in a lab.

Like a part of a coral reef, a live music club in a city is a habitat that is essential to the local musical culture and the prosperity and development of all its diverse creatures.

"The most exciting phrase to hear in science, the one that heralds new discoveries, is not 'Eureka!' but 'That's funny'."

Isaac Asimov (1920–1992), science fiction author and professor for biochemistry

Democracy, Artistry and Band Balance

Part 1: Basic Conditions of Free Art Production

How many artists spoil the broth?

From time to time I meet artists who explicitly emphasize that democratic decision-making processes disrupt the production of art. This opinion is based on the assumption that the purity, energy and impact of an artist's clear vision and plan of action might be hindered by the influence of other people. Too many cooks spoil the broth. A popular picture: the artist works on his/her ideas in ivory-tower solitude. The creative output is then presented as unadulterated, pure, strong art – a heroic act.

This is a curious cliché and a fundamental misunderstanding of processes that underlie production and the invention of art in our society.

To assume a contradiction between clear individual vision and cooperative results is a fallacy. This supposed incompatibility is in fact a fruitful paradox, which demands intelligent differentiation and constant, complex work on social balance in societies, communities, groups and bands – and on inner balance.

This existential context deserves a closer look from both a macro and a micro perspective.

The freedom of artistic expression cannot be taken for granted – citizenship on planet music and in a country

First of all, a basic and often neglected fact: freedom of individual artistic expression in a society cannot be taken for granted! It depends on country, circumstances and times in history. As artists – and citizens – we should always be aware of our rights and defend them vigilantly and thoughtfully. But we should champion them not only on behalf of ourselves but also others in our society,

even those whose ideas we do not share or who might not be aware of these reflections. It is crucial in a democracy to respect the community – in cooperation AND competition.

I consider myself, first and foremost, a free citizen of planet music – a resonating paradise or as my grandfather called it: heaven on earth. The world of music is a paradoxical utopia, existing and not existing at the same time. You can find in it colorful jungles of notes, underwater worlds of sounds with bizarre patterns, curious creatures and cities of resonance, which may disappear at any moment like a Fata Morgana. It is just moving air, tasted by your eardrum. A passport is irrelevant in this beautiful strange world. The reputation, influence and sustainable inner balance of an inhabitant of planet music depends more on his or her sensibility, sensuality, inventions, attitude and actions than on a constitution or a passport.

But let's leave heaven and go back to earth where I live in Switzerland with my Swiss passport. Our constitution says in a few succinct words: "Freedom of artistic expression is guaranteed."

The freedom of assembly and economic freedom, in particular, the freedom to choose an occupation and to pursue a private, economic activity, establishes the legal foundation for creating art and making a living from it in our society. Naturally, there are other necessary conditions, such as the protection of intellectual property, author rights and performing rights but I will focus here on basic political factors.

There is an essential hidden point in this legal permission to freely create art. The freedom of artistic expression means not only that artists are free to express themselves but also that what they express may not be used as an indictment against them. We as a democratic society are allowed to present our positive utopia in public. As we know from communist and totalitarian countries, even an artist's completely apolitical statement can be abused as a means of exerting pressure or even "convincing" the artist to collaborate with the authorities and/or subscribe to a specific ideology.[1]

1 There are many other interesting aspects in the constitutions of different countries and in the UN multilateral treaty, the International Covenant on Economic, Social and Cultural Rights from 1966. They are worth knowing.

A funny, almost Zen-koan-like paradox is revealed here, since it is incumbent upon a constitution, respectively the executive law, to define artistic expression. But art is inherently non-definable, subject to constant development and hence free. The battle over definitions, interpretations and intentions is complex and the devil lies in the detail.

On my travels through many countries with different rules, laws and circumstances, I experienced the existential meaning of these concerns. At home nothing should be taken for granted either.

Let us illustrate this with two very different cases. The first one is very basic and quite astonishing: My mother was granted the right to vote in 1971, the year of my birth. The male population of Switzerland finally voted in favor of women's suffrage after having long opposed this basic condition of democracy.

The second case refers to the absurd caprices of interpreting the free expression of art, but it is no less tragicomic. In my native Zurich, the artist Harald Naegeli, the so-called "Sprayer of Zurich," was arrested in 1984 and sent to prison for damaging property. In 2020, almost forty years later, he received the Art Award of the City of Zurich for the now world-renowned stick figures that he sprayed on the walls of Zurich's buildings. Being imprisoned for "property damage" of that kind seems a bit disproportionate; it is a revealing indication of the status of our democratic state in those days and its interpretation of the freedom of artistic expression in the form of a stick-figure utopia.

The positive outcome in both cases certainly speaks for our democracy but it also testifies to the long and arduous path that often precedes success!

So far, I have been fortunate enough to have had no such close encounters with Zurich's police authorities, nor is it my intention to use art as a form of provocation; rather, my goal is to invite people to embark on an existential journey of the imagination. However, even this harmless attitude towards artistic expression has met with opposition, admittedly with a much less dramatic outcome. In 2005, my acoustic group Mobile planned a music ritual that would take place from sunset to dawn on an empty island on the lake of Zurich. It was prohibited by the Zurich police chief on the rather flimsy grounds of noise pollution in an uninhabited location where the traffic noise on the road nearby was actually the main problem on a Friday night in a hedonistic city.

The easy life in a self-imposed prison

The above-mentioned tactics are, of course, not motivated by the wish to undermine the freedom of artistic expression; they have been instituted in order to protect us from each other: to protect property, to avoid noise pollution, in other words, to maintain a balance between rules and recklessness, civilization and chaos.

A small direct democracy like ours does not ordinarily pose a problem for the freedom of artistic expression, but it may well be a problem for a heroic artistic spirit because it is too easy to survive in Switzerland. As a result, many Swiss artists flirt with the enticing appeal of a great nation, which seems to guarantee the creation of great artists. While taking a taxi to a rehearsal in Berlin, I had a talk with the driver, who was Russian. Hearing that I am from Switzerland, he said he did not know a single Swiss artist while we have all heard of many great writers and composers from Russia. The immediate link-up of successful artists to their nation got me thinking.

World-famous Swiss writer and painter Friedrich Dürrenmatt was acutely aware of the tragicomic potential of the relationship between an artist and a nation. Having spent most of his life in Switzerland and recognizing

the universal in the local, he seemed to have enjoyed the paradoxes of Swiss democracy and also fruitfully exploited them in his writing.

In a speech[2] of 1990 honoring the writer, dissident and later president of the Czech Republic Václav Havel, Dürrenmatt creates the grotesque image of Switzerland as a huge prison, into which Swiss citizens escape voluntarily to be inmates and, at the same time, their own prison guards. This absurd voluntary conduct is a metaphor for a basic Swiss dilemma: you might say we are one of the world's most confining and freest countries. This makes us fearful and defensive. We take all of our rights for granted and are simultaneously mired in the agony of prosperity and in the mystification of our own past. Our wealth in combination with our highly developed democratic and federalist system with differentiated checks and balances of power on all levels of society should actually make us more alert, committed, curious and adventurous. Especially as artists we should be actively thankful for our fate, our good fortune and also a bit happy because these circumstances are such a benefit to working professionally and effectively on our art in the middle of Europe. As written in my text for the *Swiss Peace Supporter,* the magazine of Swiss contributions to international peace operations, (see p. 166) we should be fearless, neutrally engaged, positive and peaceful warriors, alert and aware of our possibilities and opportunities at home and abroad.

Merciful writing on the wall – Odysseus' soul wants to be Swiss

Dürrenmatt recognized this dilemma and pointed it out in his inimitable, unique, poetic and paradoxical way at the end of the above-mentioned speech:

2 "Die Schweiz – ein Gefängnis," speech for the award ceremony of the Gottlieb-Duttweiler award for Mr. Václav Havel, November 22, 1990.

"Dear Václav Havel, your task as president coincides with Václav Havel's task as a dissident. Mr. President, you are here among Swiss, Swiss men and women have welcomed you, the Swiss president has received you, a senior member of the Swiss Federal Council has given you a eulogy, and I, a Swiss, have also spoken, for we do a lot of talking in Switzerland. What sort of people are we, the Swiss? To be spared by fate is neither a disgrace nor an honor, but it is a kind of handwriting on the wall. Plato, near the end of his Politeia, tells us how the soul after death must choose its lot for a new life: 'It happened, though, that the shade of Odysseus was last in line to step forward and choose his lot. But since, remembering his previous hardships, he had given up all ambition, he went about for a long time in search of a life of calm retirement, and succeeded at last in finding one that the others had passed by. And when he had discovered it, he said he would have acted likewise if he had been first in line, and that his was a happy choice.' I am sure that the lot Odysseus chose for himself was to be a Swiss."[3]

The soul of the most adventurous ancient hero chooses to be a Swiss citizen in his next life because of an almost Taoist, wise insight into life. I wonder what the soul of Friedrich Dürrenmatt has chosen for his next life.

Compared to a big artist, like Dmitri Shostakovich, from a big country with big challenges and big wars, Dürrenmatt's writing on the wall might seem minor. I think it is just different. It helps us to be less heroic but more distinctive, both as citizens and individually. Swiss stability in combination with innovation, refinement and creativity are highly and often secretly influential. People from abroad profit from these qualities: Stravinsky's work and development would be inconceivable without his Swiss episodes, contacts and partnerships. Modern artists

3 From: "Friedrich Dürrenmatt: Switzerland – A Prison," in: *Friedrich Dürrenmatt: Selected Writings Volume 3 – Essays,* transl. by Joel Agee (Chicago: The University of Chicago Press, 2006).

and bands from Switzerland are and have been an important influence on international developments, for example Celtic Frost, The Young Gods, Yello or Andreas Vollenweider & Friends.

Switzerland often seems like a permanent world fair to me: the whole world passes through our country and inspiration flows without national blinkers. Democracy is essential and inspiring for free creativity, innovation and refinement, and thus for artistic entrepreneurship in worldwide cooperation and competition.

Václav Havel was one of the very few artists who took the responsibility of leading a democratic state as president and thus fruitfully combining his experiences of an artistic utopia with the real world. When I visited Prague for the first time as a young artist in 1990, this writer of absurd theater had been re-elected by the new democratic parliament as an impartial person of integrity. We should think of this today. As Dürrenmatt puts it in his speech: "You, dear Havel, received the prize, as it says in the explanatory statement, because your name stands for civic courage, honesty, and tolerance of other viewpoints, the indispensable basis for the free development of the individual in a democratic state."

Part 2: Band Balance

The band is a paradox:
golden cage and unleashed free organism

Decision-making processes and sustaining a balance between individual freedom and collective rules on a micro level, as in a band, depend less on complex social networks and more on personal relations. But the same aspects are important: freedom, protection, responsibility, risk, mutual appreciation and agreements. Band life is an extremely complex social organism.

In an ideal situation it is just plain fun to be part of a band. You find freedom and team spirit at the same time. A sworn bunch of people enjoy life and make music together without fear of tomorrow. To me, there's something transcendental about this – a sense of belonging, of being part of a whole without losing individuality.

Although a good band experiences many such metaphysical moments of now presence together, the reality is often more complex and, as in every group, the needs, developments and actions of all band members constantly have to be balanced out through intense, creative contact.

My life-long band mate and colleague, drummer Kaspar Rast, once said playing with our band Ronin – founded over two decades ago – had given him unprecedented freedom as a musician but it was also a golden cage. These two sides of the same coin pinpoint the paradox of making music as a band. Band members make a commitment with their contribution, investment and risk required to achieve the freedom of creative togetherness and of constant and consistent playing: fun and freedom through self-imposed restriction. They bet on that band and need to give and receive trust in order to believe in it.

The working band

In contrast to ad hoc bands or hierarchically structured groups with hired musicians, “working band” does not just mean constant work, practice and performances; it also means a serious personal investment. In return, a band member receives ongoing work, concerts, appreciation and hopefully the fun, focus and joy of playing with the other members of the group.

Again and again, the band needs to find a sustainable balance of input and output: it’s a high-risk game. The danger of losing work built up over years in a single day because of a conflict or other unforeseen circumstances is constantly present. So many bands in music history have split up sooner or later for any number of reasons: social, aesthetic, financial or simply the vagaries of everyday life.

A band is an extremely fragile organism; it is also one of the most inspiring and creative forms of being together as human beings. In the long run this only works if the band members cultivate good communication and if they are clear, decided and balanced in their team work. Effectual differentiation and distribution of tasks within the band ultimately serves the common goal of ideally effortless cooperation in making music together. This should be based on an honest evaluation of each member's interests, strengths and capabilities. If this succeeds, a band member becomes more than an individual on stage and can do things that would never be possible alone or in a setting where everybody is hired for a specific task.

A freelance musician or individual artist with no ties might be freer in choosing collaborations and projects at short notice, but that freedom can never replace the privilege of contributing to the fortuitous effortlessness achieved by a group organism through long-term togetherness, the surprise of ongoing outfoxing yourself and your band mates in a friendly way, the inspiration and enlightenment of *awase* playing together.

This is one of the reasons why, relatively early in my career, I stopped playing in ad hoc bands. I didn't want

the pressure of forcing developments in a short time; I didn't want to surrender what you can only achieve through continuity. I longed for deeper relationships and understanding among players.

Freedom of choice or freedom of restriction: both have their advantages and disadvantages. It's your decision. You can't have your cake and eat it, too.

We are all apes: destructive and constructive band energies

A band is only as strong as the weakest member or the weakest connection between two band members. Conflicts lurk everywhere. Band members, the connections between them and every group as a whole have weaknesses and sometimes not only brief conflicts but also ongoing conflict patterns. It is worth investing time and energy in surmounting potential conflict to avoid ultimately unsurmountable trouble. Togetherness is an opportunity to cultivate tolerance, attentiveness and mutual support. Both band members and bandleaders need to acknowledge conflict and learn to cope with criticism that is constructive, fair, creative and proactive!

Band life is thus training for life in general. If every person in the band behaves in a solution-oriented manner, these processes can be very fruitful albeit sometimes hard and painful. I experienced cases where conflicts in the band created destructive forces and it was no longer possible to solve the problems. This is difficult to accept and very challenging since a democratic spirit wants to work at a solution until one is found. I had to learn that not every conflict can be solved. Usually this is not one person's fault but the result of truly incompatible personalities or interests.

My mother, an experienced psychologist in transactional analysis and systemic therapy, worked a lot with teams in companies. In our discussions about group energies, she once pointed out that every group has inherently destructive and constructive energies. They are two sides of the same coin. I was shocked to realize that a group of cool people could also be self-destructive. Ordinarily, this is not deliberate, of course, but rather the reality of complex social and personal energies in groups. In the beginning of my career I tried to solve such challenges psychologically by finding a balance of all interests and needs. Later I learned to understand that social energies like power, status, appreciation, team spirit, cooperation, competition, jealousy and violence also entail many aspects that are essentially nonverbal and beyond analysis. Primatologist Frans de Waal's amazing and inspiring books gave me a better understanding of these aspects, since humans are primates, too. Initially interested mainly in conflict behavior fueled by power, rivalry, competition and violence, he discovered that even in quite competitive and violent chimpanzee tribes, cooperation, empathy and social strategies of building alliances are essential to survival. Cooperative strategies and empathetic behavior are as crucial for survival as competition and egoism. It is no wonder then that these social skills are also imperative in making music together; they must be cultivated, trained and sustainably implanted.

A good atmosphere and effective communication are always fragile. As my teacher for vocal song accompaniment and former head of the Zurich University of the Arts Daniel Fueter once said to me: "It takes years to build up polite, friendly and positive communication in a group but it can be ruined in one day by a wrongly written letter." Fruitful teamwork and leadership is not only based on good intellectual and psychological analysis but also on such social qualities as shared humor, altruistic behavior, generosity, positive attitude, role model behavior, fair and fearless confrontation, surprising appreciation, comprehensible personal demarcation – a never-ending creative list. Find your own resources and techniques!

Nobody's fault becomes everybody's problem

Playing together is one of the most satisfying aspects of making music and one of the main reasons why music even exists and why I love it so much. And yet it is one of the most difficult things to do. Effortless tightness, togetherness, flow and organism playing are the true proof of musicianship and a gift of music to experience ourselves as partners or as a holon – an individual being within a bigger whole.

We are responsible for ourselves but also for the whole band organism. Responsibility is also a crucial feature of freedom and choice. True freedom means taking responsibility and taking responsibility fosters freedom. This applies to citizens of a democratic state and smaller units like a band, a club or an association.

When something is "nobody's fault," this can also mean that nobody takes responsibility. This in turn obstructs the decision-making process and may lead to unresolved situations, in which responsibility is passed around like a hot potato with the potential of passively destructive forces generating a feeling of helplessness. In addition, the subtext of "nobody's fault" may well be a more explicit and destructive accusation: it's "somebody else's fault!" Individuals may become victims of the search for a scapegoat but the group itself suffers as well since belief in a solution is seriously damaged.

Decision-making requires a constructive, intelligent and positive acceptance of responsibility. This in turn means finding a balance between responsibility for oneself and a sensitivity to the needs of the whole. Equilibrium of that kind is never fixed or static; it is in constant flow, a continuous process that calls for flexibility in body and mind, in the band and the community.

A crucial requirement in this respect is the ability to listen – to yourself, your partners and the world at large. For more about the significance of listening, read the article on aikido (see p. 16).

Every band is a singular, creative unit

There are several different band models and every band has its specific concerns, social patterns, challenges, strengths and weaknesses. In our bands we also have ongoing discussions about what the band is and how it should be organized.

I would like to share some experiences and ways of working with my own bands in my simultaneous roles as a member and a leader. I hope it will be of relevance for creative people in general working on several levels with groups of different sizes and other band-like organizations.

My band model is based on a clear leader and the cooperation of all members, taking into account their individual interests and qualities, which can, of course, change. There are no "sidemen," as members of bands with clear leaders and changing members are called. Legendary bandleader Miles Davis never used a band name but either exclusively his own or his own in combination with the size of the band, like quartet, quintet, sextet, etc. Legendary bandleader Prince always used band names which showed the community and lineup of a certain phase: The Revolution, The New Power Generation or 3rdEyeGirl. Some bands have only a name and no single artist's name, like The Beatles, Queen or Weather Report. Even in such fabulously famous bands the social and aesthetic dynamics are super complex and different in every case, as we learn from anecdotes, books and documentaries. The internal organization, social conflicts and cooperative and competitive aspects of group dynamics are an endless story…

Ways of working

My bands depend on individual, strong characters with a lot of interest and experience in music. It is ultimately and essentially "our" music – the product of mutual understanding that can only come by playing together for many years.

Nonetheless, I take the main responsibility and risk concerning organization, communication, finance and composition. I deliver prepared pieces, usually developed long in advance, with a clear idea and concept and complete scores including listening versions. This does not mean that they cannot change in rehearsals. They are open to everybody's input and can also change over the years through repeated performance in our Monday series and other concerts. We also rehearse them again and again to keep them alive and receptive to new discoveries and learning processes. But we have the rule that a new Modul needs to be fully understood before starting to change it or incorporate new personal input. A modest, even tentative initial approach to the piece, its coherence and the composer is appropriate even for myself in the role of player and interpreter. So many Moduls have a long history of interpretation and changes in form, phrasing, dynamics, sound and especially dramaturgy.

I have always wanted to find a means of uniting the very subtle culture of interpreting classical music and the very free treatment of pieces in jazz. Modular compositions in combination with a "para-tribal" working band is my answer. Here, oral and written culture are combined as well. The band members are jointly responsible for the performance but I am solely responsible for composing and preparing, keeping records of the details of development and keeping sight of the bigger aesthetic picture over the years.

As mentioned, a clear vision is not incompatible with cooperative and collective strategies. This can be understood as a fruitful and challenging paradox. Everyone makes a commitment, invests time and works on the music while also taking my vision into account.

I have been playing in bands, my own and others', since the age of 10, which is when I first met drummer Kaspar Rast. We were in the same band project at the Zurich Music School (MKZ) and started playing together in our local football team FC Seefeld at the same time. So the experience of team playing started very early and on several levels. In the last thirty years in professional groups and since 1998 exclusively with my own bands, I have continuously tried to find ways, tools, strategies and offers to keep bands together, to reinvent them and also to respond to the challenges that arise. As a result, my two bands Mobile and Ronin still exist and we have recorded many albums, but I never know what tomorrow may bring. Like the music itself, a band can fall apart and vanish in a flash.

Band balance with freelancers: Ronin and Mobile are functional, programmatic and poetic names

We know the independent band as a bunch of dudes, a swarm of sophisticates, a cluster of cats, a coterie of cool individuals, who together define the character of a bigger, unique organism. Interestingly, the term "band" goes back to military music and over time came to refer to voluntary membership in a group.

My bands have names that are functional, programmatic and poetic. Ronins are warriors who do not serve a master; the two kanjis in Japanese literally mean "wave man." These warriors are delivered to the undulating waves of fate. This is also a metaphor for a freelancer who is responsible for his/her own fate. Ronins were losers, robbers, people in the shadows but also the freest, most sophisticated and self-responsible martial artists in Japan – like the legendary Miyamoto Musashi. To me, "wave man" implies something else as well, namely resonance and soundwaves. Our ronins are independent people in whom music resonates.

We speak of a mobile face and a mobile mind, meaning expressiveness and open-minded flexibility. "Mobile" is also the word Marcel Duchamp proposed when artist Alexander Calder asked him to suggest a name for his sculptures – his free-floating, often monumental and yet seemingly weightless structures suspended in space. The exquisitely balanced parts create a beautiful whole that is simultaneously fragile and strong. For decades, there was a huge mobile suspended high overhead in front of the Kunsthaus Zürich. It struck me every time I visited the museum, and I visited it often: my mother had taken me to every exhibition since I was a small child. I was reminded of the effortless power of these artworks when thinking about a name for my first professional acoustic group, formed in 1997 for my diploma at the Conservatory of Music in Zurich (ZHDK). Playing naturally and effortlessly also depends on the precise yet precarious balance of many factors, both personal and musical, both physical and mental!

Part 3: Rules, Roles, Principles and Strategies for Band Work

In the course of acquiring practical experience, talking with colleagues, masters and mentors, and reading, we have come up with some important rules, principles and strategies for our band work. They can improve efficiency and foster partnership, ensuring that there is more time to focus on the joy of making music together. We have learned practically everything "by doing," by trying things out.

Three essential conditions when working with and in a band:

1 Everybody needs to be around locally.
2 Everybody needs to fit socially.
3 Everybody needs to understand and like the aesthetics we create together.

This means we can rehearse, work and play regularly. It may sound simple but it is already a great benefit. Steady, continuous work over years is still completely underestimated in our business, especially in these times where every step we take is measured in economic terms.

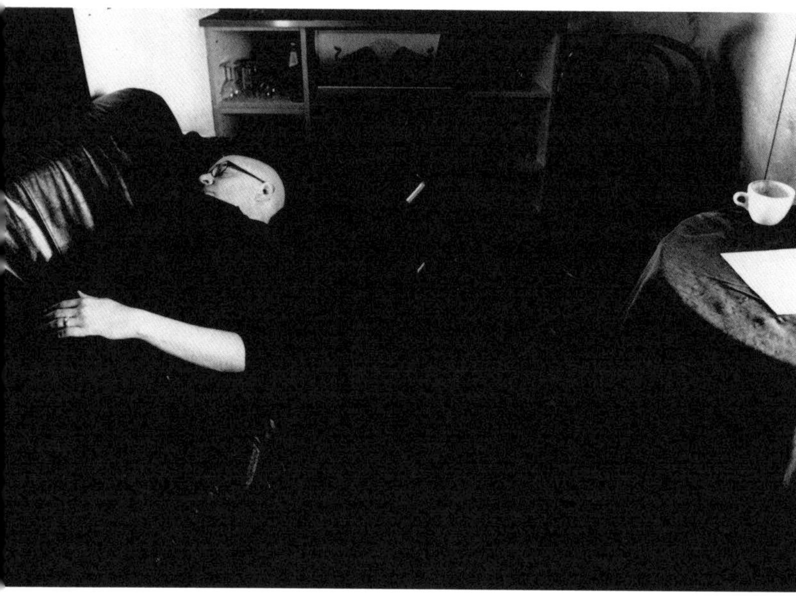

Sustainable and fulfilling results are only possible with patience, passion and consistency. We are all familiar with situations where bands are still rehearsing on stage at the beginning of the tour or in the recording studio because there was not enough time for preparation. We are familiar with ensembles of classical music with not enough time and money to properly prepare and rehearse a new composition. The premiere then takes place under the motto: "Not quite, but it'll do." Both situations are unprofessional and, in a battle, would mean death.

Take action if circumstances hinder you from moving forward.

In this case, cooperation with others can help. For example, rent a studio, found a club, a label or a festival, organize supporters, interest and money. Start with the infamous trio of "family, friends and fools" and add more rings of resonance to your project step by step. Be patient, passionate, persistent and serious. Otherwise it won't work. Keep the number of serious supporters small to be able to stay connected and to communicate personally.

Our "Montags" series with a workshop, a concert and meetings is such an example. I started out renting the new Bazillus Club every Monday evening (2004–2009) and then co-founded the club EXIL (in 2009) with four friends.

Restrict yourself to a few concrete goals.

Less is more means focusing your energy, turning down interesting offers, learning to say no politely, acting with modesty and recognizing your own limits. This is challenging for a creative person who is chafing at the bit and eager to learn!

Take responsibility for failure.

Instead of blaming others, you take responsibility as a bandleader. That does not mean that you blame yourself, but rather that you use the opportunity to take action, initiate change and improve the situation. To do so, requires "a good chin," as they say in martial arts. You have to be steadfast and stand your ground. It may even help when a leader says "all spears on me," as in the legend of the Swiss hero Arnold Winkelried, who thereby opened a gap for his own men to attack. Staying positive and poised requires strength, energy – and support from others. Regular aikido training helps me to remain steadfast mentally and physically in order to confront my own disappointments, fears and weaknesses.

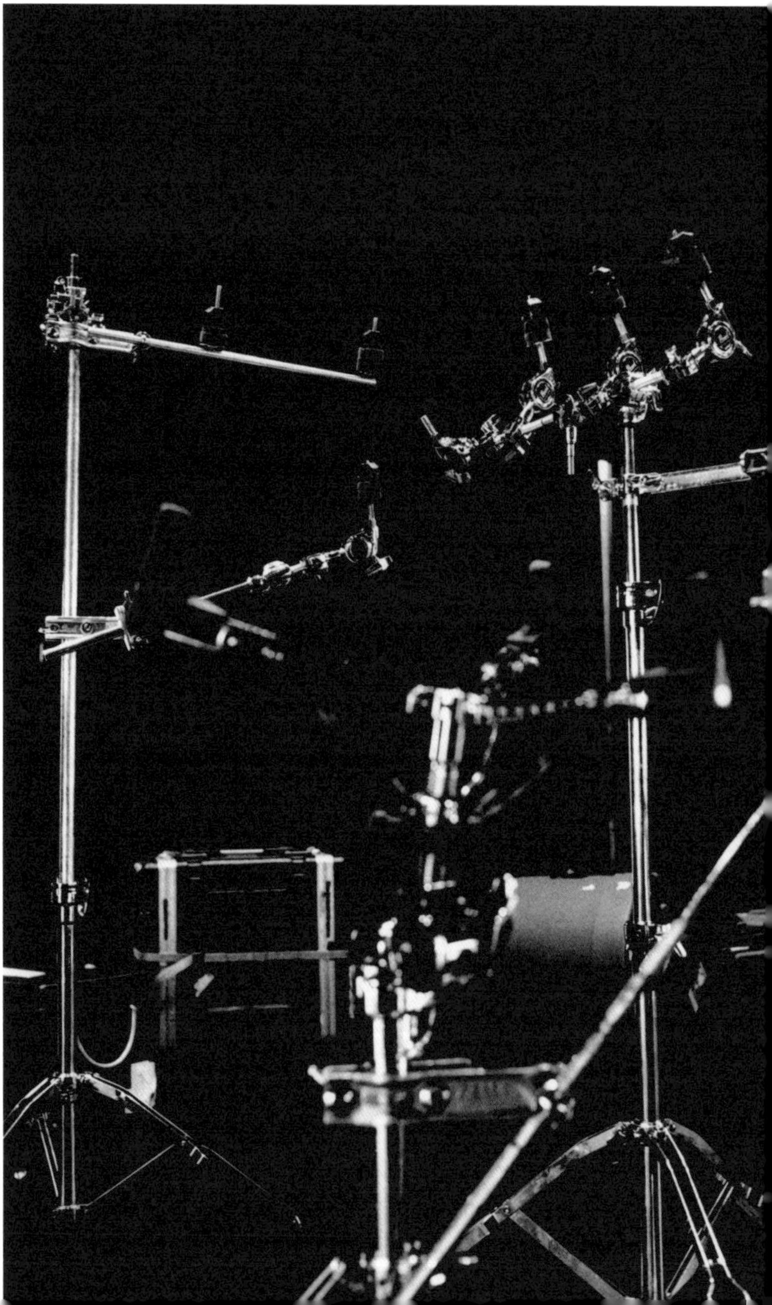

Don't take things personally.

Focus on facts and solutions. As often as not, offensive behavior and even insults are not directed at you personally but are based on misunderstandings, undifferentiated and imprecise attacks and thoughtless momentum. Instead of harping on your own grievances, be aware of the other person, who may have problems that have nothing to do with you – a sick child at home, a failed test. You just happen to be the target. Curse, blame and lament in the privacy of your kitchen table at home, but not in the band and certainly not in public. Professional discipline gives everyone strength.

Be aware of your role.

This helps to define how you need to communicate, to connect or to take responsibility at a certain moment. Are you the composer, the interpreter, the bandleader, the musical director, the producer, the dramaturg, the club owner, the colleague, the friend, the private person, the parent, etc.?

Being aware of your role helps to clarify decision-making processes and to make them more easily comprehensible to your partners. A person who has to make a decision may have several conflicting interests. Consciously separating roles and defining tasks assists in taking action and understanding the workload that has to be handled: composition, rehearsals, communication, organization, logistics, administration, financing, technics, management, booking, archive, catering/food, etc.

It is often better to decide now than to wait for the "right" decision.

Take responsibility. Don't fear decisions and envisioned consequences. Prevent processes from becoming blocked. You can still make adjustments and correct decisions that did not lead to the desired result. Don't buckle under negative criticism, energy and envy. My teenage daughter recently made it clear by referring to her world of pop music stars and their resonance in social media: if you ain't got no haters, you ain't poppin'.

Stay polite, respectful but firm and clear.

Decision-making can be understood as a positive force that helps everybody, including the person that may suffer from the decision. You cannot make everyone happy but you can – and must – treat everyone with respect.

Share tasks and information; delegate tasks if possible.

For this you need partners who can take responsibility and tackle important tasks, partners who can accept that there may be more than one way of understanding and solving a task at hand. Transparency is important but too much information can cause confusion and encourage interference from others who are not directly involved. Once again, it's a question of balance.

Institutionalize regular platforms, meetings and journals.

Keep rehearsals and meetings separate! In our case, we have band meetings once a month to evaluate and align the perception of processes regarding both the band and organization. For band vision meetings in special phases, we organize separate half-yearly meetings lasting about half a day.

loyalty
community
coherence
mpathy
cooperation
consistency
sacredness
coherence
passion
consistency
empathy
consistency
cooperation
coherence
patience
passion
community
patience
loyalty
sacredness

Creative Qualities

The bandleader should prepare meetings and keep a record of them. Solid bookkeeping, financial and otherwise, often sharpens intuition.

Find clear agreements in the group.

Agreements should be clearly formulated, reviewed with the whole group from time to time and communicated in writing, for example in an email. This does not necessarily mean written contracts but simply clear explicit agreements among members of the group.

Clearly distinguish individual, bilateral and group processes.

There are many lines of communication between the members of a group. Individual, bilateral and group processes are to be clearly distinguished. Awareness and conscious use of the appropriate lines of communication improves efficiency and discipline and helps to stay focused on the task or topic.

Communication is crucial.

Communication is the lifeline between band members, technicians, close partners, supporters and, in fact, the larger circle of interested people. It plays a role on all levels and in all tasks, even in writing the score. Nobody can survive alone in the world and as four people, there are more paths of communication than people, with the number of paths increasing quadratically. These simple facts show the complexity of human interaction and the importance of investing energy, time and conscious conduct in communication.

Communication also means listening.

Listen not only to your partners and colleagues but also to your opponents and enemies. It doesn't matter who you learn from as long as you learn.

Be a role model.

Ideally, a bandleader is a role model with integrity, passion and patience. Not infallible and omniscient but competent, coherent, clear, focused and well prepared.

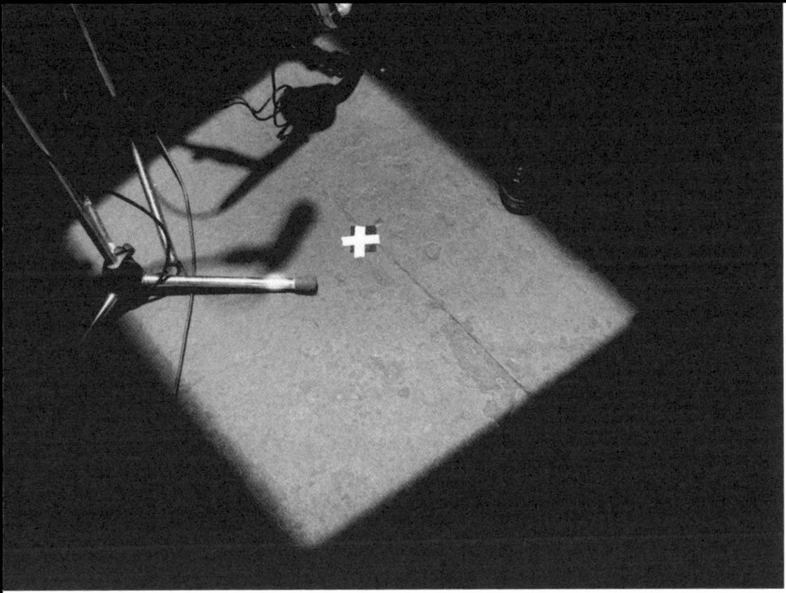

A natural authority can easily acknowledge lack of knowledge, has the strength to admit weakness and fosters cooperation and sharing. A bandleader needs to perceive and balance the interests of all members and to find fruitful hierarchies of competence on all levels of team work.

Coda: Maradona – a Solo Is Team Work

The goal of the century: mental and physical team work

In the 1986 FIFA World Cup in Mexico, Argentina's Diego Armando Maradona scored his second goal in the fifty-fifth minute of the quarter final against England. His solo run over two thirds of the entire pitch against several opponents has gone down in history as the goal of the century. I find two things interesting:

First, his colleagues Jorge Burruchaga and Héctor Enrique, running in a line with Maradona in the middle and on the left side of the field, distracted the English defenders Gary M. Stevens and Terry Fenwick. They were not sure whether Maradona would pass the ball to one of his teammates. And goalkeeper Peter Shilton had to decide in a millisecond whether to come out of the goal or not. Rarely is any mention made of the teamwork that was essential to the success of this "goal of the century."

Producer Manfred Eicher, sound engineer Gérard de Haro and the band Ronin during production in the studio of La Buissonne in Pernes-les-Fontaines in France. The ECM albums *STOA* (2006), *HOLON* (2008), *LLYRÌA* (2010) and *AWASE* (2018) were recorded and produced here. Footage of the *HOLON* production process can also be seen in the film *Sounds and Silence* (2009) about ECM's producer and founder, Manfred Eicher, by Norbert Wiedmer and Peter Guyer.

Second, the English team was understandably still very upset and under shock from the first goal scored in the fifty-first minute by Maradona – or rather by his hand and probably the biggest foul of the century – and had not yet recovered enough to organize a defense against the next attack. There were only four minutes between these two very different goals. Whether on the soccer pitch or on stage, past events and future expectations influence the mindset of the present.

Keyboardist and composer Joe Zawinul was a bandleader, involved in organism groups like Weather Report, and also a band member under strong leaders like Miles Davis. He once said that he doesn't trust people who don't read the sports section of the newspaper. He knew full well that a competitive spirit, teamwork and sportsmanship apply equally to sports, music and indeed all of the performing arts. Teamwork and unconditional presence are equally vital on stage and on the soccer pitch. Nothing else.

Quintessence: Carry Out Your Real Existing Utopia!

After all these reflections about freedom and responsibility, individual and collective contributions, you will understand why I think it is so invaluable and enriching to be able to create art and make music as a free person in a democracy together with other free people as partners. I don't see art as purposeless or oppositional. It is a real existing utopia. We are free to make art FOR something and not against something. We are free to create forms of art to express what is important to us, aesthetically and poetically. And with our art we are free to create economic and social value. This is a political statement in praise of democratic freedom and creative entrepreneurship as positive, stabilizing and driving forces in our community, our society and ultimately the whole world.

inspiration added chain

value added chain

esteem added chain

Paths of Communication

1 path

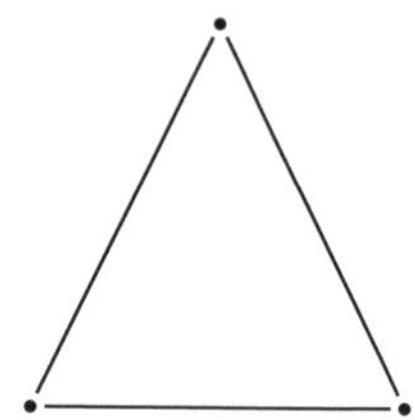

3 paths

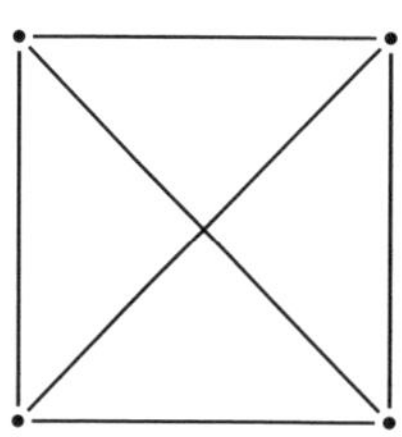

6 paths

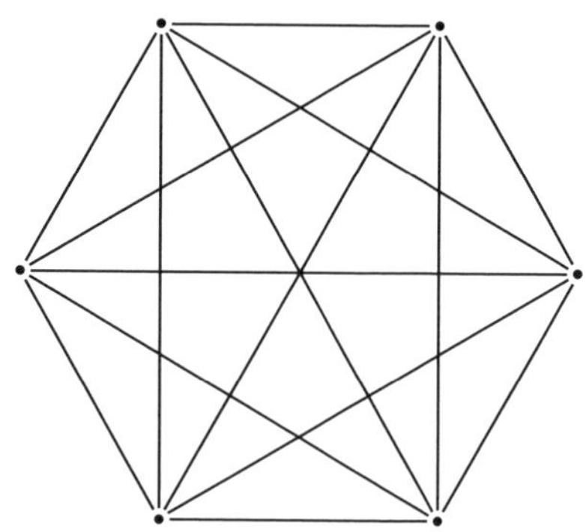

15 paths

The paths of communication between people grow quadratically with the number of people involved. Interaction becomes exponentially complex.

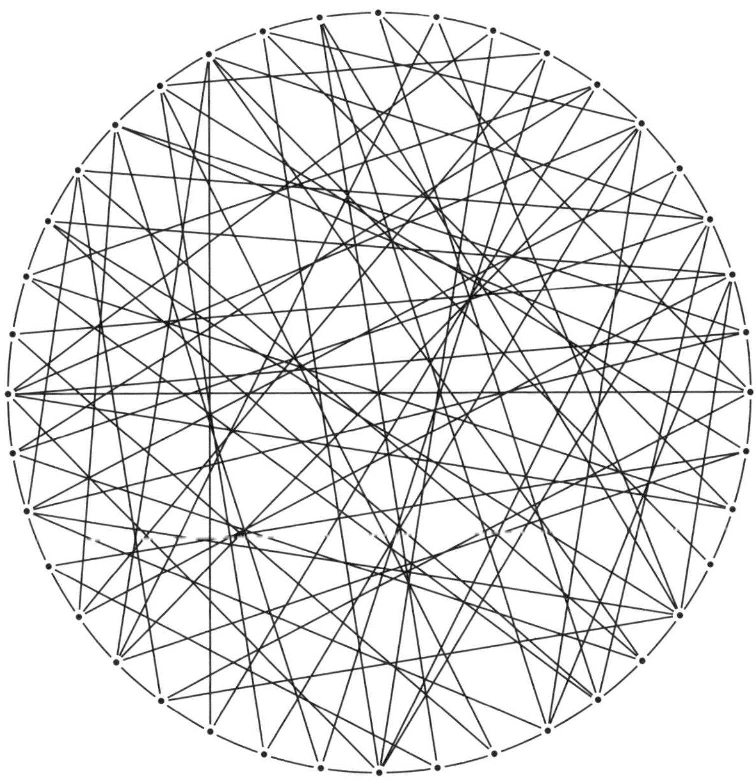

x paths

Azuki Bean Trap

I had a favorite teahouse in Tokyo, simple but refined, naturally combining the traditional and modern aesthetics of Japan. Its dim, calm and warm atmosphere made me feel centered; it was as if the whole universe was present in a cup of green tea. The tea, carefully brewed in a variety of flavors, was usually served with small sweets made out of beans. You would choose one, eat it and then taste the tea with a subtle sweetness in your mouth.

After living in Japan for a while, my wife and I realized that almost all of the sweets are made out of that bean paste, which, to be honest, tasted a bit monotonous, especially for us, having been spoiled by Swiss sweets. It must be said, however, that Japanese bean confectioners create their desserts with the same care and love that is given to everything else and they vary them to match each season, always with an exquisitely subtle blend of color, shape and elaborate wrapping. But still, to us, it always tasted more or less the same.

On one of my trips to Japan in autumn, I went back to my teahouse, looking forward to discovering new tastes in tea and even the sweets that go with it. As usual, it was served with natural, precise simplicity. I took a first sip to taste the fresh tea without sweets and then took a bite of the sweet in preparation for the next sip. Anticipating what I considered the "bland" taste of the bean paste, I was totally unprepared for the explosion of flavor in my mouth when I unsuspectingly bit into a fresh, crisp, subtly sour piece of cherry hidden in the bean paste. It was like a flash of spring, like a flash of lightning. The universe was present in the teacup and had exploded on my tongue.

That is what we should look for in every note we play – that exciting combination of subtle focus and startling surprise.

The Art of the Unobtrusive Difference

Receiving the Career Award of the city of Zurich made it possible for me and Andrea to go to Japan for half a year in 2003–2004. It was a welcome opportunity to explore our affinity for Japanese aesthetics and practices like aikido and Zen as well as traditional, ritual and modern music, food, manga, anime art, daily rituals and a great deal more. We stayed in Kobe and Tokyo but also travelled around in Japan visiting several cities, discovering landscapes and looking at monuments. While in Japan, I composed all of the Moduls for the first Ronin ECM album *STOA* (2006) and the long chamber funk piece "Modul Ritual" for the Arte Saxophone quartet, drums, percussion and piano.

Prior to that I had already devoted nearly ten years to developing my ritual groove music, together with the groups Mobile and Ronin and their members. In the process, journalist Tom Gsteiger often critically traced and described my path in different publications. In one case, for instance, he speaks about "success in creatively utilizing, and in a certain way transcending, several fields of tension simultaneously: asceticism vs. ecstasy; art music vs. popular music; funk power vs. Zen coolness, etc."[1]

1 Jazz journalist Tom Gsteiger in his interview with Nik Bärtsch, "The Art of the Unobtrusive Difference," in *Passages* 39, Swiss Arts Council Pro Helvetia, 2005, transl. from German by John O'Brien. This text is based on the interview and I would like to thank Tom for his fruitful input and precision in exploring the context and zeroing in on my thoughts.

When I came back from Japan, drummer Kaspar Rast and I inaugurated the Montags concert series at the Bazillus Club in Zurich in August 2004. The concerts moved to my own club EXIL, which I co-founded with architect Christoph Kellenberger, drummer and sushi master Tosho Yakkatokuo, promotor Michi Vollenweider and club entrepreneur Dominik Müller in 2009. Before regularly appearing with Ronin in clubs and festivals from

Movie poster from the film *Twilight Samurai* by Yoji Yamada, 2002. The film shows the Japanese samurai legend in a different light.

2001 on, we had created elaborate transdisciplinary music rituals with my music ritual group Mobile that showed a clear affinity for Far Eastern aesthetics, for instance the project Perpetual Rhythm, which was released with Mobile and Imre Thormann's Butoh dance group Bodygarage. It toured Japan for several weeks in the autumn of 2005. I have since been to Japan several times for concerts and projects.

Picture from the manga series *Lone Wolf and Cub* by author Kazuo Koike and graphic artist Gōseki Kojima, 1970–76. It is the story of a ronin with his small child. The style and story influenced many Western comic books and series.

Lost in the West

Sofia Coppola's film *Lost in Translation*, released in 2003, practically coincided with my first trip to Japan. The film was a great success and made a strong impression on the West's image of Japan. I saw it right after coming back in 2004 but couldn't share the mix of amusement and agreement that many of my friends showed in response to the "weirdness" of Japanese culture and customs. Andrea – she had already been in Japan previously at the Iwama Aikido dojo – and I had experienced a very different Japan.

The film presents the country as an odd setting for bewildered Westerners in search of themselves. It conveys a picture of Japan stamped by Western notions and projections, and portrays the Japanese as bizarre figures in this "romantic" self-search. However, the main reason I don't like the film is because of its languid rhythm. The great longing of many Western bohemians for the simplicity and slowness they believe can be found in Japan comes out both in the way the film was made and how it was received. When I was in Japan, it was the other way around; it was actually Switzerland that, from a distance, often seemed to me like an odd, mixed-up place. We Swiss live in one of the safest countries in the world, yet we're constantly preoccupied about our well-being in all possible respects. Our tendency to bemoan everything is acute, and we often display too little risk-readiness and awareness because our very prosperity has made us lose our sense of what is essential. In Japan, people are very much at the mercy of nature. For example, everybody knows they can expect a devastating earthquake at any time. It's no accident that Mount Fuji, a volcano, is the country's trademark. But there is no prevailing mood of catastrophe; instead, you feel a sense of closeness to nature and behavior characterized by serenity. It was stimulating to feel this.

Understanding is easier than practicing

Sometimes people weary of civilization see Zen Buddhism as an attractive alternative to a Western materialism that's empty of meaning. I learned Zen meditation from my mother when I was eighteen. She had already been practicing it for a long time and it didn't interest me, but then one day I asked her how it works and she introduced me to it. And, as a teenager my stepsister spent the summer holidays at a Zen monastery; she was ordained as a nun and didn't want to come back to finish school. It was a tragicomic episode in our family but finally my stepfather put his foot down and made her come home. Later I learned more from her about this technique and philosophy.

So is this Zen longing perhaps a bit of flight from the world lurking in the background? I don't think so. I pursue my affinities, even for funk music, for example, unconditionally but with self-irony. I'm not driven by any longing for *the other*. I think Zen has much more to do with philosophy than with religion – with practical, everyday philosophy. There's a Zen saying that goes: "Understanding is easier than practicing."

Unobtrusive Difference

In European jazz there's still a tendency to regard American models as "the ultimate." I was looking for something else, a different direction, facing not "Wild Westwards" but "Far Eastwards." But here, too, there is the danger of succumbing to the almost fawning, imitative love of all things Japanese, much like the adulation of New York. My ritual groove music (RGM) certainly isn't inspired primarily by ritual practices of Japanese origin. It is more a perspective than a style. However, I've noticed that people in Japan instantly respond to our RGM performances. They love ceremonial gestures and little rituals, even if they may not understand what's behind them. And through their tradition they have a definite sensitivity to musical space. In RGM the pull of space plays an important role. By means of repetition, or better, reiteration and small variations, a musical space is created where an "unobtrusive difference" gives listeners the opportunity to enjoy contemplative concentration and indulge in aimlessly rambling thoughts. Here there are certainly points of contact with Japanese culture.

The idea of "unobtrusive difference" comes from an essay by Hans Ulrich Gumbrecht. An interesting sentence caught my attention. It goes: "… always to produce identical forms anew, perhaps with an unobtrusive difference

Poster for the Mobile performance "Perpetual Rhythm" at the Hiyoshi Shrine in Otsu, Japan, 2005. Co-produced by musicologist and Biwa master Silvain Guignard, in collaboration with Butoh dancer Imre Thormann, Noh musicians and the Gagaku ensemble of the Osaka Gakuin University.

that reveals the skill invested in the reproduction, is – in maximum contrast to the Western drive for originality – the aim of all design in Japanese culture."[2]

2 Hans Ulrich Gumbrecht, "Die Innenwelt der Aussenwelt der Innenwelt," *Neue Zürcher Zeitung,* January 10, 2005, p. 23.

Backwards Ennobling

A negative cliché about the Japanese is that they only copy everything. This is obviously false and related to their respect for Western culture. Respect, a very important quality, is also bound up with the ambition to do better and sometimes manifests itself in the form of excessive nationalism. This turns a virtue into a vice. The Japanese don't just copy, they ennoble. And above all, they are the only "backwards ennoblers." With all their virtuoso craftsmanship, they consider the step backwards to what is simple and raw to be the highest art. You can see this, for example, in a comparison between Chinese and Japanese teacups. The latter always show a tiny "defect," which makes every cup a unique piece – the "unobtrusive difference," once again.

Fruitful Paradoxes and a Flower

Another disconcerting aspect of Japan for Westerners is the enormous tension between archaic tradition and a futuristic tomorrow, almost as if there were no present. This is also a subject of vehement debate in Japan itself. But the Japanese come to terms more easily with what we might perceive as contradictory, as ambiguous and paradoxical. For example, kanji, the Japanese characters, cannot always be unambiguously interpreted and their ambiguity is even considered a positive attribute. Japan

may be puzzling to us because we think too much. The search for intellectual depth is a typically European phenomenon. In Japan it's not necessary to have a profound conversation in order to express sympathy; it can be enough to go for a walk together and look at beautiful flowers.

Obviously, we can learn from other cultures, and they from us. On this earth there is no more an Evil Empire than there is a Kingdom of the Good. There are just different types of cultures, networks and communities that humans have formed.

Authenticity: what is universal, cultural, individual in a phenomenon?

When it comes to learning from other cultures, there is always the question of authenticity. Where does real understanding of another culture begin, and where are we just dealing with folkloric stereotypes?

Once, at the Berlinale in Berlin, I attended a Japan Evening at the Sony Center. The presentations were a noisy hodgepodge of archaisms and glamour. After this motley commercial event I visited Martin Krahl, who worked with Mobile in the third part of the Blue Trilogy. Although he has never been to Japan, he is also a sword art practitioner, with the rank of Grand Master in Japanese sword combat. In his apartment there was an ikebana arrangement he had designed that showed much more "spirit" than the spectacle I had just witnessed in the Sony Center.

It is important not to claim exclusive possession of so-called authenticity, like assuming that only an Afro-American person with the correct cultural background can play jazz authentically. Cultural racism can easily slip in through the back door. What is universal, what is cultural and what is individual in a phenomenon?

Think, for example, of keyboardist Joe Zawinul: he grew up in Vienna but created a sensation in the USA playing next to musicians like Cannonball Adderley and Miles Davis before starting the group Weather Report with Wayne Shorter: what exactly is his cultural background? I was wondering why it seems that he has to justify his origin in interviews. That's unnecessary. He can phrase like the devil, no matter whether he comes from Timbuktu or Hasle-Rüegsau! It's musically irrelevant. He produced *Amen* by singer Salif Keita from Mali, one of the best music albums of all time. The cultural and individual distillate of these artists on that record is of universal value and validity.

Stage design for "Area Blue," the first part of the *Blue Trilogy* by Mobile, 2000–2002. The musicians played for thirty-six hours from 6 pm Friday evening to 6 am Sunday morning in a circle of sand at the Blauer Saal in Zurich. The project was a collaboration with the video artist Trix Barmettler, who created video sequences with samurai movies by Akira Kurosawa. The actor Toshiro Mifune is seen in this video still.

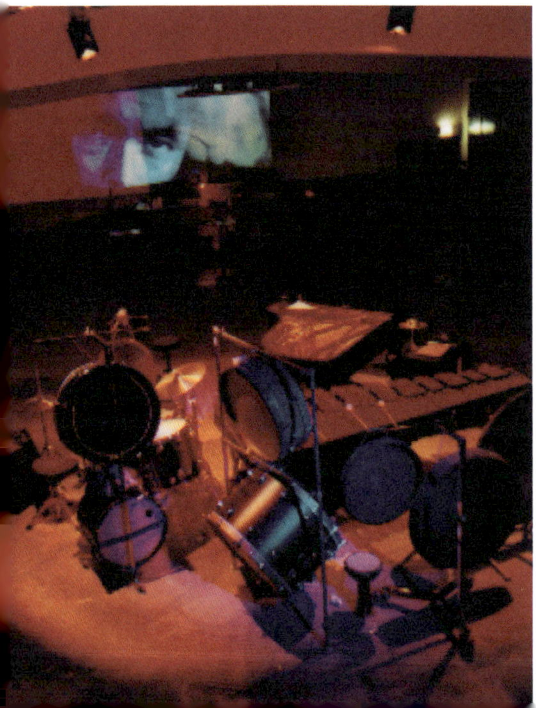

rules

roles

translate

reflect

Butterfly Holometabolic Metamorphosis as a Poetic Strategy

Bio-Poetic Phenomenon

During a creative life, an artist has to go through various transformations. Similarly, familiar and new poetic codes must constantly find a balance in order to remain agile and vibrant.

A caterpillar's life is all about eating. Within a few weeks, it can munch its way through enormous quantities of plant material. Some specimens consume up to 27,000 times their body weight in a lifetime. Once the caterpillar has acquired the necessary body mass, it will pupate. The pupa is formed underneath the "skin" of the caterpillar, which cracks open and shrivels away. Seen from the outside, nothing moves. Inside the pupa, the caterpillar releases enzymes that liquefy almost all of its body. What remains of the caterpillar inside the chrysalis is mostly a very protein-rich "soup." But this liquid contains a few cells (so-called imaginal cells) that become active, reorganizing all the proteins and turning what was once a caterpillar into a butterfly. Significantly, scientists have discovered that a newborn butterfly can retain a memory of its life as a caterpillar.

To be able to fly, artists need to go through similar stages, from caterpillar to pupa to butterfly. As a butterfly, they need to forget and remember the past at the same time.

Partnership and Perception

Andrea Pfisterer and Nik Bärtsch Talk About Music, Movement and Mind

Digital drawing by Yves Netzhammer from the series *Concave Thoughts*

Nik: When I was eighteen, I asked my mother to introduce me to Zen meditation since she had already engaged with it for many years. She then gave me the book *Zen Mind, Beginner's Mind* (1970) by Zen master Shunryu Suzuki, in which he advises using the mindset of a beginner not just for meditation, but for learning and training in general. This has been a simple and profound inspiration for practitioners of Zen and for many other arts and activities. The idea is to keep up the open, curious and modest attitude that we usually have when we start studying something.

When something fascinated me as a child, my mother always encouraged me to explore it and make something of my own out of it. For example, when I was about eight years old, I was utterly intrigued by the jungle, its animals, plants, stories and wonders, also nourished by Tintin, the hero of the comic book adventures created by Belgian illustrator Hergé, who also coined the term *ligne claire.* I ended up turning my room into a jungle with the help of my mother and my stepfather. We painted the walls with fantasy animals and filled the room with old tree trunks on which we hung real bananas. The forest was truly the creation of a Beginner's Mind!

Recently we heard another interpretation of the term by Zen monk Thich Nhat Hanh, who says that it clearly reveals what a person "wants to be." Thanks to his own Beginner's Mind, he already realized as a child that he

wanted to be a monk. According to his interpretation, it is "the deep intention, the deepest desire that one person may have." This means that we will devote ourselves more intensely, passionately and patiently to something if we sense that it is really a need, a predilection and a "calling." In my case, that something is making and sharing music. I already felt that way as a child. I am enthralled by sounds, rhythms, by all musical phenomena; music gives me a sense of security and, at the same time, a sense of the unknown. My grandfather Walter Anderegg, a passionate music lover, used to say: "Music is heaven on earth."

But let's go back to the first meaning of the Beginner's Mind, since we want to talk about the relationship between music, mind and movement, especially aikido. We will address the second meaning of the Beginner's Mind later when we talk about the joy of learning and diving into the unknown.

Andrea: I had already done some aikido at the university in Zurich when I first started studying biology. I was instantly fascinated by the immediacy, by the beautiful spiral and effective movements. Then when I moved to the Netherlands for my Master's degree I looked for an opportunity to train aikido. In the telephone book, I found the dojo (training location) of Sensei Lewis Bernaldo de Quiros in Haarlem. The first time I went to the dojo, a senior class was practicing, so I just watched. The atmosphere on the mat was intense and concentrated. I saw that the students were not just repeating the movements, but were really studying them and Sensei was observing and giving hints. I realized that this was something I could keep on learning for my whole life. I was really thrilled by this insight. Being able to indulge, to keep on perfecting, to always be curious about this art – this was something that made it very attractive to me.

I was lucky to have found this particular dojo; I am still learning now, every day, on my own and as a teacher and student in my dojo, but the classes and camps of Lewis Bernaldo de Quiros are still an important support on my journey.

N: I had a similar experience. I started aikido relatively late – I was twenty-nine – and for three reasons: I had long been fascinated by the Japanese approach to combining techniques of movement with aesthetics and philosophy in the martial arts, although I was a strict pacifist. It seems so paradoxical to me. So I wanted to find a non-competitive martial art based on nonviolence and cooperation. One day I was mugged in the middle of the city in broad daylight, but in an underpass. What shocked me most was not the man's brutality but his tempo, timing and presence – and my complete lack of all three in that situation. I felt completely helpless, powerless and outfoxed. This triggered my decision to start studying aikido and not just talk about it.

I turned to the telephone book – like you! Maybe there's a cosmic telephone book?! – chose the nearest dojo, called and started training that same evening. And I had exactly the same reaction as you did: this can be a lifelong dedication to in-depth learning. Just as I had been doing for years in music but now starting again from scratch. My body fell apart and had to be put together again. I so enjoyed being a beginner, experiencing the process all over again!

Freeze, Fight, Flight – Reaction Patterns and Alternative Responses

A: In aikido we practice again and again how to deal with challenges in a physical, nonverbal way. Aikido is a form of communication – intelligent and partnership-oriented physical communication. The basics are simple movements and exercises, which we practice every time we are in the dojo, for years. In this way, they gradually become so ingrained in our bodies that we move without thinking.

We all have reaction patterns that we fall back on when under stress: freeze, fight or flight. In a physical attack situation, this would be: just freezing up and being punched, punch back or run away. Depending on the situation, any of the three reactions might be appropriate and they are important patterns for survival and stemming from our evolution. With aikido we can "unlearn" these reactions, make them less prominent, move them more into the background of our repertoire and learn a fourth approach, an inspired, creative and appropriate response: connecting with an attack, deflecting its impact and taking down the attacker, or immobilizing him/her, while still taking care of both individuals. Aikido techniques are born of an ethical approach that involves seeking a joint resolution to conflict rather than increasing it.

Conflicts in life invariably trigger a biochemical and hence a physical reaction. Aikido practice is molded into our bodies through long-term training. These responses, thus refined and automated, are more readily available when needed in any life circumstance. A more intellectual approach such as communication training, psychotherapy or life coaching largely emphasizes a "detour" via logical thinking and analysis.

As an alternative response to a noncombat conflict situation, aikido accepts the conflict, then moves in from a state of balance and calmness, taking up a broader perspective, respecting the opponent's perspective, joining it and turning it into something both parties agree with. Our ancient warrior energy is transformed into a peaceful consciousness.

N: Usually, as an artist in a performance, we are not physically under attack but we are under extreme pressure and deeply committed to a process of communication. Being on stage and performing in a relaxed, awake, connected manner with our partners on stage and with the audience is comparable to a fight. We often feel extreme urgency, stress, pressure, tension. We have a reduced capacity to communicate with ourselves and the world. So this peaceful warrior energy you mentioned is essential.

In martial arts and in all performing arts, facing and reflecting one's own fears, needs and self-image is fundamental. We have to train physically and mentally in order to become free and creative in acting, connecting and responding – instead of being dictated by the above-mentioned freeze, fight, flight, or FFF-behavior, as it is called. The interconnectedness of mind and movement is obvious here. Today every good youth team in sports has a physical AND a mental coach; it is positively bizarre that neither of these exist in the world of professional music. Once again, Shunryu Suzuki says this clearly and simply: “Calmness of mind does not mean you should stop your activity. Real calmness should be found in activity itself. We say it is easy to have calmness in inactivity, it is hard to have calmness in activity, but calmness in activity is true calmness.”

Thanks for the Attack!

A: For most people an attack/conflict is probably seen as something negative, something to be afraid of and definitely something you want to avoid. In aikido we learn to be thankful for the attack and to even become curious about learning how to deal with it. We understand that we need the attacker for our own personal growth. When we experience that by staying connected with the technique, e.g. a wristlock, which can be quite rigorous and painful, it “miraculously” turns into something that is not painful anymore. Or being thrown to the floor by a strong technique can be devastating at first, you might get hurt, but there is also the experience of getting up again – and again.

There are many life situations where it is not possible to run away or freeze, for example, a sickness or death in your family. What we have learned from the physical experience of connecting with an attack, connecting with pain, can be helpful in such situations. It’s a conscious decision to turn it into something positive.

Nana Korobi Ya Oki is a Japanese proverb that translates as “Fall down seven times, get up eight.” It means that we will fall down in life many times, not just two or three, but many more times. We must not be discouraged by falling down, it is part of the practice of life. We get up and continue on our way.

N: I find it especially inspiring that "continuing on our way" is partner-oriented in aikido and part of the flow. Instead of fighting somebody or something, we can choose to act and work in a cooperative and intelligent way. In aikido, this fluid, flexible, respectful movement is called *awase*, the Japanese word for "blending, melting together, mixing." It is a term for connecting, staying in contact, staying interested, becoming one in a movement. 1 + 1 = 1.

A: Yes, this is an essential ingredient in aikido. *Awase* is embedded in a sequence of moments to describe a "contact process": *ki musubi* (making contact, creating attention), *yobi dashi* (entering, triggering an attack), *awase* (blending, melting together) and *zanshin* (balanced mind, a state of awareness, relaxed alertness). Ultimately, these qualities are intermixed and available when needed; we are able to translate these qualities of togetherness into other life situations.

Listen and Shoot Like Lucky Luke

N: In training, when our sensei Lewis Bernaldo de Quiros wants to create awareness and draw attention to exactly this sequence, he often says “listen to your partner!” When we listen with all our senses, the whole interaction can become more “musical” and fluid; it is like entering into a dialogue or playing or dancing together. Here, listening means being receptive with all our senses in order to really perceive the whole and not only our own view. At first, “just” passively listening and doing “nothing” feels totally paradoxical and confusing. But there is a difference between listening and hearing. Hearing is indeed passive while listening can be interpreted as a nonjudgmental, active, basic condition which, with practice and time, enables us to react intuitively and faster than our thinking. Like Lucky Luke, who shoots faster than his shadow. This is exactly the challenge we face when we play music live and interact, especially when we improvise: we have no time to think. We must lead and follow, initiate and cooperate at the same moment, be surprising and reliable in the same sequence, fresh and traditional at once, balanced and flexible in mind and body.

This steady, balanced flow of creative and responsive presence under pressure must be trained; it has nothing to do with inspiration or talent or spontaneous action. As you mentioned, our evolutionary background needs to be put in relation to new physical and mental repertoires. Primatologist Frans De Waal succinctly summarizes the results of studying our closest relatives: “Humans are also animals.” We are not abstract mind machines on a branch of the evolution tree far away from other animals.

Martial arts and music are similar phenomena when it comes to performing and long-term learning: we need to integrate age-old behavior patterns and our capacity to learn. Butoh dancer Imre Thormann, with whom I had the chance to collaborate, told me: "Maybe the long-term development to upright walking is not finished yet."

I once asked my Feldenkrais teacher Ueli Tank why humans can't learn to move like a cat that lands on its feet when falling from a tree – what a martial art movement! He countered: "Can a cat learn to play the piano?"

We cannot perform better or "safer" by just practicing a lot of techniques and preparing performances intellectually with analytic strategies. As holistically talented animals, we have to go deeper into the togetherness of body, mind, emotion and movement.

Kubrick's Bone

N: Being conscious of our behavior is only the first step. When we train to expand our presence, we discover an integral and holistic way of connecting more to ourselves and at the same time to one or more partners in space and time.

A: For a long time it was not known that we have a sense that enables us to feel our own body. In his book *The Man Who Mistook His Wife for a Hat* (1985), neurologist Oliver Sacks describes the case of a woman unable to recognize her own body because she has lost this sense entirely. Obviously, we assume that we can recognize our own bodies but as a shiatsu therapist, I have noted that many people lack a deeper connection to their bodies. They see them as something necessary to carry their brain, their intellect around. The body is either neglected or merely something that gets in the way: Why can't I sit at my computer for more than seven hours, why does my back hurt, why do my eyes burn?

Or we think we can optimize it with fitness, surgery or a solarium. Martial arts and many other body arts offer a holistic approach that enables us to take advantage of the beneficial consequences for our health. They help us to "inhabit" our own bodies, to use all of our senses to *swim* in our environment, to be in constant exchange

with it. Years of training not only improve physical aspects, but also sharpen our mental sensitivity.

N: According to Siri Hustvedt, in her book *The Delusions of Certainty* (2017), the idea that abstract concepts and thinking are an embodied form of internalized movement is acquiring traction in numerous disciplines, including philosophy, psychology, anthropology, linguistics, sociology and the humanities. Maybe this is connected to what the ancient Greek philosopher Anaxagoras meant by saying "Humans think because they have hands." Or when Stravinsky says: "Our hands find things that our brain does not." In the legendary opening sequence of Stanley Kubrick's *Space Odyssey*, we see how the hand of an ancient ape picks up a bone and discovers its potential by moving it. The bone acquires a different function.

A: Kubrick's bone turned into a drumstick or the wooden weapons used in aikido. In training, the constant improvement of our technique depends on and is driven by subtle changes we make to the less tangible mental and energetic levels: 1. being first of all connected to our own center; 2. being open to our surroundings, to the feedback of our sensations; 3. being focused and keeping an ongoing focus throughout a technique and even throughout the whole class; and 4. being calm and relaxed

even when under the pressure of an attack or multiple attackers. By training these mental, kinetic and energetic aspects, our technique will also improve almost naturally.

Expand Your Now

N: As you say, there are also energetic and kinetic ways of describing fundamental life phenomena, instead of a division into body, mind, soul, spirit. In the word ai-ki-do we find ki.

A: Ki, simply put, is the life energy that flows through us all. It can be felt on levels of individual energy, physical interaction and presence. I can perform a technique formally, without my ki. Then it is merely a technical execution, which uses leverage and timing for the result. But if I put ki in it, I am more expansive, inclusive, my whole presence radiates in the room and the technique becomes more powerful and irresistible. It resonates with partner and space.

Developing a sensitivity for ki is also an integral part of training: being able to sense the presence of an attacker, the ki of the attack about to be launched, is a necessary prerequisite for an adapted response. Ki is also the basis of shiatsu, where the therapist's touch, stretching and rotation help the body to regain an energetic balance.

If you train in aikido, shiatsu or another art attentively and with dedicated intention, your ki will develop naturally and, along with it, the ability to sense ki. This is also an essential ingredient in stage performances.

N: Absolutely. Playing correctly is not enough; it is important to connect and expand the ki, "expand the now." The now is a fragile nothing. If you want to catch and analyze it, it vanishes. Keyboard legend Joe Zawinul loved boxing and mentioned, in a BBC documentary, that when he stopped training, it affected his performance. In his own words, "When I am on tour and I don't have the opportunity to box, things are getting difficult. The timing is off, the speed is off. You don't see as fast, you cannot react. As a matter of fact, you do see it but you cannot do it. And that's the secret." This is a statement about moving mentally and physically in a musical speed space. The now is too fast for analytic thinking. You have to think with the body. To stay in the flow and groove and even be creative in it is a question of body balance and timing.

A: A treasure in this context is the following text by Zen master Taisen Deshimaru-Roshi quoted from his book *The Zen Way to the Martial Arts* (1991): "In Budo the concept of *sutemi* is essential. [...] abandoning the body, letting go of it, forgetting the ego and following nothing but the cosmic system. Abandon attachments, personal desires, ego. [...] Everything must come from here and now. The body moves naturally, automatically, unconsciously, without any personal intervention or awareness. But if we begin to use our faculty of reasoning, our actions become slow and hesitant. Questions arise, the mind tires, and the consciousness flickers and wavers like a candle flame in a breeze.

In Budo, consciousness and action must always be one. When you begin aikido or kendo you repeat the wasa, techniques, over and over, and the *kata,* the forms. You repeat them endlessly for two or three years, until forms and techniques become a habit, second nature. At first, when you're learning them, you have to use your personal consciousness. It's the same in learning to play the piano or drums or guitar. […] In Zen as in Budo, we must achieve direct, immediate unity with the truth of the cosmos. Our thinking must think beyond our personal consciousness, with our body and not just our brain. Think with the whole body."

Responsibility Shift from the Teacher to Yourself

N: So when we compare sports, stage performances and martial arts, we find they have a lot in common. But there are also interesting differences, such as the shift from competition to artistic and spiritual development, which is also implied in what Deshimaru says above.

A: Compared to sports or today's competitive martial arts, traditional Japanese martial arts do not aim to compete with an opponent or a competitor; we compete with ourselves. As Donn F. Draeger puts it: "The dojo becomes respected as a place of severe confrontation between oneself and one's self" (in: *Classical Budo*, 1973). We want to be better than yesterday; we are faced with our own insecurities, our inner judge, our reluctance to let go of the known. This may be more difficult to measure when there is no hard competitive test. The right amount of challenge is required to prevent getting frustrated about not being good enough or deluded into thinking we have already mastered a certain task.

Initially and for a long time, the teacher has the responsibility of determining the right amount of challenge. Therefore, it is very important to find a capable teacher who can guide us for a large part of our journey. As we proceed on the learning path and the responsibility shifts more to ourselves, it is vital to be relentlessly but gently demanding and honest with ourselves.

N: Erna Ronca was the most important teacher I had for smooth and effective movement on the piano, for my touch and sound on the piano and for preparing me for my own responsibility as a pianist. She has further developed the technique of playing out of the center, guided from the elbow and with weight shifting in flow. She was a student

of the British pianist Hubert Harry who studied this technique with his teacher, Romanian pianist Dinu Lipatti. At the same time I practiced the Feldenkrais Method and then also Gyrotonics and Gyrokinesis.[1]

Later I started to train aikido with Hanspeter Dietz and with you in the spirit of Lewis Bernaldo de Quiros and Morihiro Saito Sensei. I realized that there were clear parallels in teaching music, martial arts or Zen: passing on the technique and attitude along the line, every time with a slight change and development, based on a long deepening process.

A: I learned to observe carefully while studying in the Iwama dojo in Japan with Morihiro Saito Sensei, the longest serving student of aikido founder Morihei Ueshiba. The lessons were in Japanese, but oral instructions were kept to a minimum anyway and Sensei only corrected sporadically. My Beginner's Mind was so strong that it drove me to travel to Iwama alone, as a novice still with a white belt.

N: This is quite remarkable since in Japan even a first degree black belt is called "a serious beginner."

A: Our teacher Lewis Bernaldo de Quiros lived and studied in Japan with Morihiro Saito Sensei for nine years. The deepening process and development that I experienced

1 Feldenkrais Method in a group with teacher Ueli Tank and Gyrokinesis Method with dancer and trainer Niki Good.

through Lewis Sensei included his experience in the Alexander Technique, emphasizing smooth and healthy movements while sustaining the sharpness and effectiveness of Saito's lineage. In addition, Lewis's analytical mind and clear teaching spoke to my "scientific soul."

Science and Art: Translating Creative Strategies

A: Science is another area where the Beginner's Mind plays a big role. At our kitchen table we often discuss scientific research or phenomena in ecology that are more connected to my academic background. What fascinates you as a musician about this?

N: An inspired scientist is deeply dedicated to a specific subject matter, consistently seeking to learn and explore. My step-sister Nora Somaini, a theater director, an ordained Zen nun and a drama professor, once told me that she finds people especially beautiful and attractive when she sees them working with full dedication. That also applies to science, like your books about biological phenomena. When I read about the creative work of scientists, it gives me the chance to reflect and develop my view on the nature of composing and making music. Studying creative strategies in other fields can be very fruitful. I learned a lot from linguistics, especially Wittgenstein's late work, which helped me understand how a coherent musical language can be developed, shared and communicated. When asked about the meaning of words in relation to music, Igor Stravinsky replied: "Sometimes I feel like those old men Gulliver met on the trip to Laputa. They renounced language and tried to communicate with objects. A composer is always in this position because he has no verbal control over his music. The only real comment on a piece of music is another piece of music."

The book *Vanishing Act* by nature photographer Art Wolfe (2005) about animal mimicry gave me clues to a more contextual form of improvisation as a band organism. And there's another one from your bookshelf by journalist and environmental activist Claire Nouvian about current research on deep-sea creatures. It's titled *The Deep – The Extraordinary Creatures of the Abyss* (2007) and it activated a chain reaction that led to the title of the Ronin album *LLYRÌA*. But not only that, it ultimately led to a meeting, while on tour in the United States, with the discoverer of the real Llyrìa animal, marine biologist George Matsumoto of the Monterey Bay Aquarium Research Institute.

I find the precise work and engaged curiosity of scientists inspiring. A journalist once called me a scientist of groove. This may sound paradoxical again: intellectual science and sensual groove. But I embrace this combination and like to emphasize the common spirit of these two worlds: the dedication, the passion and the patience. I think serious scientists are also sensually attracted to their subject matter. I admire professional curiosity, curiosity as a profession. Darwin is one of the best examples of this. His passion, patience and curiosity profoundly changed how we look at ourselves and the universe. To me, Stravinsky is the Darwin of music history. Like Darwin, he didn't see himself as a revolutionary, but more as somebody who changed the nature of perceiving music. He suddenly discovered rhythm, groove and pattern organization in a new way although they had always been there.

A: I have always been curious about the world around me – since my earliest childhood. I loved collecting and saving all kinds of insects, worms and skeletons, not always to the delight of my parents. But I also had this love for curiosity itself, and that's what has always fascinated me about doing research. We might choose a field of study to learn what is known about it, but I was curious about what is NOT known, about formulating questions and designing an experiment to find possible answers. And then accepting the fact that a possible answer may not be the "truth" but just the most likely explanation for a certain phenomenon. That also means a willingness to abandon the explanation, should a simpler and more elegant one become apparent.

N: After my music studies I spent three years studying philosophy, linguistics and a bit of musicology. Mainly I was interested in philosophical aesthetics but during my studies my interest drifted completely to the philosophy of language. Even so, after the midterm exams I stopped and focused exclusively on music. On the one hand, the work for the university and my music career at the same time had become too much for me, and on the other hand, I had discovered how complex it is to create a healthy balance of mental and physical activities. Thinking is an intense activity and can challenge the body very much. In ancient times, people would walk and think or talk at the same time – a fruitful combination that fosters conversation and philosophizing. It is not our nature to sit for long periods of time and doing so often contributes to mental immobility. The invention of the chair created more and different problems for mankind than the wheel. My chiropractor and acupuncturist Thomas Lüthy – for me kind of a voodoo guru – told me that extended sitting at the computer and the spread of mobile phones has dramatically increased the number of people, and even children, with back problems. You shifted from the work of a scientist to devote yourself to movement, body therapy, aikido and shiatsu.

A: Influenced by the study of aikido, I had started training in shiatsu when I was a postdoc student at the university. I gradually realized that I wanted to give more attention to these other important aspects of my life. I needed to let go of the academic life.

The rigorous questioning, the analytical mind can be very helpful in practical domains. I am used to reading medical research about acupuncture or shiatsu for example. But in shiatsu therapy and also when teaching aikido, especially with children, I often work on keeping my analytical mind in check and letting myself be guided more by my intuition and by the energy and needs of the clients and students. These are manifested in their bodies, so I had to practice and learn how to perceive them.

A Modul Is a *Kata* Is a *Koan*

N: A participant in one of our workshops once said that ritual groove music should be available in pharmacies and covered by health insurance. There is a kernel of truth in this idea. Ritual groove music is a form of therapy for me. I need the two energies of kinetic groove and meditative presence to survive. We are familiar with this holistic approach of including movement in art and creativity education from other concepts, as proposed, for example, by Johannes Itten, a master at the Bauhaus.

Training creativity in a holistic way effectively sharpens all our senses. In Japanese martial arts, a tool for acquiring this body knowledge is the *kata*, a formalized movement learning sequence. But it is more than a physical exercise.

A: Yes. Deshimaru, as cited above, talks mostly about *kata* as form. It is also an agreement between the training partners. Donn F. Draeger writes about *kata* in ancient martial arts: "Kata are filled, as it were, with physical *koan*, or conundrums, situations that evoke technical crises. They are devices through which the trainee's mind is shocked into action. Physical *koan* are to be met head on and conquered in the sense that they are overcome through adherence to prescribed form; and even when this is not achieved, a degree of controlled skill is developed. Whether skill develops poorly or not is of little consequence, for it is the quality of endeavor, endeavor made without artifice and with a sincere heart that matters. Through meeting and solving the physical koan it is suggested that what is learned is comprehended not by analytic thought but by a unity of will and dedicated effort. Kata now becomes the expression of the trainee's mind and body, a mirror that reflects the degree of their

> integration. *Kata* brings the trainee to realize that his mind and body have been going in divergent directions to a considerable degree, as evidence of which the mind often calls for the performance of a movement by the muscles that the latter fail to carry out."
>
> A *kata* is the signature and distillate of a certain style or school.

N: A musical Modul can be used like a *kata:* it is a sequence with a specific topic, for example a cycle shift of patterns in five and seven. We can practice its basic topic alone or in a group and constantly increase the challenge until a free treatment of the material is possible. It is a tool to sharpen our skills and communicate with our partners on the basis of a clear agreement, comparable to standards in jazz, which everybody in the scene is familiar with.

You said that aikido is a form of communication. What we train here can also change our capacity to communicate. I see the ritual groove music and its philosophy as a form of nonviolent communication and inspiration, a creative and open system to share forms, strategies, processes and ideas of cooperation. It is not designed as an avant-garde attack but more as a partner-oriented invitation. I emphasize the groove aspect as a social energy since, like composer Heiner Goebbels once said, groove has a collective ownership. It is not someone's invention but a sensual and basic energy that allows new experiments based on social sharing. Groove and flow as kinetic phenomena cannot be forced. They have to appear naturally by the pliability (lissomeness) of their originators. They are created by focus, trust, mental and physical balance and natural, smooth movement – a state of meditative presence.

We all know the three levels of observing a performer. We suffer when we see a performer working hard and at the limits of his capacity. We are impressed by an eclectic and virtuoso performer who demonstrates a level that we will never be able to reach. And we are simply inspired and encouraged for our own life projects by a performer who naturally and effortlessly shares an intense moment of quality, togetherness and art. This effortless mastery is a mystic paradox: so much training, awareness and consciousness behind an action that is perceived as natural and simple.

A: This is exactly the same in aikido. When facing an attacker all that counts is this presence. Being completely present with all our senses, being ready for everything, yet at the same time not expecting anything. Any thought about the opponent not holding his *bokken* the right way or looking frightening will slow me down, and the response to a possible attack will be too late. Facing somebody with neither affection nor fear, neither pride nor aggression.

In our workshops we often speak, in that context, about being neutrally engaged. Again a paradox: The knowledge and experience of lifelong training and of real conflict situations are embedded in our bodies but we need to forget them to be able to listen and then to move, to play freely with what we know.

Individual and Collective Learning

Participants in our annual summer workshop Music Training, Meditation and Aikido are mostly musicians interested in this broader context. Aikido is often new to them. So staying simple and clear in our exercises, reducing them to the core principles and studying them through the simplest exercises is essential. This is also largely what training in the dojo is about. The goal is to enable musicians, performers or others to transfer these exercises and experiences to their everyday lives. The most important principles are groundedness, relaxation, connection and expanded awareness.

N: This transfer is crucial. As mentioned, aikido also helped me apply these learning processes to music training. The idea of a music dojo came from seeing this in aikido: sharing interest and dedication independently of your level. The beginners and experts can learn from each other. They both have a serious responsibility for their own learning and for learning together. This creates a form of collective learning with a Beginner's Mind.

Poetic Police

After listening to the sound check at a festival in Germany, the local piano tuner asked me if I did martial arts. I said yes, aikido. Pleased to hear that, he told me he was learning a special form of aikido with his master who lived nearby and he would love to arrange a meeting with him. I was politely defensive in reacting to this sudden invitation since I was on a concert tour and focusing on that was my priority. Besides, I didn't want to disturb a master I didn't know, especially as I was not yet very advanced in aikido. But the piano tuner insisted; he thought his master might also like my music. I deal with piano tuners all over the world, but this one was quite unusual, a big strapping guy, almost intimidating. I finally gave in anyway, although I felt a little nervous about what awaited me. He drove me to his master's house after the concert. We stopped in front of a modest terrace house, where he rang the bell on the second floor. To my surprise, the gentle, energetic man who opened the door was small in stature. He welcomed us politely, showing us to the kitchen where he offered us tea. On the way, we walked past the living room where his daughter was camping in a tent. I instantly relaxed in the friendly and creative atmosphere of this apartment.

We started to chat and it turned out that the man was a professional guitar teacher for children and a professional martial artist at the same time, or we should say: he was a true poetic warrior, as I would learn. We had a wonderful, inspiring time in this small kitchen, drinking tea and talking about the connection of music and martial arts. He played beautifully on the strings of his guitar and then showed me his technique for drawing the string of a Mongolian warrior bow, which didn't budge a single centimeter when I tried. He told me that the force and impact of an arrow shot by such a bow can be stronger than that of a machine gun.

He also told me that he trains the local police force in close combat. Comparing combat traditions over the centuries, he explained that in Japan many martial art forms flourished between 1603 and 1868, a period of relative peace although ensured by the military government of the Tokugawa shoguns. Former warriors were now cultivating martial arts, calligraphy, tea ceremony or poetry, all in the same spirit. Then he asked me an unforgettable, rhetorical question: "Which police officer today can invent a poem off the cuff?"

At that instant, I understood the common ground between the fine arts and the martial arts. They have the same immediacy; they both cope with confronting violence, love, life and death.

Ki and Presence

Instead of separating the different aspects of body and mind and of feeling, moving and thinking, we can see them as different emanations of the resonating life energy ki.

While it is valuable to localize and analyze these different aspects of being for certain processes in our existence, they can also be understood holistically as resonating presence.

A performer needs to go into the state of resonating presence to become a medium for the music. To sharpen and expand one's presence means to expand the now in space and time.

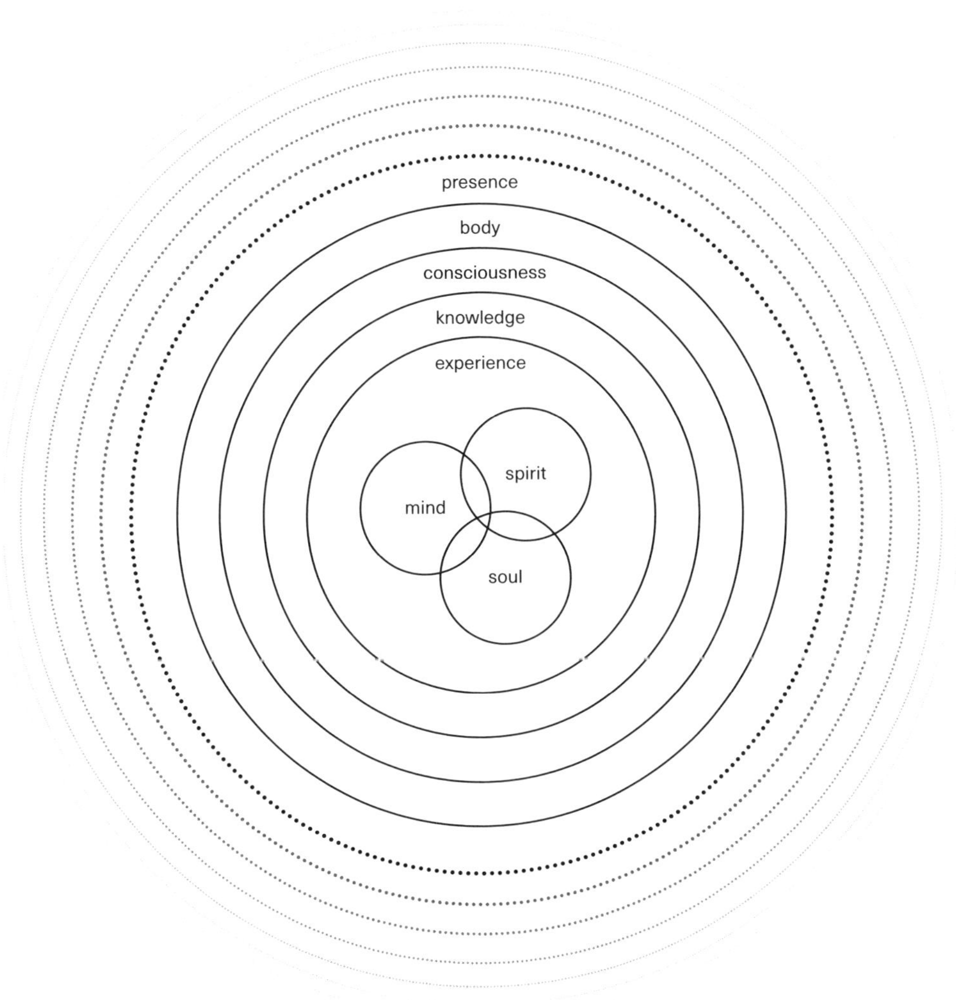
presence
body
consciousness
knowledge
experience
spirit
mind
soul

Circles and Cycles

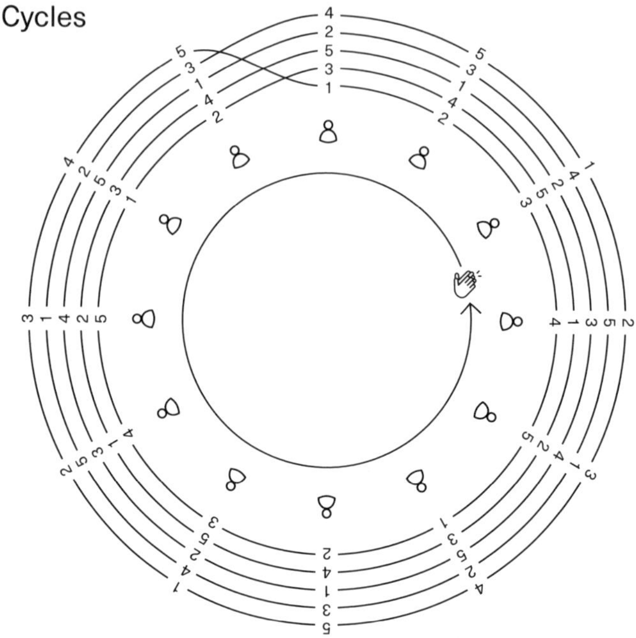

Training setting for group circle games, here with twelve people. The task is to pass on to the next person in the circle the clapping, the counting (here up to five) and/or the ball(s). It is also possible to work with shakers on a next level (see also p. 162 for the shaker meditation instruction).

The goal of the game is to stay balanced, present, *awase* and flow-focused while keeping the connection, time, tempo, rhythm and cycles. In order to develop this, it is important to keep it simple at first and train each circle alone (throwing, clapping, counting, shakering) before varying.

The game can be varied on several levels (Figure 1):
– various combinations of clapping/counting/ball throwing/shakering
– by choosing different directions for clapping/counting/throwing
– by increasing multitasking (e.g. one hand is shakering, one hand clapping on the side of the body in one direction and counting goes in the other direction of the circle)
– by using cue signs for changes of direction: such as saying “and” before the regular counting number to change the direction of the counting circle
– by increasing the number of balls in the circle
– by including stepping the main pulse
– by increasing tempo and/or meter and/or rhythm combinations (e.g. counting in quarter notes and clapping in dotted eight notes)

Passing balls or clapping freely can also be trained separately to establish the paths of communication in connection to all possible partners. One or several balls can then not only be passed to the next person in the circle but to every partner in the circle. It is essential to first establish the connection before throwing the ball, otherwise somebody will be hit. This can also be combined with all the rhythmic variations above (Figures 2 and 3). The connection between group members can also be trained with additional tools like the aikido *jo* (see next pages).

It is essential for these exercises to be trained without competition in the spirit of partnership and egoless interest in flow and groove. It is necessary to always work on a group level, which allows all members to take part and develops the circle as a real higher organism.

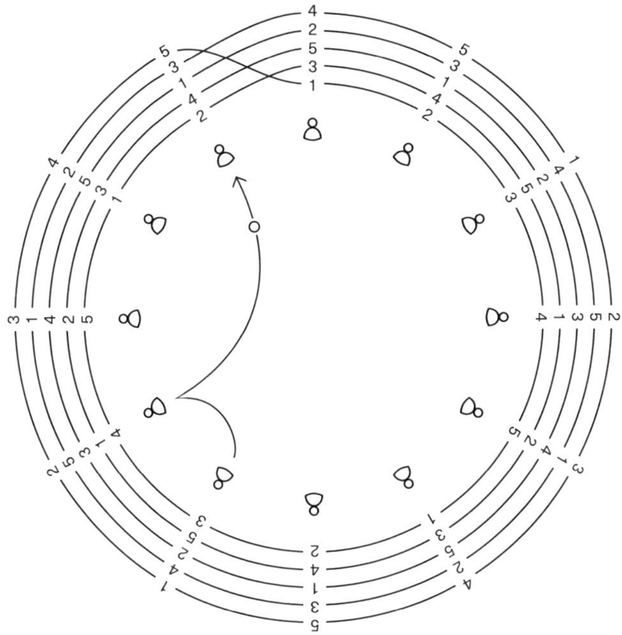

1-5	counting
	person
	clapping
o	soft juggling ball

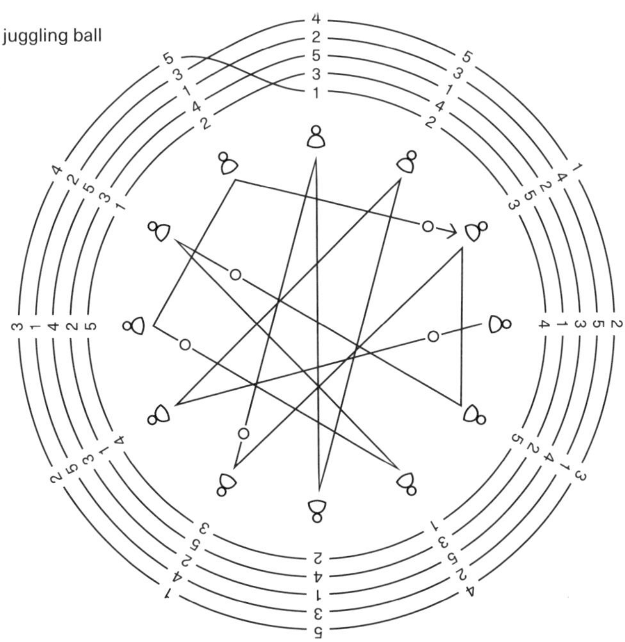

percussion
handmade in
Germany

"A good stance and posture reflect a proper state of mind."

Morihei Ueshiba (1883–1969), aikido founder

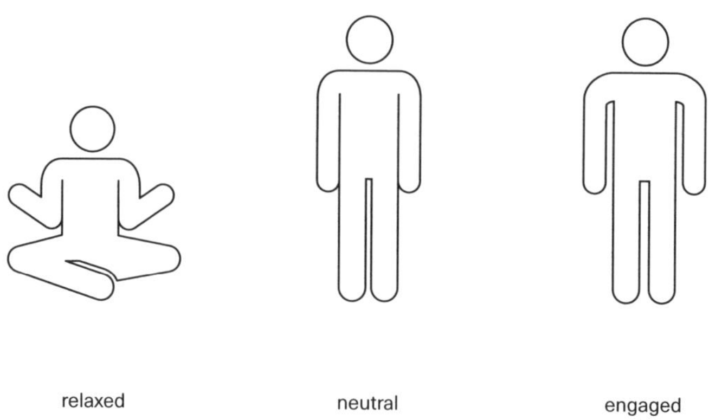

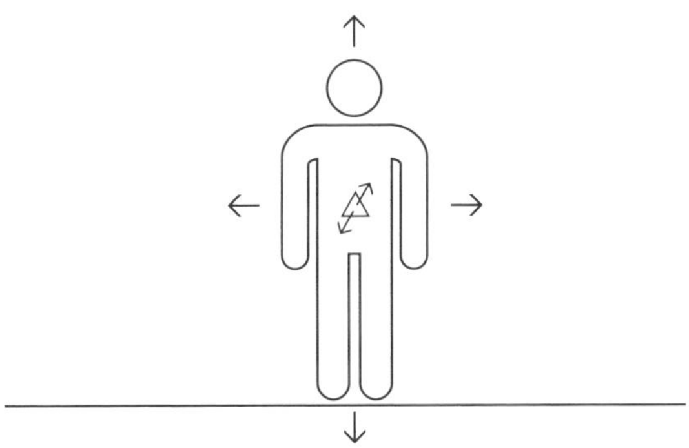

posture

The eight directions of expansion: up, down, left, right, forward, backward, outward, inward

Three Levels of Flow

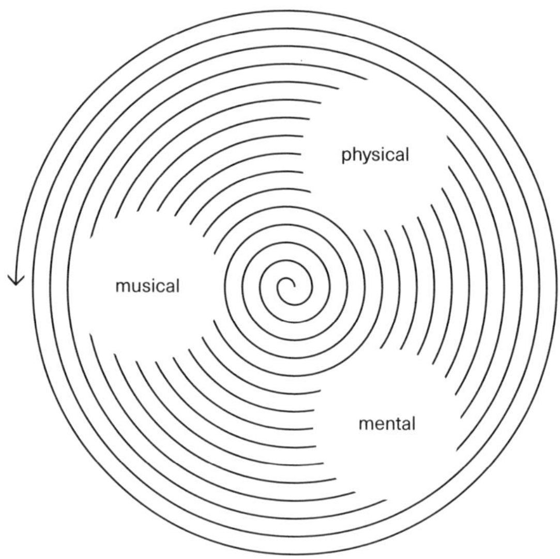

We perceive processes of flow on different levels. In the stream of organically emanated music, in lissome physical moving, in focused thinking. The perception of these flow phenomena influence each other. An interruption on one level can infect another level. A mistake in playing, for example, can confuse the movement, the mind and then also the flow of music. Irritations and surprises always happen, they can be integrated into the flow of music, movement and mind when the general flow is strong and stable. Therefore it is essential to merge the mental, musical and physical flow for present and joyful performing.

Blob
Body Learning

Bio-Poetic Phenomenon

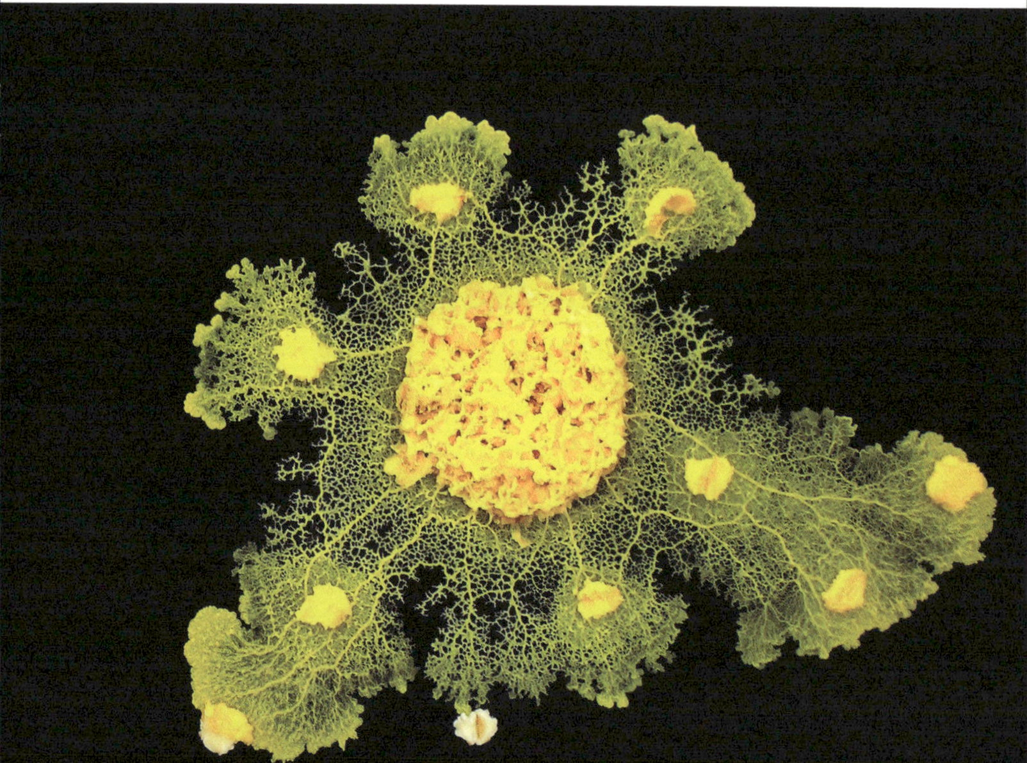

It comes in many shapes and sizes, changing from microscopic amoeba to a mushroom-like body that can be several feet across, but the blob is neither a fungus nor a plant. It is a one-celled, “many-headed” slime mold. It has no eyes, and yet it can detect nutrition. Without mouth or stomach it can digest food. Without legs or wings it can move up to 4 cm per hour.

It can form a network of connections to food sources and find the shortest way out of a labyrinth. Without a brain, it can learn to move over obstacles and if two blobs are put together, knowledge is transferred from one to the other.

Just one cell and yet it can perceive its environment, integrate this information, make decisions and learn. The blob may bring new insights on the origins of intelligence and cognition.

Creativity does not always mean analyzing and responding intellectually but above all discovering a space and situation with intuitive body awareness.

"The purpose of today's training is to defeat yesterday's understanding."

Miyamoto Musashi (1584–1645), Japanese swordsman, philosopher, strategist, writer and ronin

Fan of Possibilities

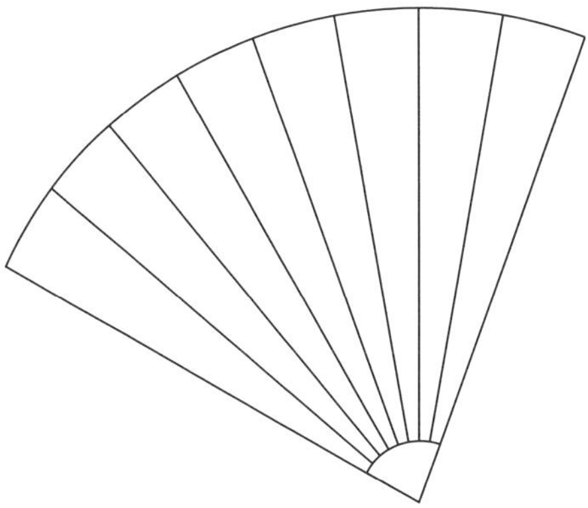

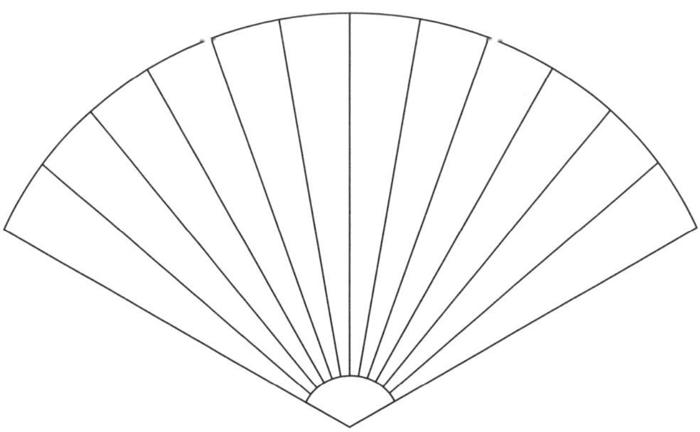

Training, practicing and rehearsing helps to create more and more perspectives on a matter. To be creative means to be interested in finding new possibilities in a familiar situation. We can open our mind to fan more wind of action.

stillr

giv

mo[illegible]er

awase

now globe

extension

initiation

movement in movement

focus

awareness

eripheral

1+1+1+...=1

take balance

curiosity

flow

zanshin

view

ki

invitation

center(s)

1+1=1

ss in movement

listening

connection

partnership

balance

neutral engagement

ent in stillness

Llyrìa
Ancient Evolution
Inspires Modern Creativity

Bio-Poetic Phenomenon

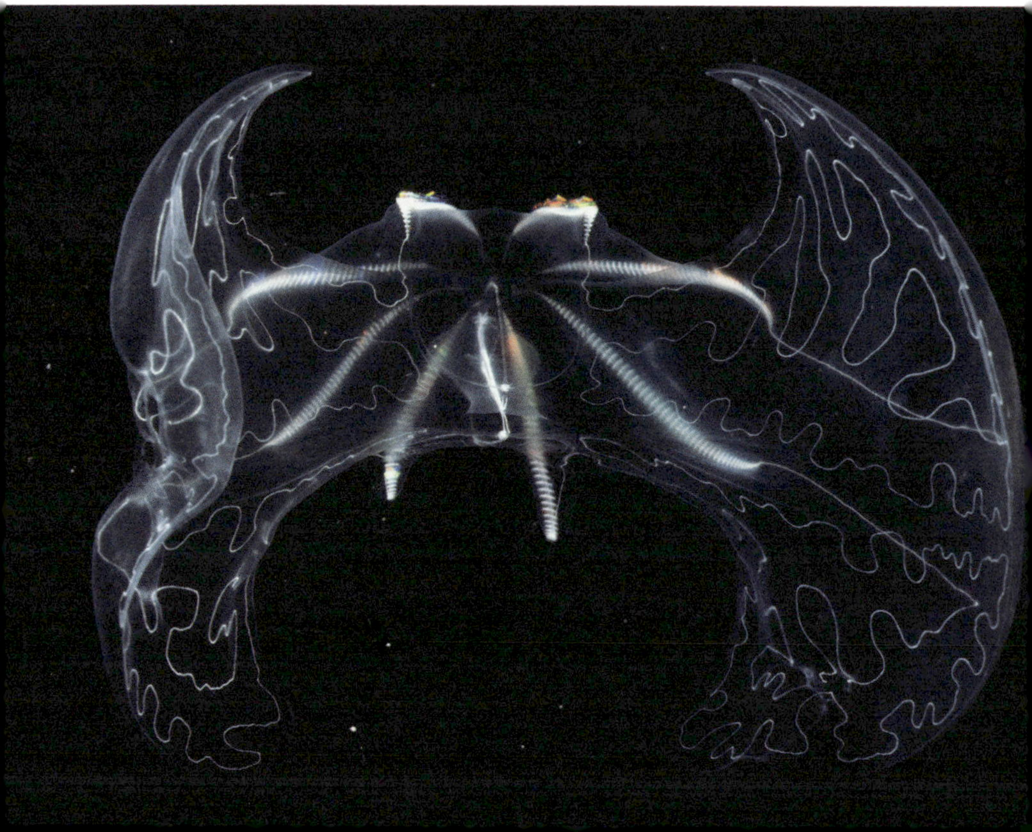

Every day, researchers at the Monterey Bay Aquarium Research Institute (MBARI) find new species in the deep sea of the San Andreas Fault. Recently, an enigmatic life form was discovered at depths ranging from 500 to 3000 m in a freezing cold habitat of complete darkness, vast emptiness and high pressure.

Almost nothing is known about this creature, how it behaves, how old it gets. It leads a weightless, transparent and bioluminescent life in complete darkness with a pressure of 300 kg/cm^2 around it.

This creature, known as Llyrìa, is a species of comb jelly (ctenophore). It possesses eight rows of tiny comb-like plates that flap back and forth to propel it through water. As the comb jelly swims, the rows of columns diffract light, thereby producing a shimmering rainbow effect. Naturally, this can only be seen when light falls on it, which is extremely rare in these surroundings. A hidden beauty.

A close look at a comb jelly's nervous system reveals that it is very different from all other species of the animal kingdom. This led a team of neurobiologists at the University of Florida to propose rewriting evolutionary history: one for the comb jelly, and one for everybody else, from jellyfish to us.

The evolution of music still contains many unknowns but by sharing the scientist's curiosity-driven spirit of exploration, a composer can discover new music creatures in the deep sea of creativity day after day.

From a Single Source

Composition, Interpretation and Improvisation as a Creative Cycle

When asked recently about current tendencies in new classical music, so-called indie classical, the New York music critic Alex Ross replied that composers have begun to perform their own music in concerts again. Jazz musicians traditionally play and interpret their own compositions, generally with their own bands. The members don't see themselves as specialists for the interpretation of their original works, but rather as a tight-knit group of like-minded artists, polishing something that promises to yield a shared musical result. So most jazz composers are also their own interpreters – and of course they improvise, too. This is obviously different in a concert of classical music. Interpreters play music by composers and there is very little improvisation. Why this difference in the musical practice of classical music and jazz and what does it tell us about the creative process of today's jazz?

The disappearance of extemporaneous playing

The Romantic music in the nineteenth century saw the onset of a slow process of specialization. A clear separation between composing, interpreting and improvising marked the development of musical practice. What Bach, Mozart or Chopin did as a matter of course, viewing their practice as different aspects in a musician's life,

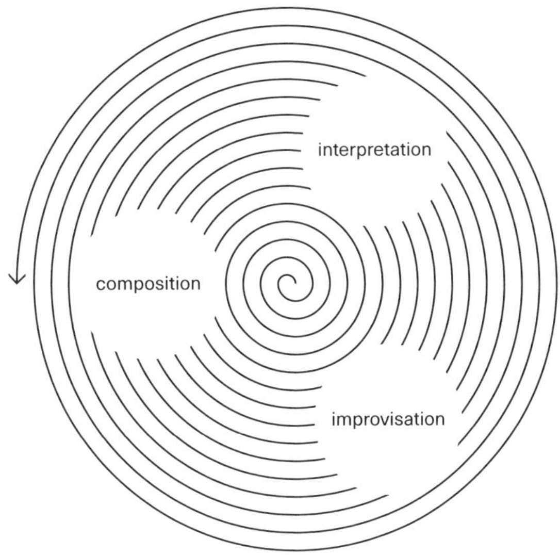

Source spiral: different musical processes and strategies like composition, interpretation and improvisation are nourished by the same source and influence each other.

no longer applies to most modern composers and interpreters. Before this process of specialization, improvisation in the form of spontaneous preluding, cadencing and rhapsodizing were a normal and highly appreciated expression of musical practice. The names of great improvisers up until the age of Romanticism are largely identical with the great composers that we know to this day: Bach, Mozart, Beethoven, Chopin. Even Anton Bruckner, a composer of eminently clear forms, was legendary for his organ improvisations in the era of High Romanticism.

A nascent awareness of musical styles as a historical factor led musicians to query in which style they should improvise. Previously, musicians warbled, fiddled and plucked mostly in their own styles, similarly to what we see in many folk music genres today, where stylistic concerns are eclipsed by the delight in making music.

Has the diversity of styles, from Bach to Boulez, turned improvisation into a sheer unsurmountable enterprise for interpreters and composers? Does the sensible solution really lie in the division of labor outlined above? It would certainly appear so. There are, of course, several renowned twentieth-century composers who are also professional interpreters, but improvisers have nearly vanished from the scene, with the exception of such musicians as George Gershwin, who transcend stylistic boundaries.

Moreover, the processes and results of composition have become more and more complex. Somewhere along the road to radical abstraction in New Music, improvisation as a natural creative resource, a conscious treatment of extemporized musical freedom, fell by the wayside, coupled with a growing tendency to treat "the work" of a composer as sacrosanct. Interpreters concentrate on the interpretation, bowing to the work in which every note has been clearly set by the composer's will. Only recently, after having seen several theater productions in Berlin, the great classical interpreter András Schiff wrote in the *Neue Zürcher Zeitung* (December 27, 2014) that fortunately, the interpreters of classical music don't take the same liberties as theater directors and actors do and are therefore less ruthless in their approach. Jazz cultivates the gap between interpretation and improvisation, combined with new forms of playing, new instruments and sounds, swing and groove, and such aesthetic and stylistic elements as hipness and an underground image.

Score part of “Modul 55” by Nik Bärtsch

Today, improvisation as a musical strategy is therefore fostered in selective contexts of the current musical landscape. Does so-called free improvisation or "contemporary" extemporization, as it were, require experience, knowledge and skill? Or is it as Keith Jarrett, one of the world's most renowned improvisers, says? He defines the beginning of each of his improvisations as a metaphysical zero point, from which he unleashes a new and uninfluenced idea. Are there (still) improvisers of unlimited potential, or are all improvisers simply cunning stylists who achieve freedom and flexibility only through technical skill, set pieces and stylistic know-how?

Would Mozart, arguably the most comprehensive improviser of his time, have been able to improvise as freely as Jarrett (or as ferociously as Cecil Taylor) if only he had chosen to? The futility of this question becomes apparent as soon as we transfer it to a current context and juxtapose two entirely different musical styles: Can a traditional musician from the Aka pygmy people be influenced by a piano étude by György Ligeti? Maybe a misleading question, but Ligeti was influenced by the music of the pygmies. Although structurally of comparable complexity, their musical worlds are the product of entirely distinct cultural techniques and reverberate specifically with experiences that are relevant and fruitful to their own respective style – Jarrett can interpret Mozart, but Mozart cannot interpret Jarrett. "Can" is used here in the sense of the French *savoir,* which means "knowing" or "being aware," in this case, of a musical context and its history. Interestingly, when talking about this concurrence, Keith Jarrett describes classical music and jazz as parallel worlds: "You have to lock the one into a closet for the other to be able to come out." (*Tages-Anzeiger,* May 8, 2015). One would think that his wide experience with improvisation on tonal music would have been helpful to him when playing Bach and Mozart, but strangely enough, this doesn't seem to be the case.

So, even one of the stylistically most accomplished improvisers of our time draws a clear line between classical interpretation and jazz improvisation.

Apparently, the improviser faces the same task as the composer – and, by implication, the composer's executive hand, the interpreter: never take anything for granted; question everything. Paraphrasing Socrates' famous sentence, Morton Feldman asks: "How do I know what I don't know?"

As professional creative artists, Jarrett and Ligeti are fully aware of the limits of their musical knowledge – both technically and physically (*pouvoir,* being able to or having the skill to) as well as intellectually and philosophically (*savoir,* knowing). Every improvising musician has role models and influences, and may even be engaged in a dialogue with them, just like all composers. Thus, they know what they know and what they are capable of. Stravinsky once remarked that every new composition is a commentary on those created previously. The same goes for every improvisation. There is no ivory tower for improvisers, nor for composers. But creative composers or improvisers want to know what they don't know, so that they can explore the boundaries of their experience as well as the alluring void that lies beyond it. If we combine Jarrett, Feldman and Socrates' dictum, we end up with an exciting, enjoyable and even logical endeavor: Since I know that I know nothing, I can start improvising from nothing – listening, moving, acting–reacting, developing. Martial artists would call it thinking through the body. They practice all their lives – not to present a smooth performance of what they have learned, but to instantly conjure a crucial surprise out of nowhere, in other words, to do something they have never done before.

This intuitive energy comes from the depths of evolution and is as inherently potential to music as a feel for rhythm and melody. Without the survival strategy of improvisation, we would never have a chance to rise to the challenge of the unexpected. Improvisation is a creative energy that we can nurture and train. It is a benchmark of our own playing and mastery of our instrument but also of making music with others; it can change our perception and creatively modify our playing. So it may be true that everyone can only work with what they know, but from this material, they can invent unknown and unheard-of creatures. Our abilities should unearth what we don't yet know. Improvisation is the art of outwitting ourselves.

Interpretation as a uniting practice

What is the difference between improvisation and composition as creative, dramaturgical and architectural practices? Let us take two of the most influential modern piano works of New Music and jazz and compare their interpretation history: György Ligeti's piano études and Keith Jarrett's authorized transcripts of his legendary Köln Concert. Ligeti sees himself as a composer, whereas Jarrett is known as an interpreter and improviser. Ligeti's oeuvre is interpreted with increasing splendor, joining the ranks of important piano cycles, while any interpreter of Jarrett's improvisation would face the risk of creating a rather peculiar form of reproduction: No one, neither listener nor player, would be able to identify the genre. Jarrett's cycle is an evening of improvisation, played entirely from the dynamics of the moment, whereas Ligeti's cycle is a notated and elaborate composition in the tradition of standardized reproducibility. This comparison, perhaps absurd at first sight, acquires traction when we consider that many of Chopin's works, for instance, are solidified improvisations, which were often notated after the fact. It is highly probable that he performed them a little differently whenever he played them live or that he continued to refine them in successive performances.

Maybe one key to clarifying this connection lies in the culture of conscious interpretation. Every age has its own culture of interpreting compositions and styles. There are schools and lineages of interpretation; there are even downright guru lines, clans and battles in the arts pages about sovereignty in questions of interpretation. In so-called serious music, this subtle art has become a field for experts, for the great soloists and conductors of the twentieth century. Since the end of the twentieth century, jazz has laid claim to this hegemony as well with musicians and critics philosophizing about what is true jazz and what isn't. Determining whose music is still to be considered jazz and whose isn't tends to be influenced by their own understanding of tradition. Instead of polemically dividing true jazz musicians from false ones or traditionalists from modernists, it might be more interesting to ask whether interpreting and inventing music are really such different practices.

The indie-classical musicians mentioned at the beginning of this article solved this problem by simply declaring themselves to be post-genre musicians. They are less interested in whether a composer, interpreter or improviser belongs to avant-garde or tradition than in whether they produce appropriate, coherent and autonomous music that transcends genre. Biographical coherence leads to truthfulness of action; they have no qualms about combining indie rock with classical music or other i nfluences. Why should an interpreter who loves baroque or classical music not be allowed to compose or improvise in these styles, even though this might smack of "retro"? Michel Foucault said that as critics (and that is what we all are), we should look for signs of life in phenomena, rather than donning the red robe of a judge. So maybe the motto is not an all-out "anything goes," but an open-minded "everything is allowed."

In *Culture and Value* (1984), philosopher Ludwig Wittgenstein advances the idea that art constitutes a kind of monastic observance: If you want to interpret the signs of a cultural situation correctly in order to communicate with it intelligibly, you have to know the rules of observance, as in a religious covenant of initiates. Today, we would call this a code. Without the ability to specifically interpret signs, I have no chance of understanding and applying the meaning of the corresponding semiotic system. Interpreters of Ligeti's études have to know the rules of his music. But the more contemporary the work they are dealing with, the more they have to actively contribute. Paraphrasing Stravinsky, we could say: Every interpretation is a comment on the one that preceded it. An interpreter has to do exactly what Jarrett said in his preface to the authorized score of "The Köln Concert": "And yet, even this choice (of certain notes) cannot communicate the intrinsic meaning of this passage as an improvisation, because only listening will determine the meaningfulness of the music. So what we have in front of us is the image of an improvisation (comparable to the print of a painting), but all we see is its surface – the depths remain hidden. (The depth originates in the listener.) As a consequence, I would like to recommend this recording as a reference to every pianist who intends to play 'The Köln Concert.'"

If we replace the word improvisation with composition, one might say that the same statement results: The score of a piece provides the architectural plan of a musical creature whose living body will be revealed in sound – but only if we belong to the right order, the right band or the right tribe capable of decoding it. So there are actually several reasons why "The Köln Concert" as a standard twentieth-century work could be more often interpreted in the great concert halls.

The origin of "The Köln Concert" is the exact reverse of Ligeti's études: The materialization of the work is followed by its notation. But the musical logic of the work's genesis remains the same: The work can only come from its sound, from the interpretation of its "notes" and the manner in which they expand a code by interpreting it.

At the opening of Jazzfest Berlin 2015, artistic director Richard Williams said that the festival wanted to inspire everyone to think about what jazz is today and what it could still become. For me, jazz is more like a practice and an attitude than a style with commandments and prohibitions. This attitude and this practice assume that composing, interpreting and improvising are different forms of the same creative energy through which we learn to understand and play music. They cannot be separated, regardless of the musical current with which we are involved. They all spring from the same mystical source.

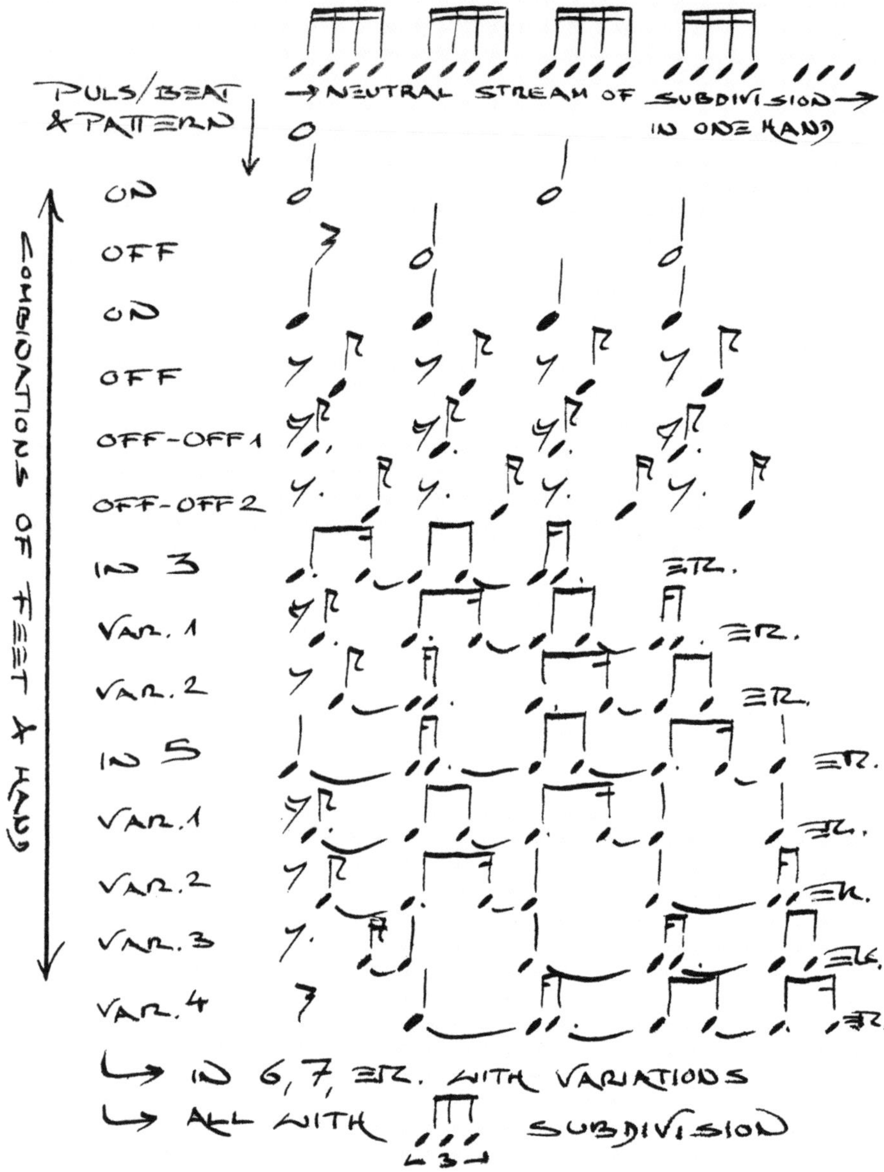
PULS/BEAT & PATTERN
→ NEUTRAL STREAM OF SUBDIVISION →
IN ONE HAND
COMBINATIONS OF FEET & HAND
ON
OFF
ON
OFF
OFF-OFF 1
OFF-OFF 2
IN 3
VAR. 1
VAR. 2
IN 5
VAR. 1
VAR. 2
VAR. 3
VAR. 4
ETC.
↳ IN 6, 7, ETC. WITH VARIATIONS
↳ ALL WITH SUBDIVISION
3

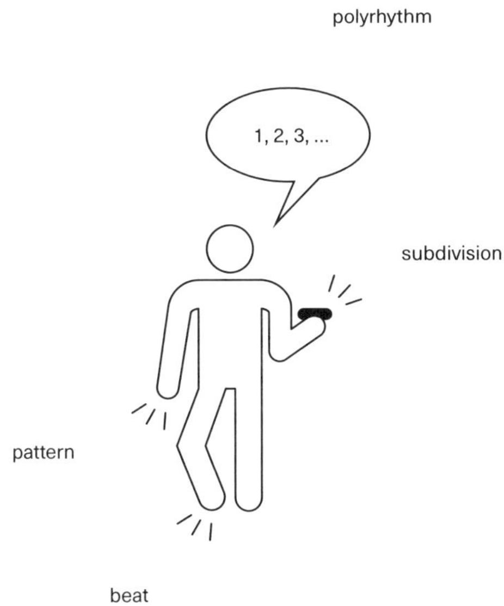

The shaker is a simple and effective instrument which immediately shows the relation of movement, mind and music when we see and hear someone playing it.

Shaker training can help to understand the deeper meaning of tempo, time, timing and phrasing and of the relations of subdivision, pulse, meter, rhythm, beat balance, cycle and form (see also next page).

First we train a movement that supports the natural and neutral stream of subdivisions. Forward and backward moving sounds similar, the time has a clear direction and the movement should be lissome. Always train both hands!

Then one can introduce combinations of clapping the body with the free hand and/or tapping the feet and/or the counting or singing. There are many possible combinations and variations.

It is important not to force combinations, to let the flow happen and to train on the right individual level. The goal is to gain more lissomeness and presence and to increase the capacity to master complex rhythmic combinations in various situations and on one's personal instrument.

As mentioned in the group circle game on page 130, shaker playing can be combined with these exercises.

Rhythm Levels and Relations

Basic Organization of “Modul 32”

Subdivision:	4 × 1/16, straight
Pulse / Beat:	quarter note
Meter / Bar:	7/4
Feel-unit:	2 × 7/4 = 14/4
Rhythm:	5 + 3 + 3 + 3 = 14/4

Beat Balance:

Cycle:	6 × 7/4, harmonic, melodic and rhythmic cycle For the final form listen to the whole track on the album *STOA* by Nik Bärtsch’s Ronin.

Form

Intro:	2 × (6 × 7/4)
Cycle:	6 × 7/4, open, continue on cue
Transition:	6 × 7/4
Polyrhythm Platform:	rhythmic cycle: 3/4 versus 7/4, open

Tempo:	♩ = 80	80 = absolute measurement of beats per minute
Time:		flow feel in relation to tempo by player(s)
Timing:		placement of musical event in the flow by player(s)
Phrasing:		way of playing subdivision (binary or ternary or in between), attack and phrases

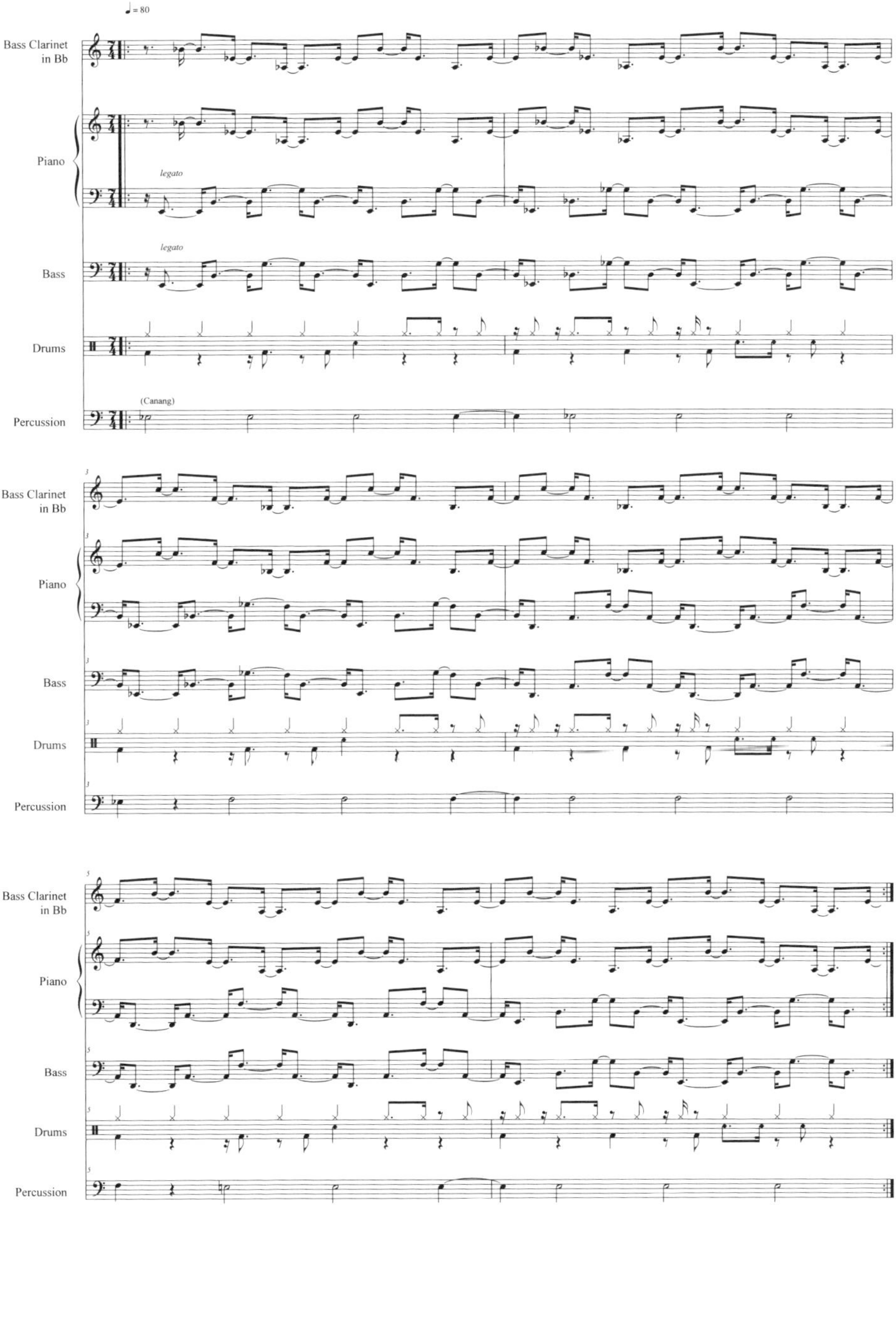

Score part of "Modul 32", Main Cycle, by Nik Bärtsch

Swiss Musical Warriors on a Peace Mission

About International Touring as a Swiss Musician

It is well known that peace building starts with ourselves. We must start on our own doorstep before trying to contribute to world peace. But the farther we are from home, the more we are perceived on the basis of our origins. When I was in Japan, the first thing people wanted to know was not who I was (be it musician, martial artist or private visitor) but where I was from.

Whether others in the world see me as a messenger of peace often depends on things over which I have little control. For example, my country of origin. On my concert tours in over fifty countries, usually with my band, I was mostly classified as perfectly harmless politically, and never as dangerous, thanks to my Swiss citizenship. That's the last thing you want as an artist. Your art should be daring and striking; it should inspire and move people. On these trips I was fascinated to discover that I can make even bolder artistic statements if I am considered politically neutral. Thanks to Switzerland, politics and history don't get in the way of the musical message.

Some concerts took place in locations that are considered politically sensitive, for example Transnistria, Tehran and Washington. At the start of the concerts people were very surprised that such harmless Swiss people could generate so much energy and enthusiasm with their music. As if the virtues of a small democracy, such as peacefulness, politeness, modesty and mutual respect, could not go hand in hand with unleashed energy, groove rhythms and deep soul. What is "Swissness" compared to the "Russian soul" or the "American spirit"?

To be taken seriously by people in different countries, a clear presence in body and mind was always essential. Peacefulness, politeness, modesty and respectful interaction require a clear mind and a trained body. My band is called Ronin, named after Japanese warriors without masters. They weren't mercenaries or soldiers, but outlawed martial artists, and therefore both physically and philosophically independent.

How many politicians do you know who strike you as alert, in top condition and exceedingly polite? Whose mental and physical demeanor commands respect from enemies and friends alike – similar to the aim of serious martial artists. In Switzerland, where there is fortunately little violence, we tend to disdain state leaders who have themselves photographed in martial arts dress for calendars. After a long period of domestic peace and international neutrality, we have become accustomed to viewing violence as bad and backward, a sign of machismo and a lack of education. This view recklessly suppresses and hides the fact that peaceful coexistence is never the status quo, but rather an ongoing struggle by peaceful means to find the right social balance – locally, nationally and internationally. We can fight as peaceful, polite, humble and respectful people, and with dignity instead of a two-handed sword. But this dignity requires total concentration, unwavering presence and all-encompassing love.

This approach, cultivated by the martial arts, is crucial in concert performance. If you are not fully concentrated, if you do not respect the music, the space and the people in it, you are doomed. You will go under in the truest sense of the word. In aikido we call this approach engaged neutrality. It is an active neutrality that commits to the world instead of playing ostrich.

awar

meditation

rhythm voodo

holon

contin

communit

zen funk

mysticism

modul

sportsmanship

blend

ronin

em

Ritual Groove Music

aikido mobile
interlocking
ess cycle
awase
clockwork
hishiryo
vement
mesmeric
toa groove
pattern
dori
playfulness
home base
tribe
modular
odiment

NIK BÄRTSCH'S MOBILE RITUAL GROOVE MUSIC

NIK BÄRTSCH'S RONIN RANDORI

NIK BÄRTSCH HISHIRYŌ PIANO SOLO

NIK BÄRTSCH'S RONIN
ECM
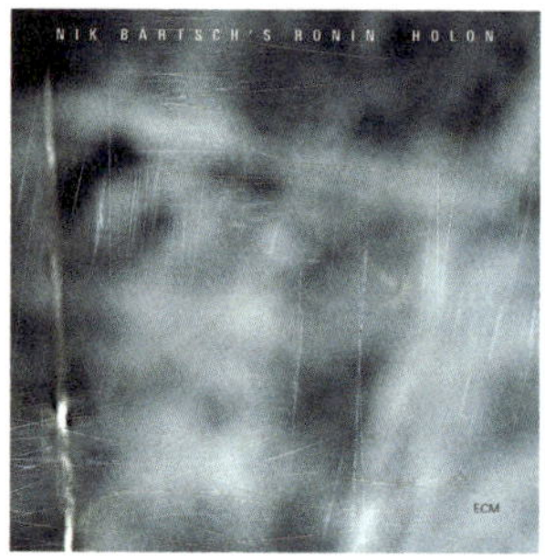
NIK BÄRTSCH'S RONIN HOLON
ECM

NIK BÄRTSCH'S RONIN LLYRIA

Nik Bärtsch
Entendre
ECM

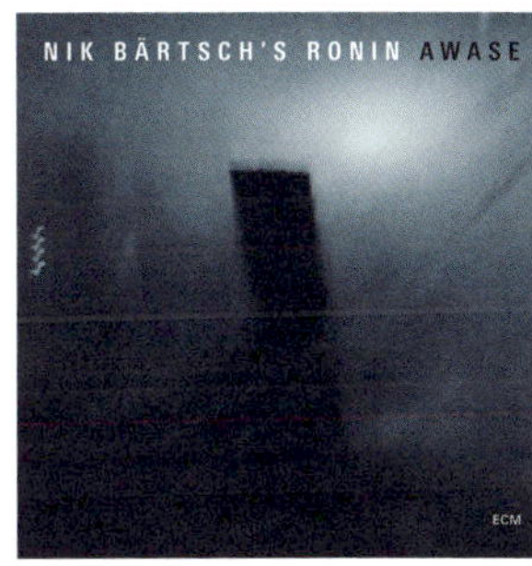

Ritual Groove Music Series 1–13

Nik Bärtsch's Mobile, *RITUAL GROOVE MUSIC,* 2001, Ronin Rhythm Records
Nik Bärtsch's Ronin, *RANDORI,* 2002, Ronin Rhythm Records
Nik Bärtsch, *HISHIRYO,* Piano Solo, 2002, Ronin Rhythm Records
Nik Bärtsch's Ronin, *LIVE,* 2003, Ronin Rhythm Records
Nik Bärtsch's Ronin, *REA,* 2004, Ronin Rhythm Records
Nik Bärtsch's Mobile, *AER,* 2004, Ronin Rhythm Records
Nik Bärtsch's Ronin, *STOA,* 2006, ECM
Nik Bärtsch's Ronin, *HOLON,* 2008, ECM
Nik Bärtsch's Ronin, *LLYRÌA,* 2010, ECM
Nik Bärtsch's Ronin, *LIVE,* 2012, ECM
Nik Bärtsch's Mobile, *CONTINUUM,* 2016, ECM
Nik Bärtsch's Ronin, *AWASE,* 2018, ECM
Nik Bärtsch, *Entendre,* 2021, ECM

Ecstasy through Asceticism

RITUAL GROOVE MUSIC, the title of my first CD, also points to the fundamental concept of my musical thinking. The music shows a close affinity to architecturally organized space and is governed by the principles of repetition and reduction as well as by interlocking rhythms. A piece of music can be entered, inhabited like a room. It moves forward and transforms through obsessive circular movements, superimposition of different meters and micro-interplay. The listener's attention is directed toward minimal variations and phrasing. The band becomes an integral organism – like an animal, a habitat, an urban space. One must think with ears and hands.

Normally, I work in three distinct formations. The group Mobile plays purely acoustic music, performed in rituals of up to thirty-six hours, including light and room design. The Zen-funk quartet Ronin is more flexible and plays the compositions more freely. As a solo performer I perform my compositions on prepared piano with percussion.

Despite the tightly organized compositional construction, improvisation plays an important role in our music.
On the one hand, accentuation, ghost notes and variations within a composition are tossed back and forth between the musicians; on the other hand, a particular voice within a composition might have more freedom than the others.

Nik Bärtsch's Mobile, *RITUAL GROOVE MUSIC,* 2001, Ronin Rhythm Records
Moduls: 5, 11, 4, 12, 4 II, 2, 12 II.
The first album was recorded after the thirty-six-hour music ritual "AREA BLUE" at Blauer Saal, Zurich, in September 2000. It was a point zero and fundamental statement, similar to *The Black Album* by Prince, *Black Square* by Kazimir Malewitch or a black garment by Christa de Carouge.
Lineup: Nik Bärtsch, piano; Kaspar Rast, drums; Mats Eser, marimba, percussion; Don Li, bass clarinet, alto saxophone.
All music composed and arranged by Nik Bärtsch, and produced by Nik Bärtsch and Mobile. Executive producer Peter Bürli, Radio DRS 2.
Recorded direct to two-track by Hanspeter Ehrsam at Radiostudio, Zurich, September 2000.
Mastered by Glenn Miller at Greenwood Mastering Studios, Nunningen.
Liner photo by Palma Fiacco. Design by Nik Bärtsch, Rio Grafik, Benjamin Pfäffli and Valeria Bonin.

Nik Bärtsch's Mobile, 2000: Kaspar Rast, Mats Eser, Don Li, Nik Bärtsch

Nik Bärtsch's Mobile, 2002: Kaspar Rast, Mats Eser, Nik Bärtsch, Raphael Camenisch, Ania Losinger

In doing so, that voice forms an independent Modul that can interact with the strictly notated interlocking patterns in continuously changing ways. Groove habitats or void musical space of raw poetry emerge.

My thinking and music are based on the tradition of urban space. They are not distilled from a national or stylistic tradition but from the universal sound of cities. The city in its roaring diversity requires an ability to focus and concentrate on the essential: to measure one's actions, to remain silent at the right place. This music draws its energy from the tension between compositional precision and the self-circumvention of improvisation. From self-imposed restriction stems freedom.

Ecstasy through asceticism.

Ronin, Freedom and Self-Responsibility

Excerpt from *Samurai-Geist* by Thomas Preston

There are two paths a samurai can walk: that of a clan member, and that of a ronin, a lonely warrior. The former is highly esteemed in Japan, the latter is bitterly detested.

The despised warrior without a clan is viewed by clan people as a hungry wolf, roaming through the country, with no ties or obligations, no duties or support, no protection, no respect for people's material well-being. Despite his virtuosity as a swordsman, a lone fighter is unable to withstand gangs or clansmen eager to fight. His readiness to die could be tested any time: not in a great battle between two mighty clans where he might

The Ronin Rhythm Productions logo by Pia Affolter, designed as an homage to a ronin with a bird whistle

Nik Bärtsch's Ronin, *RANDORI,* 2002, Ronin Rhythm Records
Moduls: 15, 8_9 I, 8_9 II, 8_9 III, 10, 13, 14, 11, 15_9.
The title of Ronin's first album, *RANDORI,* is Japanese for "bringing order into chaos." In martial arts the term describes a freestyle fight in which sparring partners are trained to apply technique to a random succession of attacks.
Lineup: Nik Bärtsch, piano, Fender Rhodes, Yamaha DX-7, drums (tracks 2 and 9); Kaspar Rast, drums and udu; Björn Meyer, ebass. Guest: Andi Pupato, shaker, Indian bells.
All music composed and arranged by Nik Bärtsch. Produced by Nik Bärtsch and Ronin.
Recorded by Björn Meyer, Greencube at Tonus-Music Labor, Bern, December 2001.
Mixed and mastered by Andi Pupato, Björn Meyer and Nik Bärtsch.
Liner photo by Martin Möll. Design by Nik Bärtsch, Benjamin Pfäffli and Valeria Bonin.

Nik Bärtsch's Ronin: founding members Björn Meyer, Nik Bärtsch and Kaspar Rast. The photo was taken by band photographer Martin Möll at the new train station Stadelhofen by architect, structural engineer, sculptor and painter Santiago Calatrava Valls in Zurich in 2001. The design of the bridge at this train station has the best flow and groove in town. The band always chooses special locations in Zurich for their photos.

die a famous hero but in trifling rows over a mouthful of rice or a sip of sake. If a ronin wants to survive, he must, wherever he goes, remain extremely careful. He has no social status whatsoever and is not respected by anybody. People treat him with the same level of caution as they would a wild animal that attacks whenever frightened.

Most of these ronin are not happy with their destiny. They spend most of their time struggling to ingratiate themselves wherever they can, hoping for a clan in need of warriors. They are cursed with shabby clothes and inadequate food, longing for the honour and security of being a clan member.

If only those destitute samurai could view their situation without prejudice! They might see that, at the cost of tolerable poverty, they have acquired a rare treasure: freedom.

They are free to learn about the world, free to discover and fulfil the true purpose of man. They can toughen themselves in the wilderness; they can study budo wherever a master is available; they can visit monasteries and practice meditation.

The price they pay for liberty is the occasional empty stomach, a little poverty and loneliness. But it is not easy to rid yourself of the clansman's crushing burden.

Beyond Thinking

"Intuition and action must spring forth at the same time. In the practice of Budo there can be no conscious thought. There is no time for thinking, not even an instant. When a person acts, intention and action must be simultaneous. If you say, 'Aha, a monster, how can I kill it?' or if you hesitate at all, only the forebrain is working; whereas forebrain and thalamus (the primitive, central brain) and action must all coincide, in the same instant, identical – just as the moon's reflection on the surface of the stream is never still, while the moon itself shines and does not move. This is hishiryo consciousness."

Taisen Deshimaru (1914–1982), Japanese Soto Zen teacher

Nik Bärtsch, *HISHIRYO,* Piano Solo, 2002, Ronin Rhythm Records
Moduls: 8_9, 13, 14, 4, TM, 5, 6, 11.
Lineup: Nik Bärtsch, piano, prepared piano and percussion.
All music composed and arranged by Nik Bärtsch.
Produced by Nik Bärtsch. Executive producer Peter Bürli, Radio DRS 2.
Recorded and mixed by Hanspeter Ehrsam at Radiostudio, Zurich, January 2002.
Mastered by Glenn Miller at Greenwood Mastering Studios, Nunningen.
Liner photo by Martin Möll. Design by Nik Bärtsch, Benjamin Pfäffli and Valeria Bonin.

> Nik Bärtsch during a solo performance, photo by Mamo Delpero

“The mind is a wild monkey.”

Zen proverb

Listening: Music, Movement, Mind by Nik Bärtsch
in collaboration with Andrea Pfisterer
ISBN 978-3-03778-670-3, Lars Müller Publishers, 2021

Drawing from the series *Concave Thoughts* by Yves Netzhammer

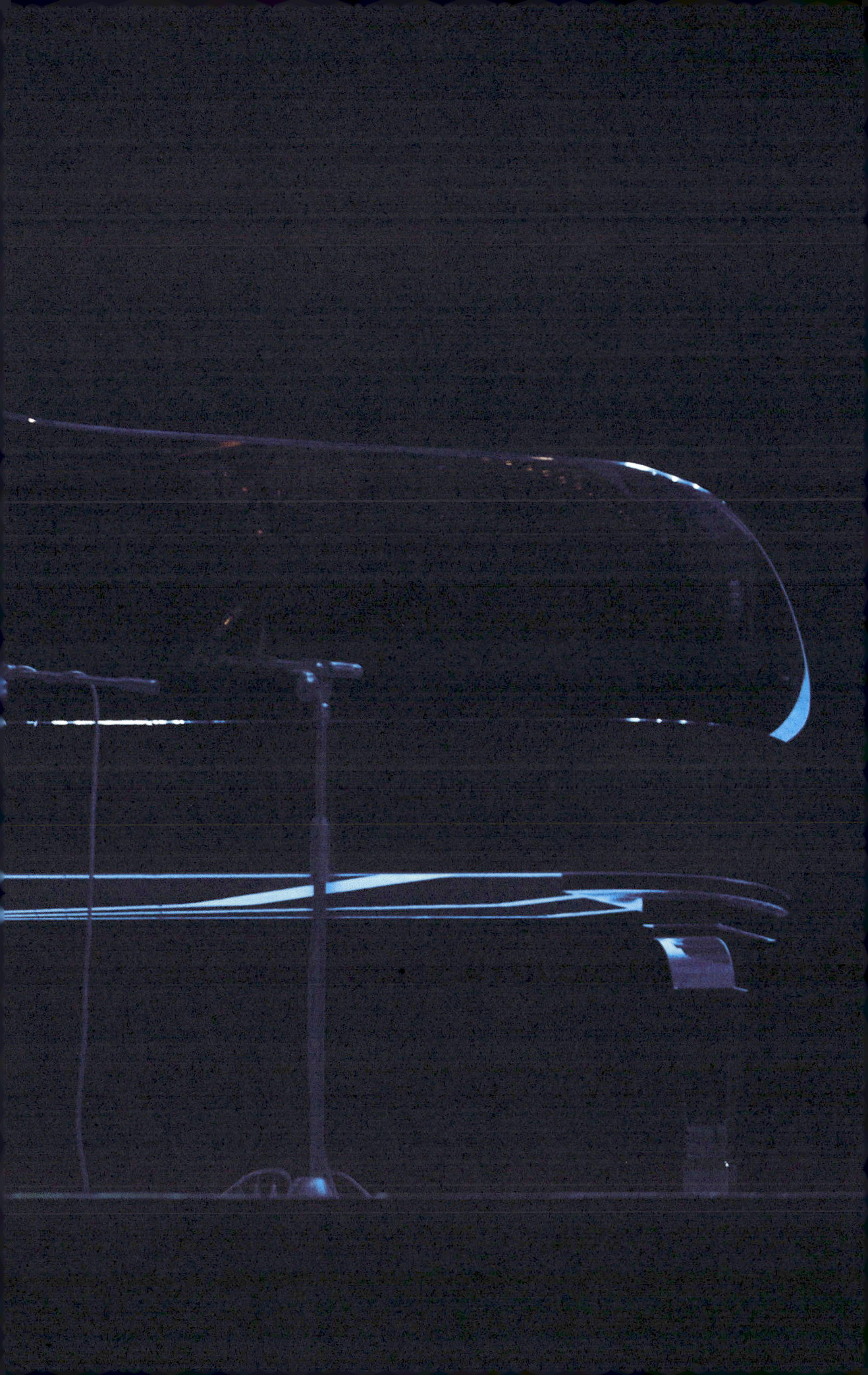

The Live Band as a Storm

The band Ronin released their first album *RANDORI* in 2002 and wanted to present this new music based on the live playing of repetitive and cycle-oriented grooves and organism phrasing. Although all tracks were also played live together on the album and no overdubs or electronic loops were used, many organizers and promoters of live shows did not believe this when they heard the album; they thought that the band was "colder" and technical in the sense of electronic ambient music and might not be interesting for an enthusiastic live audience. This was the reason why the album *LIVE* was presented in 2003 with tracks from live shows in Zurich and Bern. On the cover we see a warm tropical rain storm sweeping over the Asian ocean. Like the storm, the band hits the audience with uncompromising intensity – escape is not possible, everybody is wet from the warm rain after the concert.

Nik Bärtsch's Ronin, *LIVE,* 2003, Ronin Rhythm Records
Moduls: 14, 17, 11, 16, 8_9, 15.
Lineup: Nik Bärtsch, piano, Fender Rhodes, Yamaha DX-7; Kaspar Rast, drums; Björn Meyer, ebass; Andi Pupato, percussion.
All music composed and arranged by Nik Bärtsch, except drum beat in Modul 16 by Kaspar Rast. Produced by Nik Bärtsch and Ronin.
Live recording by Björn Meyer, Greencube, at Moods, Zurich, and Bee-Flat, Bern, May 2002.
Mixed and mastered by Andi Pupato and Ronin.
Liner photo by Martin Möll. Design by Benjamin Pfäffli, Valeria Bonin and Nik Bärtsch.
Supported by Popkredit from Zurich City Council.

Mirrored Variations

REA and *AER* were both released in 2004. They exemplify how ritual groove music works with the two bands Ronin and Mobile: the same musical concept leads to different results in different band bodies. Just as a garment looks and moves differently on different bodies with different kinetic energies and attitudes.

Nik Bärtsch's Ronin, *REA,* 2004, Ronin Rhythm Records
Moduls: 27, 22, 18, 26, 23.
Lineup: Nik Bärtsch, piano, Fender Rhodes; Kaspar Rast, drums; Björn Meyer, ebass; Andi Pupato, percussion. Guests: Sha, bass clarinet (Moduls 27 and 26), Thomy Geiger, tenor saxophone (Modul 27), Michael Gassmann, trumpet (Modul 27).
All music composed and arranged by Nik Bärtsch, except Modul 27 by Bärtsch, Sha, Hunziker, Tavano.
Produced by Nik Bärtsch. Executive producer Peter Bürli, Radio DRS 2.
Recorded by Hanspeter Ehrsam at Radiostudio, Zurich, May 2003.
Mixed and mastered by Andi Pupato and Nik Bärtsch.
Liner photos by Martin Möll. Design by Benjamin Pfäffli, Valeria Bonin and Nik Bärtsch.
Supported by Popkredit from Zurich City Council.

The new Mobile lineup in 2003: Nik Bärtsch, Kaspar Rast, Mats Eser, Sha. This photo was taken by Martin Möll at Nordheim Crematorium in Zurich (see also photo on p. 81). It was designed by architect Albert Heinrich Steiner, an urban planner, progressive modernist and professor at the ETH Zurich. In combination with the landscape architecture by Willi Neukom the location is a complete work of art. The photos for the album *AWASE* were also taken here by Reto Camenisch (see pages 222/223). The function, spirit and design of this place represent an aesthetic consciousness of the transition from life to death, which is also essential in the ritual groove music.

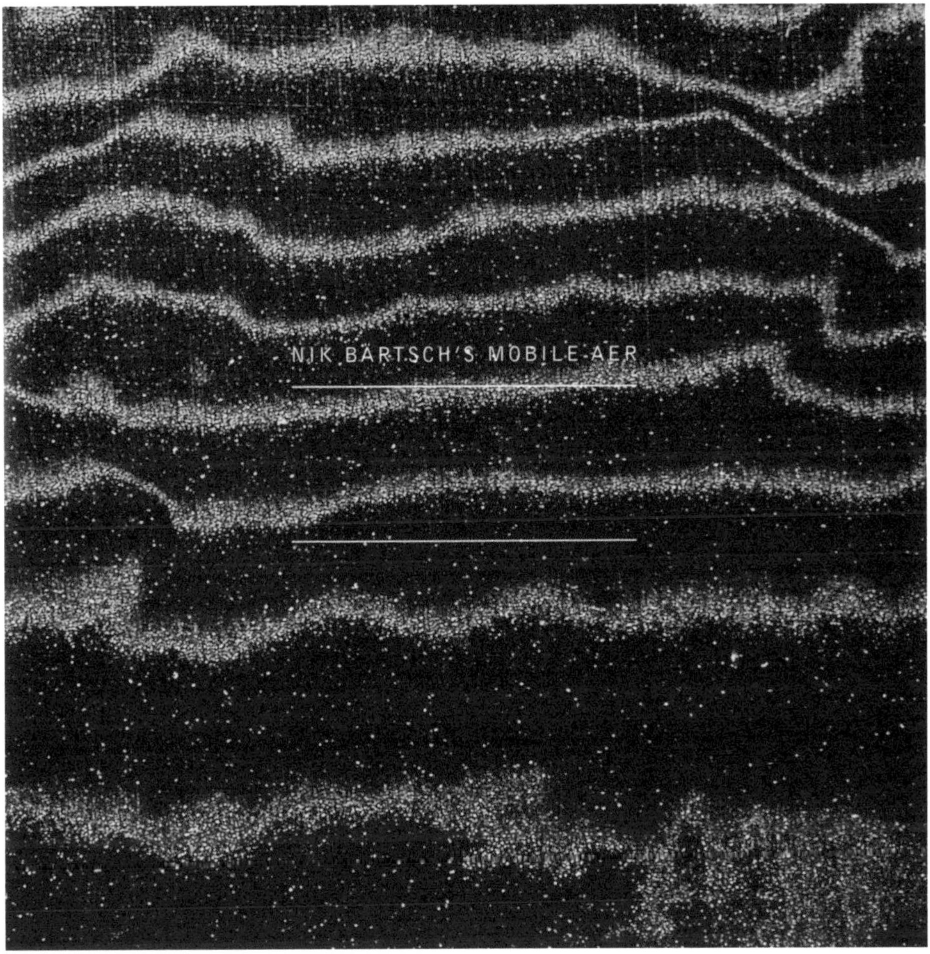

Nik Bärtsch's Mobile, *AER,* 2004, Ronin Rhythm Records
Moduls: 29, 16, 18, 20, 26, 8_11.
Lineup: Nik Bärtsch, piano; Kaspar Rast, drums; Mats Eser, marimba, percussion;
Sha, bass clarinet, alto saxophone.
All music composed and arranged by Nik Bärtsch.
Produced by Nik Bärtsch. Executive producer Peter Bürli, Radio DRS 2.
Recorded by Hanspeter Ehrsam at Radiostudio, Zurich, August 2003.
Mixed and mastered by Andi Pupato and Nik Bärtsch.
Liner photo by Martin Möll. Design by Benjamin Pfäffli, Valeria Bonin and Nik Bärtsch.
Supported by Popkredit from Zurich City Council.

> "SEE – a live musical sound picture," four-hour performance on the lake stage in Zurich in 2005, co-production of Nik Bärtsch's Mobile, OOS architects and Theaterspektakel Zurich

Stoa, the European Equivalent of Zen

Asked about the meaning of words, Igor Stravinsky replied: "Sometimes I feel like those old men Gulliver encounters in the Voyage to Laputa, who have renounced language and who try to converse by means of objects themselves. A composer is always in that position: he has no verbal control over his music... The one true comment on a piece of music is another piece of music."

The painting *Appetenz* by Berlin artist Armin Staudt depicts a primeval animal, muzzle to the ground, in a geometric space of black on black. "A composer improvises aimlessly the way an animal grubs about," says Stravinsky. The animal in the picture looks so alive, archaic and wondrous precisely because of its clearly composed surroundings. Depending on the direction of the light, the colors slumbering beneath the surface of the painting break into seismic song. The pictorial composition outwits itself.

A band should mature into an integral organism – then it is alive, like an animal, a biotope, an urban space. It creates overtone blossoms, ghost notes, spectral sounds, flights of perspective.

The rule of the Japanese martial arts is: think with your body. Anaxagoras tells us: man is the wisest of animals because he has hands. As the animal in *Appetenz* sniffs the ground because it has a nose, so Ronin play

Nik Bärtsch's Ronin, *STOA,* 2006, ECM
Moduls: 36, 35, 32, 33, 38_17.
While Ronin were searching for a title for their first ECM record, Swiss writer Michel Mettler pointed out in conversation that the European equivalent of Zen is the Greek philosophy of the stoa.
Lineup: Nik Bärtsch, piano, Fender Rhodes; Kaspar Rast, drums; Björn Meyer, ebass; Sha, bass clarinet and contrabass clarinet; Andi Pupato, percussion.
Music composed by Nik Bärtsch. Produced by Manfred Eicher.
Recorded by Gérard de Haro, Studios La Buissonne, May 2005.
Cover photo by Jean-Guy Lathulière. Liner photos by Marc Wetli and Andrea Pfisterer.
Design by Sascha Kleis.

music because of the pleasure they take in the tactile, in the percussive construction of cities, in reasoning by resonating. They think with their ears and hands. Their pieces are spaces to be entered and inhabited.

Appetenz by Armin Staudt,
hanging on the wall of Nik Bärtsch's workspace

"A composer improvises aimlessly the way an animal grubs about. [...] All creation presupposes at its origin a sort of appetite that is brought on by the foretaste of discovery. This foretaste of the creative act accompanies the intuitive grasp of an unknown entity already possessed but not yet intelligible, an entity that will not take definite shape except by the action of a constantly vigilant technique. This appetite that is aroused in me at the mere thought of putting in order musical elements that have attracted my attention is not at all a fortuitous thing like inspiration, but as habitual and periodic, if not as constant, as a natural need. This premonition of an obligation, this foretaste of a pleasure, this conditioned reflex, as a modern physiologist would say, shows clearly that it is the idea of discovery and hard work that attracts me."

Igor Stravinsky (1882–1971), composer, pianist and conductor

Modules as Musical Holarchies

By Garrett Johnson

In his scathing 1967 critique of contemporary psychology, *The Ghost in the Machine,* Arthur Koestler introduced his holon theory, which bridged what he understood as the limiting extremities of views in the two predominant schools in psychological and cognitive philosophical thought: the reductionist methods of the more popular behaviorist school, which level all human actions to the same plane as animal instincts, and the holist methods of the gestalt school, which espoused that a whole is more substantial than the sum of its parts.[1]

The holon can be easily understood by dissecting the term etymologically. The word consists of the prefix holo-, from the Greek *holos,* and the Greek neuter suffix *-on,* which in the scientific realm can be seen in terms of identifying a belonging to a larger whole, as in proton or electron.[2] Thus the term holon describes an entity which belongs to both poles of the traditional part/whole dichotomy simultaneously, which takes elements from both the behaviorist and gestalt schools.

The beautiful and simplistic paradox of Koestler's holon, which defies the very linguistic foundations of the part/whole dichotomy ("What exactly do we mean by the familiar words 'part' and 'whole'?"),[3] becomes all the more attractive when one identifies the presence of holons and holarchies[4] in perhaps every conceivable

Nik Bärtsch's Ronin, *HOLON,* 2008, ECM
Moduls: 42, 41_17, 39_8, 46, 45, 44.
Lineup: Nik Bärtsch, piano; Kaspar Rast, drums; Björn Meyer, ebass; Sha, bass clarinet and and alto saxophone; Andi Pupato, percussion.
Music composed by Nik Bärtsch. Produced by Manfred Eicher.
Recorded by Gérard de Haro, Studios La Buissonne, July 2007. Assistant Nicolas Baillard.
Cover photo by Thomas Wunsch. Liner photos by Martin Möll. Design by Sascha Kleis.

Ronin's friendly focus circle before the concert

aspect of existence. In his 1978 book, which focuses more closely on the holon, *Janus: A Summing Up,* he uses the living organism as an example of a commonplace holarchy. He breaks down the hierarchy into nine layers: the organism, organ systems (respiratory, digestive, etc.), organs, tissues, cells, organelles (ribosomes, mitochondria, etc.), molecules, atoms, subatomic particles, and ? ? ? – leaving room for the unobservable.[5] Use of such a system of analysis implies that all levels of the hierarchy exist simultaneously in a balance autonomously (self-assertiveness) and subserviently (integration), exhibiting what Koestler calls "the Janus Effect", after the two-faced Roman god.[6]

Koestler saw similar relationships and the holarchy's analytical potential in explaining structures not only in anatomy, psychology, or social hierarchies, but also in language (for example, in linguistic morphology the unbound morpheme is essentially a holon)[7] as well as in music. Koestler refers to the obvious holarchic structures evident in classical music: "... the architecture of movements, of themes and variations, development and recapitulation, rhythm and harmony..."[8] These elements of common-practice period composition can be seen as analogous to Bärtsch's modules in that they share a level of extreme transparency in terms of compositional techniques.

1 Koestler, *Janus: A Summing Up* (New York: Random House, 1978), p. 26.
2 Koestler, *The Ghost in the Machine* (New York: Macmillan, 1968), p. 48
3 Koestler, *Janus,* p. 26.
4 Koestler names the relationships between holons at various levels a holarchy.
5 Koestler, *Janus,* p. 29.
6 Koestler, *Ghost in the Machine,* p. 48
7 "... nowhere on the upward or downward journey through the linguistic holarchy do we encounter hard and indivisible 'atoms of language.' Each of the entities on various levels – phonemes, morphemes, words, sentences – is a whole relative to its parts, and a subordinate part of a more complex entity on the next higher level." Koestler, *Janus,* p. 35. An unbound morpheme, in contrast with a bound morpheme, is a fragment of language that can be combined with other lexemes (linguistic units) to create other words or stand alone and still have meaning. The unbound morpheme is also referred to as a bound morpheme. An example of an unbound morpheme combining with another unbound morpheme to create a new meaning would be the "doghouse" (dog + house).
8 Koestler, *Janus,* p. 27.

Move Your Ears

"I always leave the concert hall when I start tapping my foot." This is how Morton Feldman once put it, only half-ironically. Concentrated listening and rhythmic dancing seem diametrically opposed. But to me, music is an art of motion, and thus akin to dancing and martial arts. Far-Eastern martial artists try to unite the brain with the heart, bodily suppleness with tension: an agile mind and body will intuitively produce the right response in a fight. Musicians move in much the same way as martial artists: they create the requisite musical flow in the immediate present, as if of its own accord. (The fingers of even the most unathletic players dance on the instrument.) Their motions move listeners in a dual sense. An ecstatic groove and an ascetic awareness of form and sound in composed music are not mutually exclusive: they can form combinations that take our senses by surprise. Being an agile organism, our band makes decisions on phrasing, tension and musical direction in a fraction of a second. It reminds me of a school of fish moving across a coral reef with lightning speed. Are the fish faster than thought? An instant later they are peacefully afloat in the translucent sea as if nothing had happened. Each player in our band illuminates the whole through his improvisation. As a soloist, he loiters in the sound of the composition like a squid waiting for prey in the reef.

HOLON poster by ECM, Sascha Kleis, band photo by Martin Möll, 2008

Poetic Deep-Sea Science

While I was thinking about the process of creating new music and reading Stravinsky's views on finding, inventing and composing music, my wife Andrea showed me a wonderful book about the deep sea and its creatures. We were especially intrigued by a creature with the mystical name "Llyrìa." It was some sort of comb jelly (ctenophore) but did not yet have a scientific name, since it had just been recently discovered and scientists did not know how it behaved and what it was exactly. Watching this fluorescent animal floating in the deep, light as a butterfly under heavy deep-sea pressure, was inspiring and enlightening. It was like discovering a new musical pattern or motive in the deep ocean of music. We were enthralled by the huge potential that could be unearthed by observing this creature, and the exciting prospect of finding more undiscovered species. So we got in touch with the scientist who had discovered and named it to ask if we could use this poetic name for the new Ronin album. Fortunately, Dr. George I. Matsumoto from the Monterey Bay Aquarium Research Institute (MBARI) was interested in our exchange and permitted us to use the name, which he had come across in a fantasy novel. Later, when I was on tour in the States playing in Oakland near San Francisco, I visited him and his research center. I wanted to thank him for his work and kindness and to give him a CD personally. He showed me how he and his colleagues sail out with their research ship every day and lower their

Nik Bärtsch's Ronin, *LLYRÌA,* 2010, ECM
Moduls: 48, 52, 55, 47, 53, 51, 49_44.
Lineup: Nik Bärtsch, piano; Kaspar Rast, drums; Björn Meyer, ebass; Sha, bass clarinet and and alto saxophone; Andi Pupato, percussion.
Music composed by Nik Bärtsch. Produced by Manfred Eicher.
Recorded by Gérard de Haro and Nicolas Baillard, Studios La Buissonne, March 2010.
Cover photo by Jean-Guy Lathulière. Liner photos by Martin Möll. Design by Sascha Kleis.

deep-sea robot to the ground in Monterey Bay to discover new species. Current estimates about the number of species yet to be discovered vary between ten and thirty million. So I wonder: how deep is the music ocean? How many new patterns, motives and cycles will we find?

Empathy and Phrasing

> "The aspects of things that are most important for us are hidden because of their simplicity and familiarity. (One is unable to notice something – because it is always before one's eyes.) The real foundations of his enquiry do not strike a man at all."
>
> Ludwig Wittgenstein

Music is fondly called a universal "language." When we make music and listen to music together, the musical code necessary to this end usually seems self-evident. But how does such a code arise and proliferate? How does dialect or slang emerge from a language? What gives rise to characteristic phrasings, embellishments and rhythmic alloys shared by an entire group of musicians? And how do rules of style take hold?

In addition to its tours and performances, for six years Ronin has held a concert every Monday evening at its own club in Zurich. This long-term experiment encourages and demands constant musical evolution – the result of interaction, attentive listening and critical, even ironic musical and verbal dialogue. On these Mondays we eat and play together. In this way Ronin has, over the years, independently created its own phraseology and proceeded blithely but consistently on its own path as a socio-musical organism. As the band's composer, I precisely set down most of the pieces in notation; but in live performances it becomes, at some point, impossible to tell what is composed, interpreted or improvised. The band has to discover the right tension and the suitable dramatic structure for a piece on the spur of the moment. The band organism thus outwits not only the composition, but itself. For music exists only when it resounds, when the air vibrates, when resonance arises between notes, sounds and human beings.

The interplay between drummer Kaspar Rast and me has already been going on for more than twenty-five years. It has influenced our inner ears no less than our view of communication per se. When five musicians play together, ten different paths of communication open up between them – a challenge to deft, accurate interaction and mutual attention. The only way to find and share these paths is with a large degree of empathy, which enables us intuitively to reflect our partners in ourselves, immediately and reflexively. In addition to criticism (the other form of constructive reflection), empathy is a key prerequisite for creative collaborations. It is a cooperative survival strategy, as old as time itself, and thus deeply rooted not only in our thought but in our bodies. That is what makes this gift so valuable and productive for our interaction. Joint phrasing, after all, cannot be captured in notation. It can only be gained through training and patience, through mutual respect and interest, through the ability to resonate with each other.

Then familiar phrases, curious and vivid turns of phrase, webs of ghost notes and rhythmic punch lines will arise as if by themselves.

"In 2001, after watching a stunningly beautiful film at the Monterey Bay Aquarium in California, I took my first dive into the deep. In that one moment, and without expecting it in the least, my life changed direction. […] What a universe! I watched the film four times in a row, scrutinizing the screen incredulously, searching for some clue that inevitably would betray even the best special-effects artist. My thoughts looped, just like the film: 'This isn't possible … These animals aren't real … These effects are magnificently executed … totally unheard of: Tim Burton must be behind all this!'"

Claire Nouvian (*1974), French environment activist, journalist and film director

Ronin lineup from 2010: Rast, Meyer, Sha, Pupato, Bärtsch. This photo was taken by Martin Möll on the original ramp at the huge former Toni creamery, which was converted into the new campus of the Zurich University of the Arts, now called Toni-Areal. The building's transformation was designed by the architects at EM2N. The ramp can also be seen on the title page of the score for the album *LLYRÌA* on page 233.

Live Around the World in Fifty Concerts

It is essential to hear Ronin live to understand the band's work. So for the ECM *LIVE* double album, Ronin recorded over fifty live concerts between 2008 and 2011 and selected the nine best tracks from Lörrach (DE), Leipzig (DE), Vienna (AT), Tokyo (JP), Amsterdam (NL), Mannheim (2, DE), Gateshead (UK) and Salzau (DE). This album was a summary and an inside view of the band's live presence, and introduced new bass player Thomy Jordi who replaced Björn Meyer in 2011.

First Ronin sticker with the new lineup, designed by Hans Grüninger, WBG

Nik Bärtsch's Ronin, *LIVE,* double album, 2012, ECM
Moduls: CD 1: 41_17, 35, 42, 17, 22. CD 2: 45, 48, 47, 55.
Lineup: Nik Bärtsch, piano, Fender Rhodes; Kaspar Rast, drums; Björn Meyer, ebass; Sha, bass clarinets and alto saxophone; Andi Pupato, percussion; Thomy Jordi, bass on Modul 55.
Music composed by Nik Bärtsch. Produced by Manfred Eicher.
Recorded live 2009–2011 by Andi Pupato.
Mixed at Studios La Buissonne by Gérard de Haro and Romain Castera, Nik Bärtsch and Manfred Eicher. Mastering by Nicolas Baillard.
Cover photo by Geno Lechner. Liner photos by Martin Möll. Design by Sascha Kleis.

Mobile Continues the Journey

The first Mobile album released on ECM included three tracks with a string quintet. This Mobile Extended group also performed in concerts at the Elbphilharmonie Hamburg and in the music rituals “Spiral Space I & II” at the European Molecular Biology Laboratory in Heidelberg during the Enjoy Jazz Festival. The title *CONTINUUM* refers to the continuous work of the band, which launched the ritual groove music project. It also refers to minimal works by other composers, such as György Ligeti and Edu Haubensak. The new launching of Mobile, with drummer Nicolas Stocker replacing Mats Eser, testifies to the ongoing work of the band. Nik discovered an inspiring photo in the café next to his house and realized that photographer Christian Senti worked in the same street too. They decided to shoot a special band photo in the eternal moment of nowhere in the street where they had both met, in which every musician is pictured twice (see p. 218).

Nik Bärtsch's Mobile, *CONTINUUM,* 2016, ECM
Moduls: 29_14, 12, 18, 5, 60, 4, 44, 8_11.
Lineup: Nik Bärtsch, piano; Kaspar Rast, drums and percussion; Sha, bass clarinet and contrabass clarinet; Nicolas Stocker, drums and tuned percussion. Extended on Moduls 18, 60, 44: Etienne Abelin, violin; Ola Sendecki, violin; David Schnee, viola; Solme Hong, cello; Ambrosius Huber, cello.
Music composed by Nik Bärtsch and arranged by Mobile. Produced by Manfred Eicher.
Recorded by Stefano Amerio at Radiostudio Lugano, March 2015.
Cover photo by Max Franosch. Liner photos by Martin Möll and Dániel Vass.
Design by Sascha Kleis.

The "Abu Dhabi Resonance Square Ritual" was a twenty-seven-hour music ritual held at the Arts Center of the New York University Abu Dhabi in 2016. It was structured by the Islamic prayer rites and combined with an exhibition about the music rituals of Mobile.

Mobile photo by Christian Senti, every band member appears twice in the picture, which was taken in the street where Nik Bärtsch lives.

"Spiral Space I – a four-hour music ritual" at European Molecular Biology Laboratory Heidelberg, 2014, co-produced with Enjoy Jazz Festival. Light design by Daniel Eaton

One Moving Organism

Awase is a term and principle from aikido. It means a matching and blending movement, a melting together and moving together. 1 + 1 = 1. Togetherness is an essential quality in band playing. As in martial arts the momentum of togetherness is a matter of life and death in music.

Second Ronin sticker designed by Hans Grüninger, WBG

Nik Bärtsch's Ronin, *AWASE,* 2018, ECM
Moduls: 60, 58, A (by Sha), 36, 34, 59.
Lineup: Nik Bärtsch, piano; Kaspar Rast, drums; Sha, bass clarinet and alto saxophone; Thomy Jordi, ebass.
Music composed by Nik Bärtsch, except "A" by Sha. Produced by Manfred Eicher.
Recorded by Gérard de Haro and Nicolas Baillard, Studios La Buissonne, October 2017.
Cover photo by Thomas Wunsch. Liner photos by Reto Camenisch. Design by Sascha Kleis.

> Ronin photo by Reto Camenisch

Hear the Listening

Entendre, the title of the first solo recording for ECM, refers to the basic, spiritual principle of deep, aware and conscious listening that is powerfully expressed in the French word. The intense experience in the studio with producer Manfred Eicher and sound engineer Stefano Amerio focused on the piano and its sound in the room. The album is a reflection of the past, an expansion of the now and an outlook to the future.

Nik Bärtsch, *Entendre,* 2021, ECM.
Moduls: 58_12, 55, 26, 13, 5, Déjà-Vu, Vienna.
Lineup: Nik Bärtsch, piano.
Music composed by Nik Bärtsch. Produced by Manfred Eicher.
Recorded by Stefano Amerio at Radiostudio Lugano, September 2020.
Cover by Fidel Sclavo. Liner photos by Caterina Di Pierri. Design by Sascha Kleis.

Nik Bärtsch and visual artist Sophie Clements joined together for the performance "When The Clouds Clear" inspired by a Japanese martial arts poem about the moon in the water. They create live a mesmeric meditation on elemental forces and cycles. Poetic patterns and sculptural forms unite in a dramaturgy of sound and light. The project was co-produced by and premiered at the Enjoy Jazz Festival Mannheim and the Barbican Centre London in 2019.

RSI

Nik Bärtsch, piano solo poster, photo by Martin Möll, design by Hans Grüninger, WBG, 2012

Nik Bärtsch's Ronin poster, photo by Martin Möll, design by Scott Woodward Meyers, 2006

STOA poster, photos by Marc Wetli, design by Sascha Kleis for ECM, cover photo by Jean-Guy Lathulière, 2006

Nik Bärtsch's Ronin poster, photo by Martin Möll, design by Hans Grüninger, WBG, 2008

Nik Bärtsch's Ronin, album score *LLYRÌA,* photo by Martin Möll, design by Hans Grüninger, WBG, 2010

Nik Bärtsch's Ronin poster, photo by Martin Möll, design by Hans Grüninger, WBG, 2012

Nik Bärtsch's Ronin poster, photo by Jonas Holthaus, design by Hans Grüninger, WBG, 2018

Nik Bärtsch's Ronin tour flyer, photo by Jonas Holthaus, design by Hans Grüninger, WBG, 2019

Nik Bärtsch, piano solo poster, photo by Christian Senti, design by Hans Grüninger, WBG, couture by DE NIZ, tatami by Sato, 2021

Fresh Fruit in the Dark

A while ago, after one of our Monday concerts, I came home to find a branch bearing fresh fruit lying on our cherry-wood kitchen table. My wife had left it there to surprise me. I couldn't really tell what kind of fruit it was in the quiet light of the semidarkness and so I just took a bite out of one. It was crunchy, both sweet and sour and had a pit. I had never tasted anything like it before but there was still something vaguely familiar about it. The next morning my wife asked me if I knew what kind of fruit it was. It was still a mystery to me. Dates, she said, just plain dates. But they were not the kind we usually eat because they were fresh. I had no idea this fruit could be so different from what I'd been eating for thirty-nine years – since my childhood in fact. That's how I felt about the sound of the piano in my first studio session for ECM with Manfred Eicher: by telling me what he hears in a piano note, he opened up a new taste for me. I discovered rich overtones and a complex life within the note.

And that's how I often feel about the creative and artistic processes that I share with my team and colleagues. Perceiving, intuiting and conjuring the presence of subtle nuances on all levels without losing sight or sound of the dramaturgy of the larger whole – that sparks incredible energy and fills me with unbridled enthusiasm. Once at the film festival in Locarno, when they screened *Sounds and Silence*, a film about Manfred Eicher's work,

Eicher said I was obsessed by music. I told him that I am enthusiastic by nature. I love these spiritual ghosts, not the immaterial, esoteric ones but the real ones that emerge when you work with precision and devotion. We inspire each other and create life-changing chains of inspiration. In music, you hear these ghosts in the phrasing, the vibrations, the sound, in the breathing and the groove, in the suspenseful emptiness of the unplayed notes and, ironically, as if dancing, in ghost notes.

o

mondrian: c

bach: well

mo

monet: haystacks

r

com

novel series

kawara: today

nposition with grid

mpered piano

tags series

es

dul series

eries

Tree of Life

The performance "Die Leere Drehen" (To Turn the Emptiness) brought together the artist-carpenter and wood turner Ernst Gamperl, the ceramicist Thomas Bohle and myself on the piano. Gamperl's largest and most significant project to date, *Tree of Life,* began in 2008, when a mighty 230-year-old oak was uprooted by a hurricane. Thanks to Gamperl, this rare treasure was destined to find a whole new lease of life.

The sheer size of the tree made it unsuitable for standardized workflows, presenting Gamperl with a new set of challenges. The trunk segments, which weighed in at around twenty-four tons and whose diameters ranged up to 2.7 meters, could only be salvaged by heavy-duty cranes, meaning that the initial pre-cutting work had to be carried out on location. However, the basic idea of only exhibiting the objects created from this tree in their entirety – once it had been fully transformed into finally sixty-seven vessels and sculptures – remained. The large-scale exhibition at the Gewerbemuseum Winterthur in 2019 marks the beginning of this phase.

In our collaboration, Gamperl, Bohle and I simultaneously created live three individual compositions: a wood sculpture, a ceramic sculpture and a music sculpture in the spirit of artistry and craftsmanship.

The performance was initiated and produced by Hans-Joachim Gögl and the Montforter Zwischentöne Festival in 2018. It was also performed at the Gewerbemuseum Winterthur in 2019 during the exhibition of Ernst Gamperl's *Tree of Life* project.

Monday Series MONTAGS 月曜日

The Montags series started in November 2004, first at Bazillus, an underground club in Zurich next to my house. Before Andrea and I went to Japan for half a year in 2003, we had already introduced an open-house tradition every first Monday of the month from 12 noon to 12 midnight. It was an invitation for friends and friends of friends to pass by, stay for as long as they pleased and meet new or familiar people. The combination of people was different every time. Long ago, I had read in a newspaper about a Jewish writer who had opened up his house once a month in New York during the Second World War, a custom that he kept up afterwards so that it became a regular and reliable place for people to find and meet each other again, possibly having lost sight of each other during those difficult times. The idea inspired me to do something similar, in my own way.

After coming home from Japan I wanted to have a more regular meeting point, not only for my friends but also for my community and especially my bands. We realized that we would never be able to grow and develop properly without regular weekly rehearsals and concerts. So

Ronin in front of one of the walls of the former Nagelhaus in Zurich's urban district 5, where the EXIL club is also located. The residential building was the symbol of local resistance toward gentrification. The network painting on the facade was created by artist Pierre Haubensak and remained until 2016, when the building was finally demolished.

The reverse side of the Montags flyer designed by Hans Grüninger, WBG. It shows the Japanese kanji symbol for moon as used in "Monday" and "month."

I rented the then new Bazillus club on Mondays and gave regular workshops in the afternoon from 2 to 4 pm, after which we would rehearse and play for the public in the evening. Together with Kaspar Rast we organized what turned into our Monday concert series for the next five years before I co-founded and built the EXIL club in 2009 with four other partners (see p. 248).

Since then the EXIL club in Zurich has become permanent home to the Montags series, our ongoing platform for continuous work on the ritual groove music, as well as a platform for a wider community interested in related musical ideas. Workshops and concerts still take place every Monday.

The afternoon workshop is now called the Music Dojo and, since 2018, the Montags evening concerts have also been streamed live by Yourstage.live, a cultural project and platform in the same spirit, initiated by Marc David Nathmann.

The Montags Music Dojo incorporates the principles and the philosophy of our music between funk, jazz and new classical music and offers group work with patterns as well as work on minimal groove and improvisation. The workshop is, and always was, open to all who are interested. The idea of the dojo – as a training center in martial arts is called – always appealed to me: beginners train with advanced practitioners, and the spirit of learning from each other with care and respect is more important than the grade.

The Montags series teaches me humility, dedication and commitment. We never know if there will be another Monday, every Monday could be the last.

The EXIL, an Exile for Music in Our Own Town

The EXIL club was created in 2008 and set up in 2009 in three months without public funding but with some private loans and the crazy, positive energy and planning of five cultural entrepreneurs: architect Christoph Kellenberger, night-life entrepreneur Dominik Müller, promoter and light designer Michi Vollenweider, drummer and sushi master Tosho Yakkatokuo – and me.

In 2002, Christoph Kellenberger and his OOS company for architecture and design had already worked with my band Mobile on the set design and dramaturgy of the third part of the Blue Trilogy project and in 2005 on "SEE – a musical sound picture," a performance on the lake. Christoph and I had been wanting to create our own music club for a while and were looking for buildings and professional partners who would be crazy enough to launch a music club based on the idea of presenting good music and events independent of style and scene but more dependent on quality and taste. Christoph gave the club its name because he wanted to create a place in his own home town where he could go into exile to find a true, sophisticated music spirit and lifestyle and to share this with other people. It ended up becoming an unusual story of a team of people, who were always fair and direct but also tough and honest with each other.

The founders of EXIL, Tosho Yakkatokuo, Nik Bärtsch, Christoph Kellenberger, Michi Vollenweider and Dominik Müller in a break during a sailing trip on Lake Neuchâtel, where they were holding a creative meeting in 2011.

After a few years, light designer, early EXIL technician and co-builder Pipo Schreiber along with booker and cultural entrepreneur Stipe Svalina joined the founding team. The EXIL project survived in part and in particular thanks to Stipe and his enormous creativity, pragmatism, street credibility and smart sense of the contemporary local and international groove music scene.

The EXIL club illustrates that, for once, creative cultural activities and economic survival do not have to be a contradiction in terms. But this succeeds only because every member of the leading team and the club team ceaselessly seek to renew and energize the presence and competitiveness of the club and its underlying concept. To me, this group of people and the whole project demonstrated that a love of culture, true entrepreneurship and team spirit can change the world – or at least a tiny corner of the world.

MORE THAN MUSIC

MORE THAN MUSIC

TOLERANT MULTICOLORED POSTCULTURAL UNDERGROUND OVERWHELMING QUEER INTENSE POLYAMOROUS LOVE CHOICE INCLUSIVE WAVY 1312 BLACK JOY ALIVE GENDER BENDER VOGUING CONSCIOUS INTO IT OUT OF IT PROGRESSIVEUNITY FREE UGLY DON'T STOP NOW FOREVER HYPNOTIC RHYTHMIC SAVAGE VIGOROUS LIVE SEC THRILLING SOPHISTICATED EROTIC HAPPINESS GAY PSYCHIC SPIRITUAL HOMO HETERO NOTORIOUS BISEXUAL INDIE POST-GENRE URBAN GROOVY ECCENTRIC MYSTIC TANTRIC FREAKY STUNNING RAVE SUBVERSIVE TRIPPING BALLS SENSUAL SEXY RHYTHMIC COLLABORATIVE COLLECTIVE CONNECTING INDEPENDENT FUNKY POSITIVE MIND BLOWING DANCING A SONG A STORY DIRECT INSPIRING FUTURISTIC TRENDSETTING MULTILINGUAL MODULAR KAWAII ARTISTIC PANMUSICAL SOULFUL HUMAN TASTY FANTASTIC ORGANIC HIP HOP FORWARD THINKING INTERNATIONAL SMART INTELLIGENT DIRECT EXCITING FASCINATING THIRSTY HUNGRY OPEN ACCOMMODATING HELPFUL COOPERATIVE POWERFUL SUBTLE DIFFERENTIATED SOCIAL SACRAL CRAZY ROCK FAST FLOURISHING COLORFUL YOUR FRIEND EMBRACING TOUCHING VISIONARY STRONG VISUAL CLAIRAUDIENT CLAIRVOYANT DEMISEXUAL TOUGH TURNING SPINNING NASTY PHILOSOPHICAL FAIR FANCY STYLISH STYLISTIC MAD MONSTROUS EXPLODING ENERGETC FLOWING FLOATING BLOOMY BOOMING SPEED MOVING CINEMATIC AROMATIC FRESH FLASHY SPARKLING AMOROUS IN LOVE TENDER RESPECTFUL SPICY FOOTLOOSE FUNNY ATTRACTIVE SMOOTH AWAKE ETERNAL INTUITIVE DRUMMING PLAYFUL SINGING SWEET SUPER PEACEFUL STOIC ENTHUSIASTIC PATIENT PASSIONATE ORIGINAL DISCRETE SECRET NATURAL ENGAGED SAFE NOCTURNAL ACTING INTERESTING ELEGANT ANIMALISTIC CHARMING CONSTANT COHERENT COSMIC UNIVERSAL BEAUTIFUL WARM SNUG MEDITATIVE WELCOMING INVITING POLYSEXUAL AMPLIFIED ACOUSTIC A RITUAL ROCK'N'ROLL AMBIENT ONGOING PANSEXUAL LESBIAN NONSTOP CHREIS 5 LIFE FRESH POPPIN' PILLS NOT TELEVISED

EXIL

Whales
Evolution of a Song through Modular Creativity

Bio-Poetic Phenomenon

The ability to sing is not restricted to birds and humans; whales and dolphins also sing. The songs of humpback whales are probably the most complex form of communication in the animal kingdom. Four to six basic units of several seconds each form a partial verse, two partial verses form a stanza, which the whales repeat for two to four minutes. Several of these so-called themes in succession then form a song that lasts up to twenty minutes, like a pop song that has a first verse, a second verse, a chorus repeated several times and then put on repeat.

The humpback whales' songs undergo steady development. All the males in a population sing the exact same song – but only for one season. The following year they have a new favorite song, which is based on the old one. The animals rearrange verses, adding something in different places or leaving something out. When the new repertoire is complete, all whales sing exactly the same song again. Through this process, the songs of a population become more and more complex from year to year.

Significantly, every few years the humpback whales in eastern Australia take over the songs of their west-coast conspecifics. They probably listen to the new sounds of individual animals that have swum over to them from the west. In a kind of musical revolution, they suddenly stop varying their old song and start singing the hit from the west instead.

According to Katy Payne, zoologist and pioneering bioacoustics researcher, "There's a psychological concept describing how fashion works in human beings called 'optimal mismatch.' It's great if you make a change that's just extreme enough so that everybody will follow you, but no good if it isn't different enough. So the optimal mismatch to set a new trend is just in that range. I suppose that's happening as whales listen to each other's songs."[1]

1 See: David Rothenberg, "Whale Song Explained," https://mindsurfing.typepad.com/connexions/2017/12/e1ahe1ch-dont-even-sing-about-it-.html (accessed: 04.05.21)

Maybe whales get bored with yesterday's hits, just like us.

However, scientists are still trying to solve the puzzle of which individual whale artists come up with new songs and why this exchange only takes place from west to east and never vice versa.

From the east coast of Australia, songs, and not the whales, migrate farther and farther east over the following years, from one group of whales to the next in a stepwise and directional fashion traversing almost 6,000 miles of ocean – like a gigantic game of humpback whale telephone or the spread of a fashion trend or pop song.

It is therefore no exaggeration to speak here of culture, assuming, of course, that culture is not an exclusively human achievement, as in music, painting, literature and theater.

Reduce Things to Three Principles

In a live-performance situation, mind and body cannot relate to more than three principles.

Choose a topic and reduce it to three principles.

Musicianship reduced to three principles:

1 Listen!
2 Only play the essentials
3 Make the others sound good

Performer Spirit reduced to three principles:

1 Expand your Now
2 Communicate
3 Don't fear to fail or die

Parenthood reduced to three principles:

1 Listen!
2 Speak through action
3 Love unconditionally

Love reduced to three principles:

1 Give unconditionally
2 Receive unconditionally
3 Switch off your cell phone

Peace reduced to three principles:

1 Respect your partner
2 Be awake
3 Risk your life for it

Origin reduced to three principles:

1 Universal
2 Cultural
3 Individual

Musical Source reduced to three principles:

1 Improvisation
2 Composition
3 Interpretation

time

tempo

timing

Reduction – Contemporary Perspectives of a Musical Strategy

Reductive strategies are central in my musical thinking as well as my daily life. In body and mind, as well as in the outside world, there are millions of interesting and interlocking ideas, concepts and possibilities. It seems that for me personally, reduction to the basics is one of the best strategies to maintain precision, to keep from losing myself in the spectrum of possibilities and to avoid panicking and falling apart as a consequence: the reductive process treats the material with careful economy, while simultaneously liberating, enlivening and deepening it. It allows one to see and hear the material better: what it says, what it sings and how it moves. Freedom arises first through (self-imposed) order, as Stravinsky once said. The questions are the same in art as well as in life: What's really important? How much of something is needed? Simplicity is often more complex than complexity.

In contrast to the mid-twentieth century (especially after the "liberation movements" in jazz and contemporary music in the sixties and seventies), I find that minimalist or rather reductionist techniques in art as well as in life provide feasible alternatives to the reigning "everything goes" mentality of the present. The relativist phenomenon and the enormous potential diversity it offers in art and in an everyday social context demands that one must know exactly under what criterion he or she is working and take full responsibility for those decisions – a good situation! The question is still the same: What is important? What is “essential”? What is fundamental to me, fundamental to the material, and how can the material be reduced to its fundamentals? Awkward simplicity lacks tension – the tension of intelligent simplicity is the ironic conflict between self-negation and self-awareness.

In contemporary music, reduction in the “modern sense” is surely one of the most interesting innovations of the twentieth century and is still a feasible alternative in all possible styles to the insistence on narrative, arbitrary associations or a belief in the quality of complexity. It forms an important bridge between visual art and music. Occasionally it leads to a cul-de-sac – either where simplicity is only suggested instead of being created and constructed, or where popular “reductive” classical music should fill empty concert halls and record company tills. Reduction is not a patent recipe for modern, good or even interesting art. Reductive strategies are obvious answers to the explosion of musical styles and the manifold diversity facilitated by the ready availability of history, samplers, home recording and DIY production. They are a response to the profusion of sound waves filling the air: forward to the roots – back to the future.

Cephalopods
Dynamic Camouflage

Bio-Poetic Phenomenon

Cephalopods are most closely related to slugs and mollusks; they have no bones and live only for a maximum of three years. Although they have neither a shell nor sharp teeth to protect themselves in an environment full of predators, these animals survive – thanks to their intelligence.

They are the only group outside of vertebrates to possess a complex, clever brain. But unlike us humans, who have only one brain to process every bit of information before they can react, cephalopods have "satellite brains" in each of their eight to ten arms. In this way they can react much faster, for example, when hunting. They can even process visual information directly in their arms, enabling them to quickly change color and pattern for a perfect camouflage. To blend with their surroundings or to confuse predators or prey, a cephalopod uses some twenty-five million color organs dispersed over its skin. With these chromatophores it can create patterns of spots or stripes, send a so-called passing cloud display through its body and also voluntarily change the texture of its skin.

When cephalopods sleep, they show signs of REM phases, during which they also show changes in color and texture.

In an experiment, it took captured squid only a few days to realize when they might be fed shrimp – their favorite food – in the evening, for which reason they would eat less throughout the day.

In other words, they can dream, perform dynamic camouflage and change behavior according to their expectations. Is this the extra-terrestrial intelligence we have been looking for?

Improvisers can adapt to their musical surroundings by being part of the picture and contributing individuality. Instead of soloing they can play the game of mimicry with joy.

mus

listen

structural er

-musical director

interpret

compose

dramatic adv

sound engineer

improv

conducto

ian
er
neer
r
or
ser

On Composing, Improvising and Performing

Part 1: About Trams, Tailors and Unstable Buildings

A ticket for everything?

A funny advertising campaign for the public transport authority of Zurich had the slogan "A ticket for everything," indicating that travelers can combine several means of transport like trams, trains, buses and ships in one ticket. This advantage was underscored by equating one type of transport with another, as in a poster picturing a tram plying the waters of a lake.

Inspired and skillful musicians take a similar approach: musicality is also "a ticket for everything," for transporting music with various vehicles. Composing, improvising, interpreting, arranging, producing and orchestrating are just some of the diverse means or strategies nourished by a common source, as mentioned in the text "From a Single Source" (see p. 150). To use the musical "ticket for everything" in a target-oriented manner, we need to think about the qualities of the musical "means of transport." Otherwise we will not reach our destination safely. An improvisation or composition can also drown, like a tram in the lake.

700 pieces in eighteen months or not even a simple little exercise in one day

Keyboardist Joe Zawinul, who has composed many famous jazz hits, says about composing: "I improvise quite a lot with my laptop and my small keyboard. When I'm on the road, I set up in my hotel within five minutes and then play for ninety. Everything is stored on the laptop. 700 pieces have been composed in this way over the past one and a half years. The pieces on the CD [*Faces & Places*] have been taken directly from these improvisations. I didn't have to play them over again in the studio; I just edited them because they are often too long. Having the original improvisation on the CD gives the music a special intensity."[1]

Quite a difference to Morton Feldman's statement about composing: "I have ideas that I throw away in two minutes that the poorest one in this room would give me at least ten thousand Marks for. And the reason I do that is because I don't want to be influenced with my own thought. That might divert me from the focus of that moment. But I don't think that that moment is essentially a kind of a one-night stand with an idea. I wouldn't say that it's a short-term commitment. I just have to

1 See: Gunther Baumann, "Composing," in *Zawinul: Ein Leben aus Jazz [A Life of Jazz]* (Vienna: Residenz-Verlag, 2002), p. 78.

Photo by Stefan Minder for the advertising campaign "A ticket for everything"

be focused and doing my best at that particular moment because it's a very serious operation. There are a lot of questions to ask, and some of the most important questions are: your attitude as a composer. Schoenberg once wrote in a letter that some days he gets up in the morning, and he can't even do a simple little exercise. Composing is so difficult. To write something lousy is so difficult."[2]

It is irrelevant to ask which of these great creators is right, especially since both emphasize the authentic need to be a cosmic catalyzer for music, like many spiritual musicians. It is interesting how their attitude is reflected in their work ethic and technique and in the results: the way they write music and how they want their music to be performed. Their personality is reflected in the musical stories they tell. How do they create their style?

2 Morton Feldman, *Essays*, ed. Walter Zimmermann (Kerpen: Beginner Press, 1985), pp. 186–87.

3 Feldman, *Essays*, p. 212.

About tailoring compositions and designing roles

A musical composition that is not carefully tailored to the context of its performance falls short. It is not an abstract pattern that shines in the platonic heaven of eternal ideas; it is a real, resonating materiality, a communicating being. To take shape naturally, it requires appropriate circumstances and numerous people embodying different roles.

A composer seems to be both fashion designer and tailor, uniting innovation, craft and the capacity to communicate. As Morton Feldman puts it, "My music is handmade. So I'm like a tailor. I make my buttonholes by hand. The suit fits better."[3] Before becoming a professor of music, he worked in his father's business of manufacturing coats for children.

Pattern-making in the fashion industry is the result of a creative process related to real circumstances. It has to take facts into account: choice of fabric, movement, people's needs, the influence of weather and, of course, money and time. The work of fashion designers and their tailors clearly requires moments of intuitive innovation as part of the creative process but in the end, the collection as a whole is the outcome of a thoughtful, meticulous process. Clarity and coherence are essential.

My mentor, fashion designer Christa de Carouge, taught me this quite naturally. To follow the development of her collections from initial sketches to final presentation in a performance could be called a rhythmical experience. Being responsible for the music in her fashion performances, I had the opportunity to study the pragmatic steps that she took to implement her creations. I realized they were comparable to creating an album or a collection of pieces in music.

Wear your composition for a while like a dress

Christa usually wore her newly designed clothes herself for a while to first feel and explore how they were "behaving" and how she felt in them. She considered them her second skin, her protection, her appearance and even her "habitat," as she called it. She did not want to sell her clothes to anyone before doing a reality check. In her studio I learned what it takes to proceed from an idea to its implementation in a reasonable amount of time: autumn collection follows spring collection, tough timing for creativity. Christa also taught me the joy of improvising clothing out of found fabrics, but designing a new collection required a different focus. Christa was creative director, fashion entrepreneur, draftswoman, tailor, pattern maker, producer, team leader and even saleswoman, but she also skillfully delegated most of these roles and worked with an excellent tailor who finally became her successor.

As a composer, I do not work on pieces in isolation either. The first ECM album *STOA,* for example, developed and written during my six-month stay in Japan, was clearly tailored for the band Ronin and its personalities. We thereafter shaped the pieces in rehearsals, played them in our weekly Montags series, then on tour and finally recorded them for the album together with producer Manfred Eicher and sound engineer Gérard de Haro. This prolonged process allowed the sense and sensuality of the compositions to sink in, to become second nature, as it were, so that they could ultimately be communicated naturally to the audience. People can wear the music like a cool, classy weatherproof dress that will not fall apart after listening to it a few times.

Would you like to walk into your composition?

The composition of music in all its varieties – jazz, pop, classical music, folk, etc. – is subject to a diversity

Christa de Carouge, ca. 1998, in her “Urban Nomad” outfit

of circumstances, environments and social settings. The process from creative beginning to performance covers an extraordinarily broad spectrum. Even the word "composition" does not necessarily mean the same thing to a classical musician as it does, for instance, to a jazz player.

Every musician has different needs, talents, skills and views on how music is created – as composer and as player. Musical vehicles like composing, improvising, interpreting, arranging, producing, orchestrating, etc. are not only different musical strategies but also have different meanings depending on the context. Therefore it is useful to differentiate and sharpen awareness of the musical roles that contribute to the final performance, such as composer, interpreter, improviser, producer or sound engineer. Everyone involved must be dedicated to making a piece sound and ultimately appear like a perfectly natural act.

A solid composition should have already received a lot of affection and care from the composer before it is entrusted to other hands for a performance.

A remarkable comment using a different metaphor on the subtle and yet robust results of a composer's work comes from eighty-five-year-old Igor Stravinsky: "Meanwhile, I confess that I would be frightened to enter some of the compositions I have heard of late, in their forms as buildings."[4]

In this respect, a composition consists of more than the musical material; it also represents the social, ethical and aesthetic ideas of composers – the way they build their musical houses, plant their musical gardens, invent their musical habitats, tailor their musical clothes.

Which compositions would you like to walk into like houses? Which compositions would you like to wear like clothes?

4 See: "Stravinsky at Eighty-five: An Interview," in *The New York Review of Books*, June 1, 1967.

Part 2: Putting Stuff Together

The difference between something and anything

Composing literally means to put stuff together: to give musical entities a fruitful context on various levels, from simple small resonances to big complex habitats. Putting stuff together coincidentally or associatively leads to chaos and arbitrariness. A coherent and sustainable dramaturgy requires a balance between form and sensuality, between convention, expectation and surprise. It consists of an inherent truth.

It is a beautiful challenge for a composer to discover, assess and develop musical material that is full of potential from *within*. Its "outside" potential is infinite. A musical structure can be associatively combined with anything – from various other musical motives to a teapot. But what lies latent in the structure itself? We need to understand the difference between the openness to anything and the focus on something. Creativity in this case does not mean to see variety but to listen with great care to the discovered material: what does *it* want? This might be

My sketch of Igor Stravinsky composing in an ice-cold junk room with an off-tune piano in Château-d'Oex in Switzerland, winter 1914. The room full of empty old Suchard chocolate boxes and next to a chicken house … (see: Igor Stravinsky, *Chroniques de ma vie*)

different from what the composer wants. As an example of finding the potential inherent in a musical motive, we can ask how it behaves in a little canon. In my piece "Modul 44" for example, the four-tone motive in the beginning is combined with its retrograde and then turned into a canon. The motive itself encourages this reduced use; the composer does not need to invent it but just to find it.

In this context, Igor Stravinsky uses the terms "contrast" and "similarity": "Contrast is everywhere. One has only to take note of it. Similarity is hidden; it must be sought out, and it is found only after the most exhaustive efforts. When variety tempts me, I am uneasy about the facile solutions it offers me. Similarity, on the other hand, poses more difficult problems, but also offers results that are more solid and hence more valuable to me."[5] Note that Stravinsky also uses the word "solid," which we usually apply to physical constructions.

A composer is a sensual and sensible scientist of music with a sharp ear, capable of finding the hidden potential of similarity and aligning a musical being.

The compass of Captain Jack Sparrow and Dürrenmatt's *Stoffe* or the dialogue between composer and material

A composer should be able to listen to his/her inner will or drive as sensitively as to the will of the material; that means being acutely attentive to one's personal cosmic compass. It indicates the intuitive poetic, aesthetic and ethic direction and is not influenced by the legitimation

5 Igor Stravinsky, *Poetics of Music in the Form of Six Lessons* (Cambridge, MA: Harvard University Press, 1947), pp. 32–33.

6 "Aber die Stoffe sind Resultate meines Denkens, die Spiegel, in denen, je nach ihrem Schliff, mein Denken und damit auch mein Leben reflektiert werden." *Der Winterkrieg in Tibet* (1969) (Zurich: Diogenes 1998), p. 13.

7 Paul Klee, *The Diaries of Paul Klee, 1898–1918* (Berkeley: University of California Press, 1968), p. 124.

8 *Im Reich der Falten – Mode und Textilkunst aus Japan,* exhibition, Museum Bellerive, Zurich, 2013.

of excellence or by criteria of quality from outside. It requires just a few essential things, embodied in what we have described as the "beginner's mind" (see p. 104).

To know our inner will as a composer means listening carefully with our inner ear. This inner ear is as important as the outer ear for the substance or material of composing; they are in contact and partnership with each other.

Writer and painter Friedrich Dürrenmatt used the German word *Stoff* ("stuff") to describe the relationship between material and author: "The materials are the result of my thinking, the mirrors in which, depending on the polish, my thinking and my life are reflected."[6]

The material talks to the author and the author talks to the material. It is a dialogue on the deepest level of attention and existence. Painter Paul Klee laconically remarked, "I am my style."[7] This should not be confused with prodigies who have one hit, one work, one idea during their lifetime. The dialogue between composer and material means to listen to both one's own affinities with a certain material and the material itself. Fashion designer Yohji Yamamoto said this in a beautifully modest way: "I learned to accept my own style."[8] The inner will might also be compared to Captain Jack Sparrow's compass in the film series *Pirates of the Caribbean*. This unusual navigational instrument does not point to the magnetic north but rather to what the holder wants. But, if you don't know what you really want or if you want too many things, the compass just turns and turns and turns. Young pirate Will Turner later asks first mate Gibbs, "How can we sail to an island that nobody can find with a compass that doesn't work?" Gibbs replies, "Aye, the compass doesn't point north, but we're not trying to find north, are we?"

Do not sail to an academic north, find your own direction. Never betray the compass!

Original score of “Modul 22,” a so-called “one page piece”: the basic idea of the rhythmic structure, structural harmonies and form are understandable at a glance.

Part 3: My Compass – Ritual Groove Music and Its Background

Convention and innovation

Before sharing some of my basic musical guidelines as a composer, I would like to talk about the relationship between analysis and creative work. A condition for being consciously innovative is to reflect one's own knowledge and craft and to be aware of its circumstances. This is a tricky subject, as we will see.

According to Claude Debussy, "Every work of art develops a law. But you don't begin with it."[9] Stravinsky also emphasizes that analysis *follows* creation. When asked what theory is in musical composition, he replied, "Hindsight. It doesn't exist. There are compositions from which it is deduced. Or, if this isn't quite true, it has a by-product existence that is powerless to create or even to justify. Nevertheless, composition involves a deep intuition of theory."[10]

These statements show the dilemma of describing the creative process of composing and its "rules." Composers *must* have a sense of balance, dramaturgy, coherence and innovation, a sense of the universal process that inspires musical communication. Composition is not based exclusively on intuition and associative capacity, nor exclusively on a good academic education. Composers must find their own position in the historic stream of music by reflecting and "feeling" past, present and future developments in their compositions.

9 Quoted in: Feldman, *Essays,* p. 145.

10 Igor Stravinsky and Robert Kraft, *Conversations with Igor Stravinsky* (New York: Doubleday, 1959), p. 12.

In this process it is essential to find a balance between conventional material, commonly known and understandable musical code, and invention. Pianist and music theoretician Charles Rosen explores this in his fabulous book *The Classical Style – Haydn, Mozart, Beethoven* (1998). To look back onto a past musical epoch makes it easier to understand the laws of common code and innovation in the present time as well. The music of the classical age shares a similar musical language, but every composer who uses that language speaks differently. In other words, composers of a certain period and style in music history work with the same conventional material, which is taken for granted in a specific time and region, but since they each invent expressions of their own, the language itself gradually changes over the centuries. This ties in with the development of language itself and even with the history and development of ideas and concepts in science, culture and society in general.

In his book *The Order of Things* (1970), philosopher Michel Foucault explores this phenomenon in the light of common knowledge. He calls unconscious and unquestioned assumptions "epistemic assumptions." They are often connected and related across different areas of society and culture, for example, music and art. In that sense the conventional material in music is a necessary condition for the existence of a coherent musical style. The convention is at the same time a springboard for its own transcendence. It defines a style by being clear and familiar without innovation, with the consequence that every innovation is noticeable. This is different from the revolutionary avant-garde strategy of breaking the rules of the past as quickly as possible and at any price. Without insight into contemporary conventions, it is not possible to transcend them and to let the music evolve.

In the text "Empathy and Phrasing" (see p. 208) I quote philosopher Ludwig Wittgenstein's remark about the relation of the known and unknown in everyday life. He says that those aspects of things that are most important for us are hidden because of their simplicity and familiarity. This is exactly what Charles Rosen points out in his book about the classical style. In the works of the composers Mozart, Haydn and Beethoven, all the chords, scales and conventional patterns are not the things we remember as innovative ideas. They are "just there." Even figures developed only one generation earlier, like the Alberti-bass arpeggios, have already been internalized. They are just the context for the next innovation. The invention of today is the convention of tomorrow.

As composers we need to be aware of the cultural code with which we are working. We need to combine two aspects of awareness, as mentioned by Wittgenstein: the hidden implicitness of familiar things and the need to know the rules of observance to interpret signs of a cultural situation correctly. It sounds quite basic but many musicians stay epigones because they don't think about the correlations of convention, innovation and change. Tradition can be a golden cage.

Experienced players of jazz or chess do not think about the rules anymore. The rules become second nature

Cover of the Ronin Rhythm Records album *ROFU*, *MANTA MANTRA*, 2020. The album includes two chamber music compositions by Nik Bärtsch for two pianos and two percussionists, played by the Makrokosmos Quartet. Produced by Nik Bärtsch. Recorded, mixed and mastered by Andreas Brüll. Design by Hans Grüninger, WBG. Pictures by graphic novel artist Gion Capeder from the graphic novel *Superman*, published by Edition Moderne in 2017.

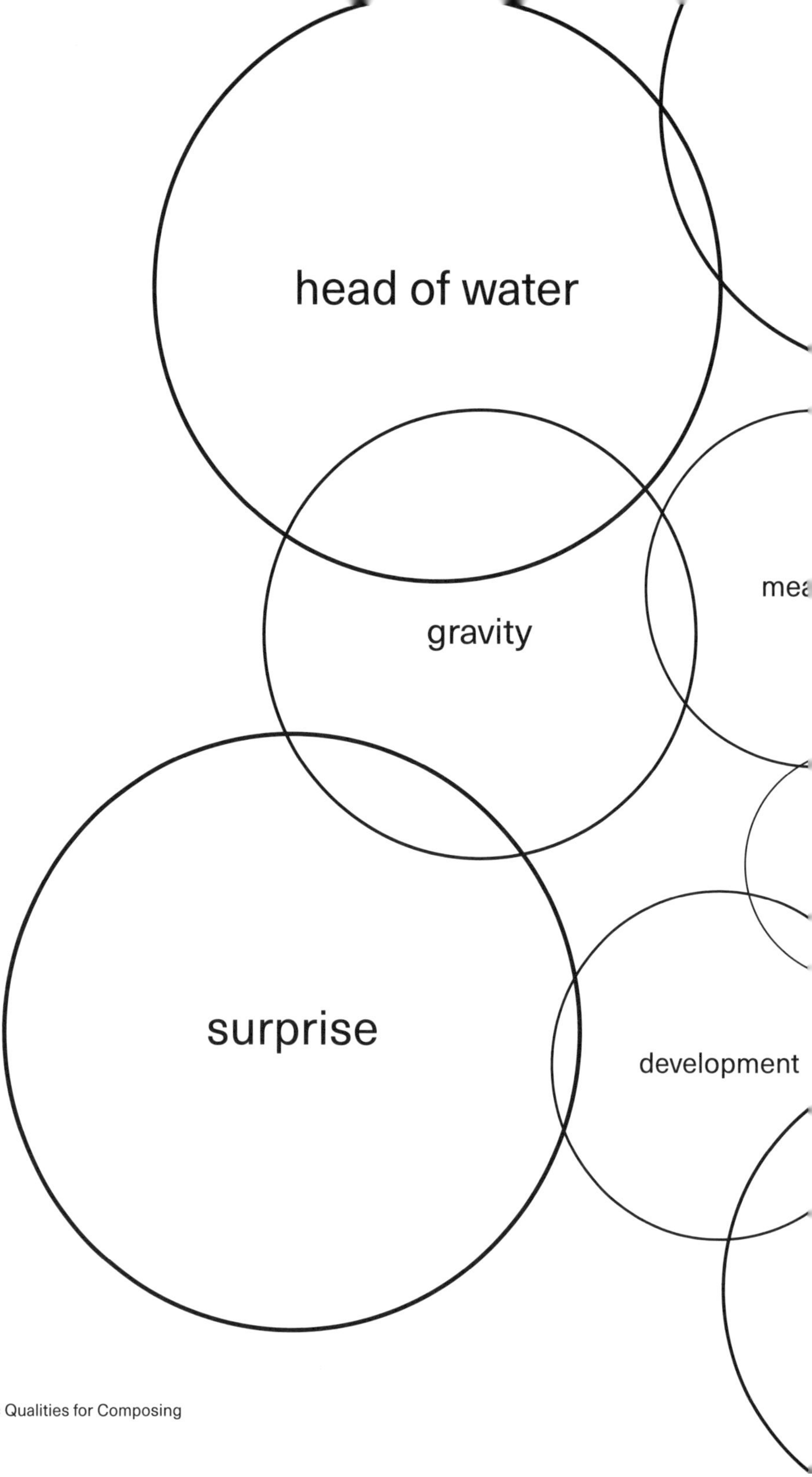
head of water
gravity
surprise
development

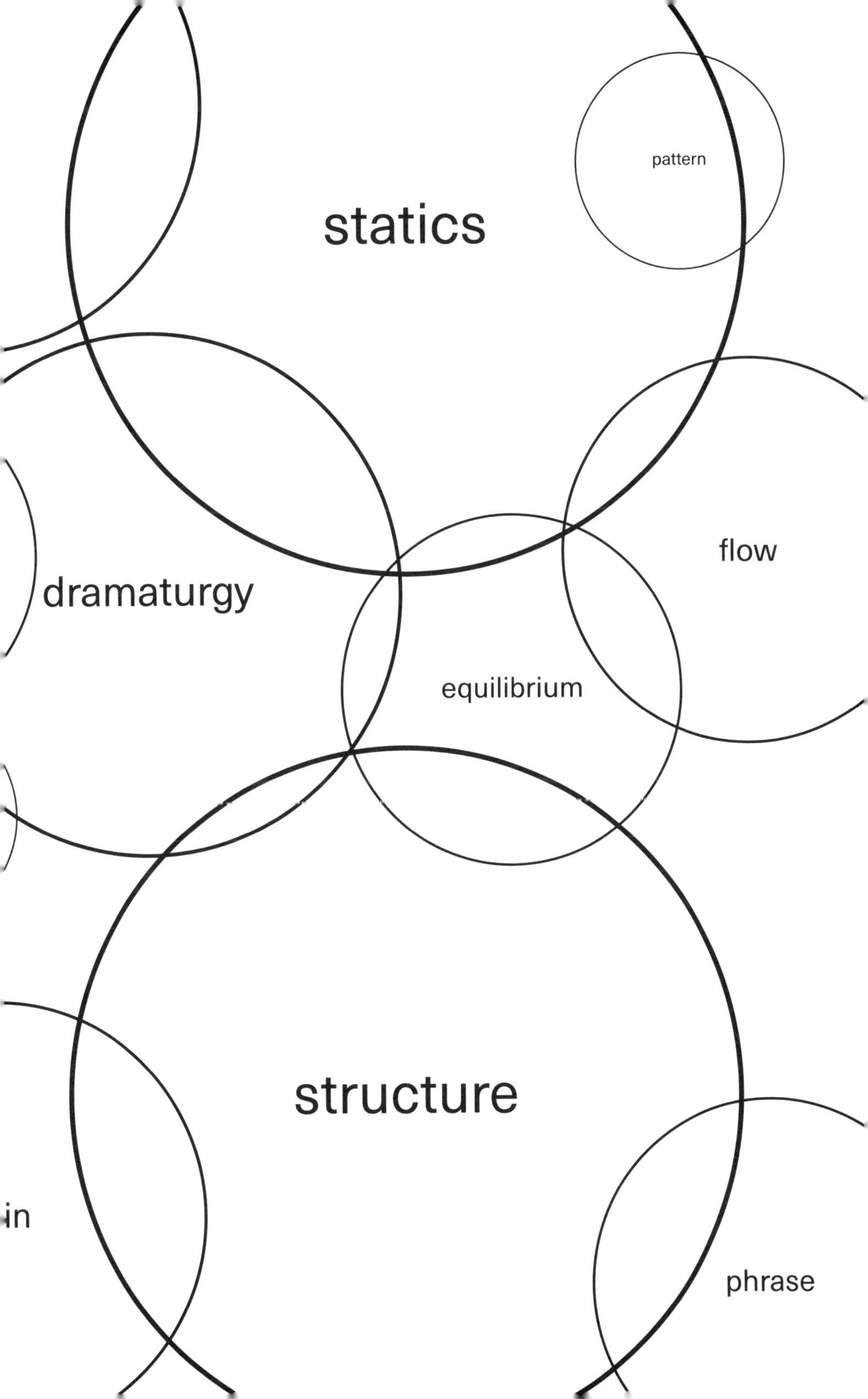

pattern
statics
flow
dramaturgy
equilibrium
structure
in
phrase

in creatively exploiting the possibilities. Unlike chess, however, a careful innovative composer needs to know these rules *and* change them, ultimately changing the entire game.

The goal of sharing inside views on my compositional thinking and techniques is to offer a more specific vocabulary to describe and understand this music and its deviations from existing common code, perhaps also encouraging you to think about the cultural codes of your worldview and your own creative work. The stamp "Ritual Groove Music," which I have chosen for my musical world, describes the general direction in which my ideas, affinities, perspectives and strategies flow. Much of this can be found in other musical times, styles and expressions. The term does not stake out musical territory but is, rather, a microscopic and telescopic means of exploring music in more detail.

It is a guide that helps me to avoid falling into the trap of convention, even my own.

The Modul: about my musical conception

A Modul [məʊ'duːl] is a composed and combinable musical molecule. It functions like Arthur Koestler's holon, an entity that exists both autonomously and in relation to a larger whole. The Modul can consist of a simple two-bar pattern (e.g. "Modul 8") or encompass several smaller modular elements as a system of interlocking patterns (e.g. "Modul 14") or within rhythmic and/or harmonic layering, which results in multimeasure cycles (e.g. "Modul 23" and "Modul 26"). Moduls can also be layered and combined with one another (e.g. "Modul 8_9") and often vary in instrumentation and form. Forms are established by repetition, the layering of contrasting meters and "rotational" cycles – or also through the more liberal use of the patterns and modular components (modular elements within Moduls).

Score part of “Modul 15” by Nik Bärtsch

Moduls can be strictly realized by classically trained interpreters (e.g. “Modul Ritual,” an arrangement of “Modul 23” for saxophone quartet, drums, percussion, piano and Rhodes) or by a band familiar with the improvised means used to interpret and vary the composed material (e.g. the band Ronin). However, the composed material remains the focus of the music. Single parts of the form can be varied in length or reorganized modularly. The form that is to be followed is cued through an easily recognizable auditory symbol – usually a clear and high-pitched bell, a scream or similar sound.

In more broadly conceived concerts and musical rituals, lasting as long as thirty-six hours (e.g. “MU BLUE,” 2002, by the acoustic group Mobile), composed sections and the more freely improvised sections are interchanged. In the open sections, the musicians' improvisations remain grounded in the composed material or relevant Modul. Moduls can then be seen as through-composed musical building blocks, enlivened by the realization and interpretation of the specific live ensemble of that moment.

This text about the Modul was written in April 2001 and revised in 2012. The writing of new Moduls still continues and some also have much longer dramaturgies with through-composed transitions and musical hinges (e.g. Moduls 52, 53, 58, 59, 66). I have chosen the technical name to show how these musical pieces are composed and organized. Like a sinfonia, sonata, étude or study, the name just indicates the existence of a piece of coherent music. And it gives the interpreters and listeners of the music the poetic and emotional freedom to find their own meanings in the music. The first piece that consciously explored this way of composing was a chamber music piece, called “Modul Ritual,” written in 1997 for my piano diploma.

My modular approach in composition was initially inspired by two courses at the Zurich University of the Arts, taught by the two Swiss composers Felix Baumann and

Martin Schlumpf. Schlumpf, himself a post-minimalist, gave an inspiring class about minimalism in music, especially about the sophisticated music and writings of Steve Reich; Baumann gave a class about twenty-first century compositions, emphasizing the modular aspect in the work of Feldman and Stravinsky. Especially in "The Rite of Spring," Stravinsky sometimes had to adapt lengths in the score since the choreography of the ballet changed during its creation. Feldman, like Stravinsky, had a strong rhythmic sensibility, although he did not show this explicitly but would sometimes groove like Stravinsky, in slow motion. In a lecture he said:

"I work very moduly, I don't work in a continuity, I work moduly. And many times I like to work moduly because then I turn it around! If I just think in terms of a module, I could take this in another place like Frankenstein, and I could put it over here … (*draws*) … I am very interested also in retrograde. And I have pieces where I don't repeat the tones retrograde, but I repeat the whole module retrograde."[11]

Working with modular cells by retrograding, inverting, augmenting, diminishing or combining them is extremely fruitful for coherent composing. Modular composition strategies like this create different formal possibilities from narrative developments on a time scale.

Modular versus linear concepts: being IN the piece or being WITH the piece

To illustrate being IN versus being WITH a piece, we can compare it with the tradition of the careful linear development of a composition, exemplified by Anton Webern, a composer of the Second Viennese School. This school crucially influenced modern composing and its philosophy. Music philosopher Theodor W. Adorno considered it

11 Feldman, *Essays*, p. 166.

an example of "good contemporary" composition, in contrast to Stravinsky's approach to composition as well as jazz and other groove music. This confrontation seems unnecessary to me. I studied Webern's music intensively, especially the piano piece "Op. 27," which I learned by heart to internalize it. I also played a lot of his dense and distilled chamber music. In his lectures on composing, Webern emphasizes how motives grow continuously and are deduced from their own origin and past, like a plant, based on Goethe's idea of the primordial plant.[12] The notion of a primordial motive is also called "gestalt," a term used mainly in psychology and biology. The strategy of composing everything out of a basic series of notes creates the greatest possible coherence. The above-mentioned conventional material and the innovation in a piece are quasi identical. There is no redundant material in time anymore, which is the dream of every radical linear composer: absolute coherence. The price for this is being trapped in linear time.

In modular tradition the formal space of a composition is organized differently. A piece can be entered like a room or a space and musical memory works with multidimensional relations and references. Morton Feldman

12 Anton Webern, *Der Weg zur Neuen Musik, Der Weg zur Komposition in 12 Tönen, 2×8 Vorträge* (Universal Edition, 1985).

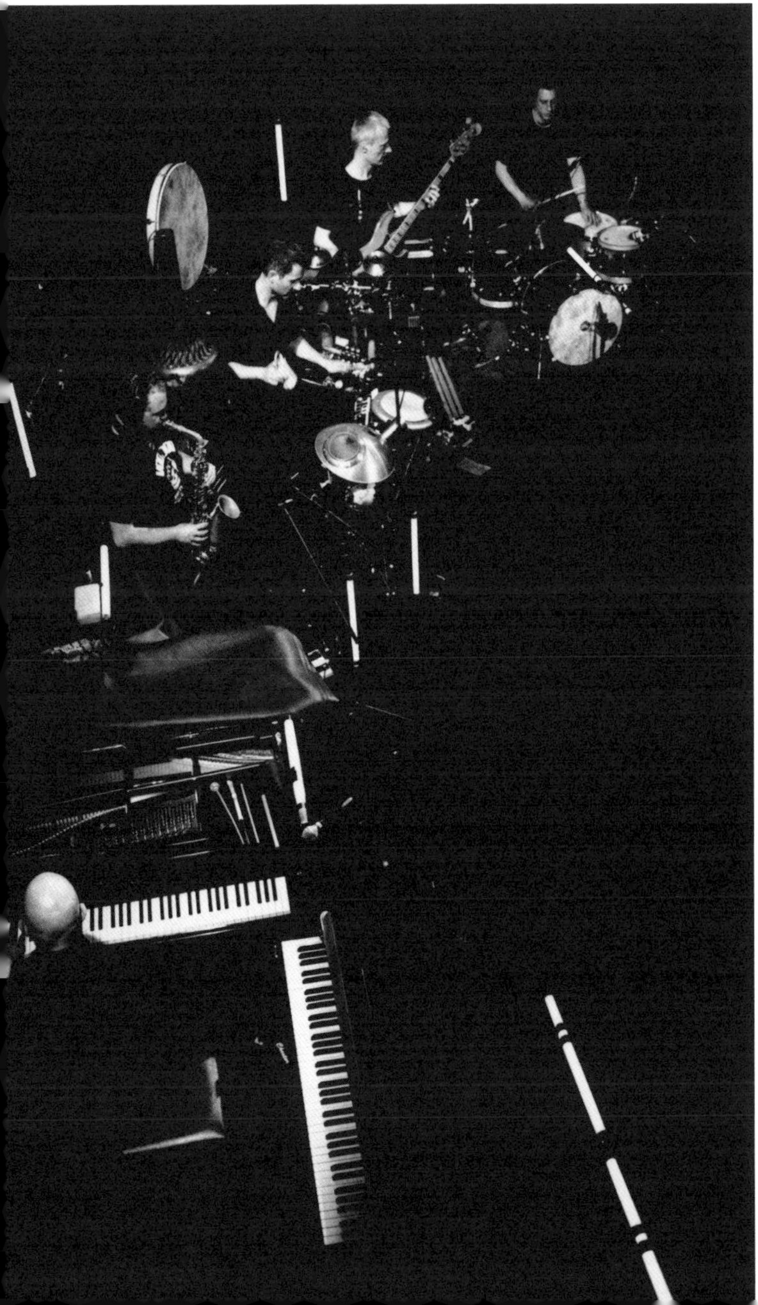

explains this by saying that time is his canvas on which he paints his notes – time *is* space. The relation of past, present and anticipated future creates paradoxical memory moments like déjà-entendu effects. We are not sure anymore what we have already heard and what is new. We are IN the piece, not WITH the piece. The musical space becomes a multidimensional organization of now-spheres transcending linear time with all sorts of musical connections. Time is only one dimension in the formed musical space. In combination with repetition and groove, modular composition creates an enormous variety for dramaturgical flow and can outfox time without losing the essential drift of directed dramaturgy.

Digression: ancestral groove lines, polyrhythms and odd meters

Let me permit myself a digression on my groove biography to explain why I feel naturally connected to modular composing and groove music.

I had an eclectic and open musical education as a child and began playing so-called “popular music” in concerts at the age of nine. I loved playing boogie-woogie. Actually, I did listen to Béla Bartók as a teenager because my mother introduced me to him by wishing that I would play one of his pieces for her birthday. This led to an exploration of his “Mikrokosmos” for piano and then to the rest of his music. It was my first encounter with classical music right after having discovered “Preludes” by George Gershwin, whose music lives organically in the zone between classical music and jazz. Until then I had been playing mostly jazz standards and Latin music, inspired a lot by Chick Corea.

Although ignorant of classical music at that point, I instantly liked Bartók’s music – the strong rhythm and groove orientation, the variety of meters and even the polyrhythms. I started to collect all the fantastic Hungaroton recordings of his music. At the same time I was immersed in all-night jam sessions at the Bazillus club in Zurich, where a freaky underground community was wildly exploring groove music. Club founder Beat Kennel always emphasized the groove organism aspect and got angry when someone started soloing too egoistically. It was in one of those sessions in the early nineties that I extracted a bass line in 5/4 naturally from a simple beat structure in 4/4, which you can hear today in "Modul 15." This led to "Go Between," a composition in which a 4/4 beat goes against this bass line in 5/8 with a piano pattern in 7/8 and a reeds pattern in 9/8, which can still be heard today in "Modul 8" and "Modul 9."

Later on, when I started studying classical music at the conservatory in Zurich, I began listening to minimalist and reductionist music and then more and more to other composers interested in rhythms, like György Ligeti, Conlon Nancarrow and also composers from Zurich, like reductionist and microtone researcher Edu Haubensak. I was also playing with other Swiss bands, like Domenico Ferrari and the Groove Cooperative and Don Li's Tonus, and listening to artists like Prince, Steve Coleman, The Meters or James Brown, who all had a focus on repetitive groove strategies.

Groove, odd meters, polyrhythms, reductionism, and Stravinsky as the forefather of these compositional developments, are a few basic points of orientation to understand the direction of my own development and interests.

Repetition, reiteration, variation, interlocking: a natural drive in groove music

Back to composing: The study of minimalism and modular reductionism in classical music was enlightening in connection with strategies of groove music, in which rhythmic patterns, interlocking rhythms and repetition

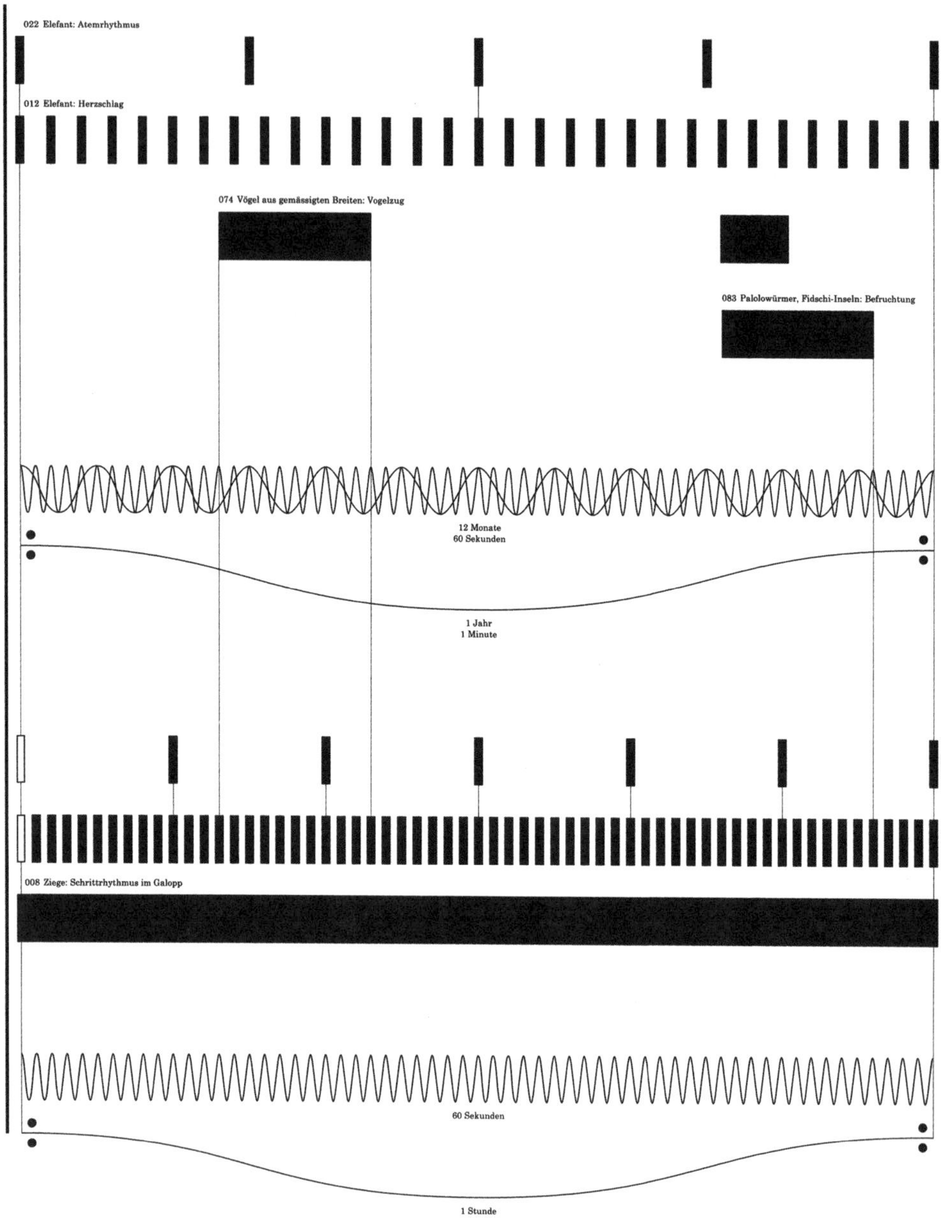

Double page section of the art book *Sinfonia Numerosa – Studies of systems and rhythms* by Christine Kälin. The book graphically shows relations of cycles and rhythms on different levels of order of magnitude. For example, the heartbeat of a hedgehog in hibernation is compared with the eruption rhythm of a geyser or the production rhythm of chocolate balls. The book was created in 2008 and Nik Bärtsch wrote and produced the composition "Universal Rhythms" as a musical interpretation of the book.

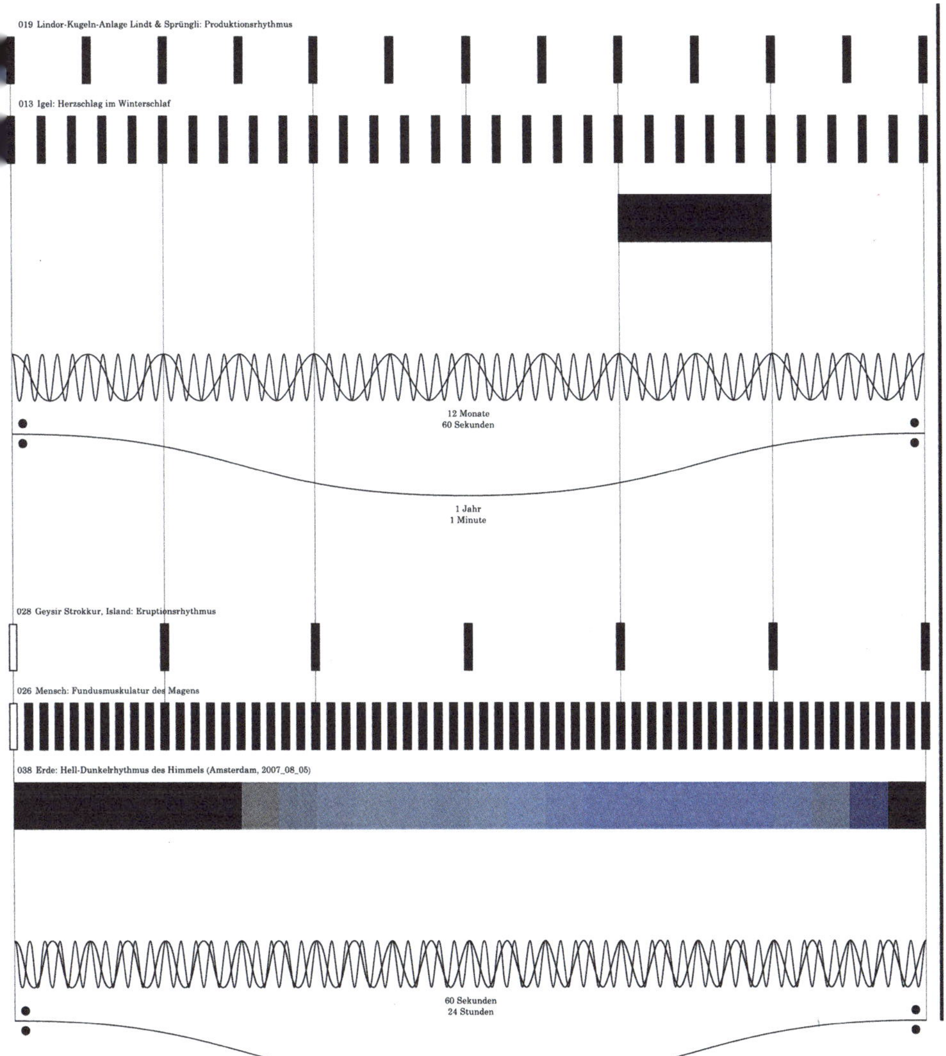
019 Lindor-Kugeln-Anlage Lindt & Sprüngli: Produktionsrhythmus
013 Igel: Herzschlag im Winterschlaf
12 Monate
60 Sekunden
1 Jahr
1 Minute
028 Geysir Strokkur, Island: Eruptionsrhythmus
026 Mensch: Fundusmuskulatur des Magens
038 Erde: Hell-Dunkelrhythmus des Himmels (Amsterdam, 2007_08_05)
60 Sekunden
24 Stunden
1 Stunde
1 Tag

are omnipresent. They lie in the nature of this music and are conventional and creative material at the same time! I already felt an affinity with this kinetic approach to music as a child; I was attracted to the drums and, as mentioned, boogie-woogie on the piano. Kaspar Rast was an influence, too. He has been a strong, super talented partner on the drums ever since we met as schoolmates at the age of ten. Drumming is to him what eating and sleeping are to ordinary mortals. Over time it became natural to dedicate my life more consciously to my own music by following my affinity compass, which pointed in the direction of rhythmic patterns, cycles, interlocking and flowing repetition.

Meaningful repetitive playing means reiteration and is not the same as electronically created repetition or looping. As Feldman puts it, "I am working with two aspects which I feel are characteristic of the twentieth century. One is change, variation. I prefer the word change. The other is reiteration, repetition. I prefer the word reiteration. So I am involved with both. I don't make a synthesis, but they are going on at the same time. The change then becoming that, which then becomes the reiteration, and the reiteration is changing. So you have these both things going on all at the same time. And it's not a calculated dialectic because I have to watch when it happens."[13]

So, as in Feldman's comment quoted at the beginning, the reiteration is handmade and tailored, like his buttonholes. Usually, his music is not understood as groove but he does not fear repetition when it serves to increase tension, energy and awareness – as in groove music, where nobody questions repetition. It is the very foundation, the raison d'être of groove. The groove massages itself, casually setting free kinetic energy and sensuality.

13 Feldman, *Essays*, p. 212.

Structural harmonies for elliptical forms: musical space-time

Modular reduction, handmade groove, reiteration and variation in combination with harmonic and rhythmic cycles create elliptical musical forms that start to become charged very naturally when the players trust the music and let it happen smoothly and nimbly. In that way, spin and drift of the musical material enter sonic space-time.

To support this organic flow I search for what I call "structural harmonies." Their sequence, flow, direction and spin are based on abstract interval structures and shifts, often mirrored at a certain axis on the piano (e.g. Moduls 22, 26, 32, 35, 46, 52, 66). My ear helps to choose suitable possibilities. I avoid traditional harmonic structures with their embeddedness in traditional functional harmony and their fixation on minor and major third contexts; I also avoid coincidental dissonance. In contrast, developments in structural harmony are "neutral" and can thus create their own harmonic balance and direction.

Mobile game hero Ida playing with the laws of perspective and gravity of Monument Valley, 2014

Structural harmonies can also be created by linear movements, recharging their inherent polyphonic energies and counterpoint potential (e.g. Moduls 18, 49_44, 56, 59).

In combination with the above-mentioned rhythmic, modular and reiterative forces, structural harmonies develop a balance, a space and a drift, somewhat like M.C. Escher's optical illusions or the virtual space of the fabulous video game Monument Valley (by ustwo Games).

Polar thinking: gravity of notes, musical forces

This structural harmonic organization in combination with awareness of the gravity of a note or interval in linear musical development is the result of polar thinking and feeling. This is completely different from a modal organization of scales and chords, which functions more statically in relation to a mode, with a root note and hierarchic organization. The polar feeling is based on complex balances like a planetary system with forces that attract and repel the various elements and with complex relations including the spin of planets.

An adequate description of these musical forces stems from Stravinsky: "So our chief concern is not so much what is known as tonality as what one might term the polar attraction of sound, of an interval, or even of a complex of tones. The sounding tone constitutes in a way the essential axis of music. Musical form would be unimaginable in the absence of elements of attraction which make up every musical organism and which are bound up with its psychology."[14] Feldman also describes the challenge of that phenomenon: "And not only am I fighting the overtone series, but I'm also fighting, not tonality, I prefer Stravinsky's word polarity. And it seems as if it's the most natural thing in the world."[15]

14 Stravinsky, *The Poetics of Music*, p. 36.

15 Feldman, *Essays*, p. 167.

I like the forces of musical gravity. Modular organization in combination with all of these fundamental musical forces based on polarities, orbits, rhythmic and harmonic cycles, polyphonic and polyrhythmic directions, results in a musical universe with infinite possibilities for composing. This cosmos gives birth to both formal and physically perceived phenomena like harmonic orbits, floating harmonies, beat balances and paradoxically moving multidimensional music creatures.

Register and orchestration: every note has a different character

Instrumentation is crucial for these musical elements to sound simple. The works of Feldman and Stravinsky also taught me to focus on listening instead of thinking about octaves in the sense of the same note just higher or lower. There is a limited number of notes and all sorts of resonances around them in our tone system, each with its own character, sound and innumerable combinatorial possibilities. An interesting chord can sound strange, weak or even “wrong” if it is transposed a little higher or lower. Some combinations of notes only work when there is enough distance between them. In addition, every instrument behaves differently in each register, in each combination and in each dynamic. The architectonic structures of a composition are not enough to ensure the stability and balance of the sounding piece. Music comes to life only when the notes really sound in their context.

Part 4: Practice and Performing

Practical results of these theoretical thoughts: group slang, bass line and drumbeat culture

The description of compositional ideas and strategies, their possibilities and effects contribute to understanding the sounding results that we hear and feel, but these sounding results are created by musical and social preferences.

Most music makes no sense without a group of musicians who really play music together as an integral organism. The subtle teamwork and detail tuning that underpins chamber music also applies to a working band in pop, jazz or folk. Every good group has its own sound. The group needs time to listen and time to explore togetherness. This process is as important as the composition itself. The members of a group need to understand the universal language of the music they want to play, and only then develop their own culture, their own dialect. In time, they even find sophisticated slang to express their own brand of musical irony, jokes and conundrums. In that way the music of a community naturally acquires depth, and it is ever more fun to make music together because the shared musical syntax starts to create its own universe of meanings, references and ambiguities. The language of music is alive, like a spoken language. Each group is an eco-system that creates its own musical habitat and philosophy with its own axioms and rules.

In the musical language of our community, the rhythm has the function of the melody. This exchange of basic musical parameters is refreshing for the ears. Groove, rhythmic interlocking and cycles are sufficiently interesting, challenging and convincing. A clear melody or solo is a distraction that competes with the rhythmic structure and is therefore neither useful nor necessary. The club and dance style Drum & Bass represents a more independent, popular implementation of this idea. Radical pieces by DJ Photek often felt more avant-garde to me than compositions of new classical music.

Thus, in our music, bass lines are often foundation and melody at the same time. The bass line is more deliberate, it must be composed and clearly elaborated and is not just the rooting or enclosure of the chord.

The drumbeat is an integral part of the composition. The drums are actually an orchestra of different instruments within the band. The character of the drumbeat, its movement and balance, is important and often has a connective function for other voices in the composition.

The band can be imagined as one big rhythm section or percussion ensemble, responsible for the beat and rhythm balances and the relation of meter, rhythm, bar, cycle and interlocking.

Therefore the "One" of a bar is not the most important point of orientation. With rhythmic and harmonic cycles and interlocking, a composition has several different "Ones" and emphases: in meter or bar, rhythm, cycles, harmony, melody, bass line low notes or bass drum notes. The right balance of all these emphases makes the piece dramaturgically interesting. "Modul 35" for example has a complex balance of such "Ones."

All these musical qualities must be represented in the performance, which in turn should stand for itself.

Qualities of performing: phrasing, dynamics, sound and dramaturgy

The four qualities of performance, phrasing, dynamics, sound and dramaturgy, are only partly noticeable in a score. They enable me to analyze and understand a performance more consciously. These qualities are part of the interpretation process and it is better to elaborate them directly in rehearsals. No score is cut and dried. It requires a culture of interpretation, which is often as old as the piece itself. The history of interpreting Bach's music exemplifies how complex it is to find "the right" way to play it. A mix of oral and written tradition, the development of instruments like the modern piano, musicological insights and the technology of recording keep changing views on how Bach should be played.

The list below presents a few ideas on an uncomplicated approach to the qualities of a performance.

Phrasing includes phenomena like: the relation of absolute tempo, time (the way someone plays within a certain tempo) and timing (when something happens); the interpretation of triplet or binary phrasing or the relative mix of both; attacks and the way they are combined; the way ghost notes are added and played.

Dynamics includes all aspects of volume and attack: loudness, relations, range of different dynamic events and the density of these events.

Sound includes the treatment of phenomena of resonance: instrumentation, room (size, type), blending, color and combination of instruments, tightness of attack and questions of amplification if it is used, in which case the sound engineer is ideally part of the group.

Dramaturgy includes shaping of form, direction of phrases and developments, awareness of musical space and the path created by the band in a performance – how to move from a to b but, ultimately, also from a to z. The whole presentation – presence, togetherness, atmosphere, light design – is also subject to dramaturgy.

Responsiveness to these qualities can be activated by attributes that are essential for every performer: connecting, listening, enjoying. Players who actively connect among themselves, with the audience and with the space is the prerequisite of being able to listen, to trust each other and to enjoy the music.

This leads to the essence of musicianship that should characterize every performance:

Listen!
Only play the essentials.
Make the others sound good.

Principles of improvising: ghost notes, band organism and more

The qualities of performing can be used for all genres of music. Improvising and working with freedom in music is an additional, essential competence, which we also discussed in relation to composition and interpretation (see p. 150). With my bands, I have developed new perspectives on improvising as an organism based on the modular music that we play. Improvising and soloing are often seen as individual contributions to a musical piece, sometimes accompanied or supported by the other members of the band. But there are many more creative and supportive possibilities for a band and an individual player.

Kodama, forest ghosts in the anime *Princess Mononoke,* 1997

A major aspect of playing as an organism is to work with small, added notes between those notated and agreed on. These additionally phrased notes are called ghost notes and their developments and networks rise out of the flow of a piece or groove. The development of a ghost note can be likened to the appearance of the Kodama, the forest ghosts, in Hayao Miyazaki's anime *Princess Mononoke* (Studio Ghibli). It happens very subtly and they remain a part of the forest.

Together with variations in micro phrasing, ghost note organizations can modify a piece making it different every time it is played while leaving its essence untouched.

Blending, doubling, shadowing and varying a main voice by one or more other band members are other fruitful ways of benefiting from the freedom to improvise poetically. They support the musical space and dramaturgy needed in performance.

This leads to a sort of mimicry, known from nature. One or more players have the freedom to move in a musical structure or habitat while remaining a part of the picture. They appear and disappear in an organic way without sticking out in the sound- and groove-scape.

A good improvisation strategy is also just to listen attentively. A thoughtful ear often helps the other players to increase presence and musical tension. A pause in this case is a something, not a nothing.

A solo player can also accompany the other players freely, in an inversion of the solo role or in dialogue with the band.

Even when a player has a more classic role and a clear individual solo, "island playing" is still partnership-oriented. From time to time, the soloist plays islands of motives in an ocean of sound. When we see the beautiful empty ocean and the occasional island or an archipelago from a bird's-eye view, time and space are not the same as when we fly over complex lands and territories. The ocean is as important and impressive as the islands. Their beauty is mutually dependent. The island player creates space and draws attention to the other players and the band as a whole.

The band can also improvise as a whole, creating musical habitats together. Nobody acts like a solo player; all of the players are responsible for the balance and stillness of the developing musical biotope. This can be based on modular patterns and combined with swarm behavior, terrace dynamics, still tension spaces and collective action triggered by cues.

Swarm behavior means collectively following a certain musical action of one band member, for example, the development of a tremolo. The lead can also change without being noticed from the outside as in a school of fish or a flock of birds. Terrace dynamics means developing sound and groove with different dynamics and densities, not by simply increasing density, volume and interplay as in a conventional solo, but by creating different terraces for them. The terraces of a plantation built into a hill illustrate this dramaturgy. It is not a matter of linear consolidation of motives and energy, and, in this way, a piece can stay interesting for a long time, while even getting softer and emptier in between, without falling into the trap of dramaturgies that require a climax. Soundscapes with still tension are areas in which only a few resonances are happening but the tension in the few musical elements and in the attitude of the players is high. It is comparable to a duel, in which two opponents stand still, facing each other and not knowing who will attack first. The air vibrates.

Cues can help to organize all these actions and of course also call out hook lines, parts or composed structures at the right moment. The result is again a sound- and groove-scape with clear rules but with an open variety of combinations and directions for the music, another modular way of working. It is as important to do nothing at the right time and place as to do something at the right time and place. To wait and listen attentively opens and launches unheard directions.

Pieces are self-contained life forms, bands are intelligent kinetic organisms

All these strategies do not put the soloist(s) into the center but understand and emphasize this role as a part of the musical picture with different grades of freedom. The transition from interpreting to improvising, from composing to inventing is fluent. Therefore it needs a lot of discipline and empathy of the players for each other and an interest to listen to each other to find together the right balance in every moment. And it needs a big respect for the material of the composition. The band transcends the composition and simply transforms it into a real performance.

The result is that the audience does not know and hear anymore what parts of the performance are composed, arranged, agreed on or spontaneously improvised.
It simply does not matter anymore.

Many Moduls have a long and complex development history of this kind. They went through an evolution spiral, a kind of self-learning process and a constant re-encounter. Although every composition has a clear idea, a clear coherence, a clear form and elaborated voices in the score from the beginning, it will develop a life of its own that is impossible for the composer to envision when he composes the piece.

The piece is always more than the composer. Pieces are independent life forms and their movements are guided by the band as a kinetic, intelligent organism.

Twenty Relevant Albums

When I was twenty-six, I sold all my CDs and LPs to make room in my apartment and in my head – and also because I needed money. I only kept then twenty personally relevant albums.

In alphabetical order:

J.S. Bach: *Sonatas for Viola Da Gamba BWV 1027–1029,* Anner Bylsma, Bob Van Asperen (Sony Classical, 1990)
Béla Bartók: *Music for Strings, Percussion and Celesta,* János Rolla, Chamber Orchestra Ferenc Liszt (Harmonia Mundi, 1992)
Béla Bartók: *Out Of Doors,* Piano Music II, Tusa Erzsébet (Hungaroton)
Ran Blake and Jeanne Lee: *You Stepped Out Of A Cloud* (Universal, Decca, 1989)
James Brown: *Star Time,* Box of Collected Recordings (Polydor, 1991)
Brian Eno and David Byrne: *My Life in the Bush of Ghosts* (Sire, E.G., 1981)
Morton Feldman: *For Bunita Marcus,* Hildegard Kleeb (Hat, 1991)
Morton Feldman: *Untitled Composition for Cello and Piano,* René Bergmann, Kees Wieringa (Attaca, 1991)
Heiner Goebbels: "La Jalousie" / "Red Run" / "Herakles 2" / "Befreiung," Ensemble Modern (ECM, 1993)
Herbie Hancock: *Inventions and Dimensions* (Blue Note, 1964)
Japon: *Musique du Nō, Shakkyō: Pont en pierres* (Radio France/Harmonia Mundi, 1987)
Salif Keita: *Amen*, produced by Joe Zawinul (Mango, 1991)
Kōhachiro Miyata: Shakuhachi – *The Japanese Flute* (Nonesuch, 1991)
Meshell Ndegeocello: *Peace Beyond Passion* (Maverick, 1996)
Photek: *Ni ten Ichi Ryu* (Virgin, 1997)
Prince: *The Black Album* (Warner Brothers, 1994)
Franz Schubert: *Impromptus D899 & D935*, Radu Lupu (Decca, 1984)
Igor Stravinsky: "The Firebird (Suite)," "Le Sacre du Printemps," Claudio Abbado, London Symphony Orchestra (DG, 1987)
Toru Takemitsu: *In An Autumn Garden,* Reigakusha (Sony BMG, 2002)
Lennie Tristano: *Lennie Tristano* (Atlantic, 1956)

phrasing

sound

dynamics

dramaturgy

Surface, Self and Practicing

Image and self-image

A word about "image." Performers have to be aware of their interaction with the world outside. In contact with other people, we are all performers on different levels of interaction, for the self is, of course, a complex mystery even in and of itself. While making theater music for my sister, director Nora Somaini, around the year 2000, I had the opportunity to watch actors in action and learned a lot about the complex hall of mirrors, facing everyone who plays a role. A colleague once nailed it ironically by saying that Robert De Niro is such a good actor that he can play a dog who does not know that he is a dog. So who or what is a musician on stage? How can we play music naturally, become a medium for the music, without being trapped by our ego or losing it altogether? The audience usually perceives our persona as a popular picture, a public extract that is different from our complex, offstage personality. Musicians don't play a role like actors do, but they do have the responsibility to serve the performance and the music and to respond to the public. We immediately understand this when we bear in mind that not every good musician is also a good performer. A powerful presence, connecting up and communicating are essential adjuncts to musical skills. Awareness of how image and self-image relate fosters the rootedness required to focus on the music.

Surface and content

I cultivate both inner drive and surface. The picture that people get, more or less fleshed out depending on the venue, is nourished by things that are honestly important to me. Inevitably, it can be distorted or reduced to a cliché. Journalists make assumptions and do not always check facts. For instance, I have been described as wearing an esoteric earring or a Japanese kimono. The "earring" was an in-ear monitor from a headphone system, worn by the whole band to hear each other better on a big stage; the "kimono" was the creation of an avant-garde urban fashion label and completely different in both tailoring and look.

When I work with partners in designing surfaces, like my website or the lighting for a concert, I do so because I love exploring the relationship between surface and content, which applies equally to choosing an album cover or simply buying a coat. One cannot NOT choose, just as one cannot not communicate, as psychologist and communication philosopher Paul Watzlawick correctly pointed out. Choice means responsibility. Working explicitly on an image would mean communicating a different me. But the problem goes much deeper: How do we even know what or who we are? Who is "me," what kind of magnetism makes that "me" a single whole?

Every person has narcissistic tendencies, it lies in the nature of being and of self-reflection. The question is rather when and how this energy manifests itself, whether we are aware of it and how we deal with it.

Transcending the ego by making music

By bowing to music we can forget ourselves and our talking mind. A Zen phrase says: "The mind is a wild monkey." It jumps wherever it likes to; it is easily bored, frightened and disappointed; it finds everything funny;

it loses concentration quickly. Music can calm this monkey mind down, can make it dance or even lull it into oblivion. I am so happy making music because it has the power to transcend the ego and activate our communicative abilities. But if you abuse it to give yourself an aura, it instantly takes revenge, retreating and leaving the unfortunate, hopelessly entangled egoist to fend for himself.

I believe in the primacy of practice: when I devote myself regularly to practicing the piano, meditation, aikido, in fact, to practicing everything, as if to practice practicing, there's no room for any dubious imbalance between outside and inside, between image and self-knowledge. "The purpose of today's training is to defeat yesterday's understanding," said legendary ronin Miyamoto Musashi.

Popular and elitist

I like many products of pop culture because they bring people together. Composer Heiner Goebbels points this out in his writings: "Groove has collective ownership." Groove is an inclusive energy. In his own work Goebbels developed an interesting tension between pop and avant-garde. These two social energies, the high and the low, do not exclude each other. Composer Morton Feldman said that he would leave a concert when his foot started to tap. Although this seems to contradict inclusiveness, I find it remarkable because I hear the "low" in his beautifully elitist music, in his extraordinary sense of rhythm and groove.

I like to think about the relationship and fusion of surface, form and content; I want to learn more about it and occasionally wonder and laugh about it, too. Inquiry of that kind propels my own aesthetics, nurtured and mirrored by strong and creative partners, with clear references and affinities and at the same time completely open-minded and blissfully ignorant of what is to come.

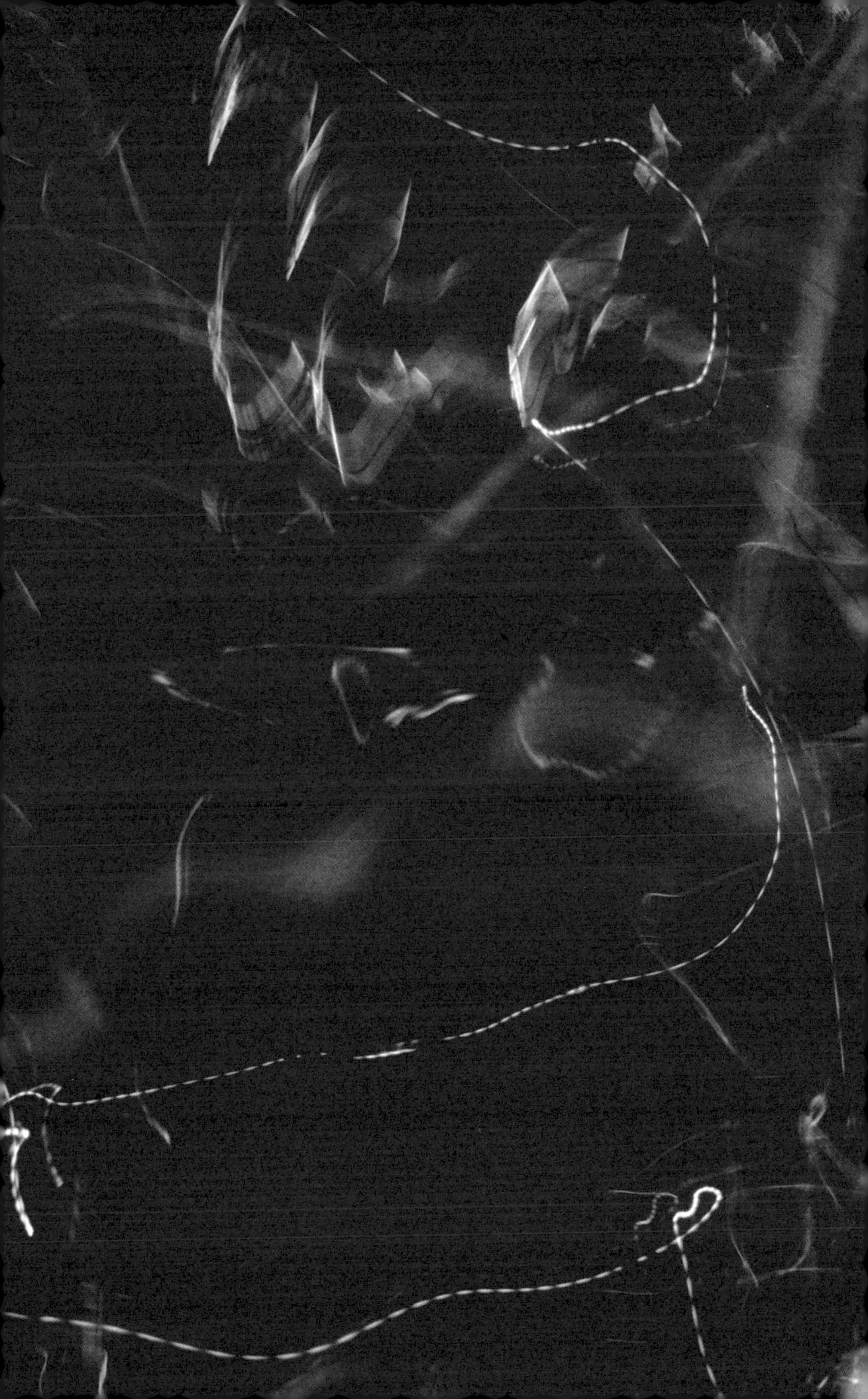

"Our hands are finding things that our mind cannot find."

Igor Stravinsky (1882–1971), composer, pianist and conductor

Digital drawing by Yves Netzhammer from the series *Concave Thoughts*

“Time is not a line, but a series of now-points.”

Taisen Deshimaru (1914–1982), Japanese Soto Zen teacher

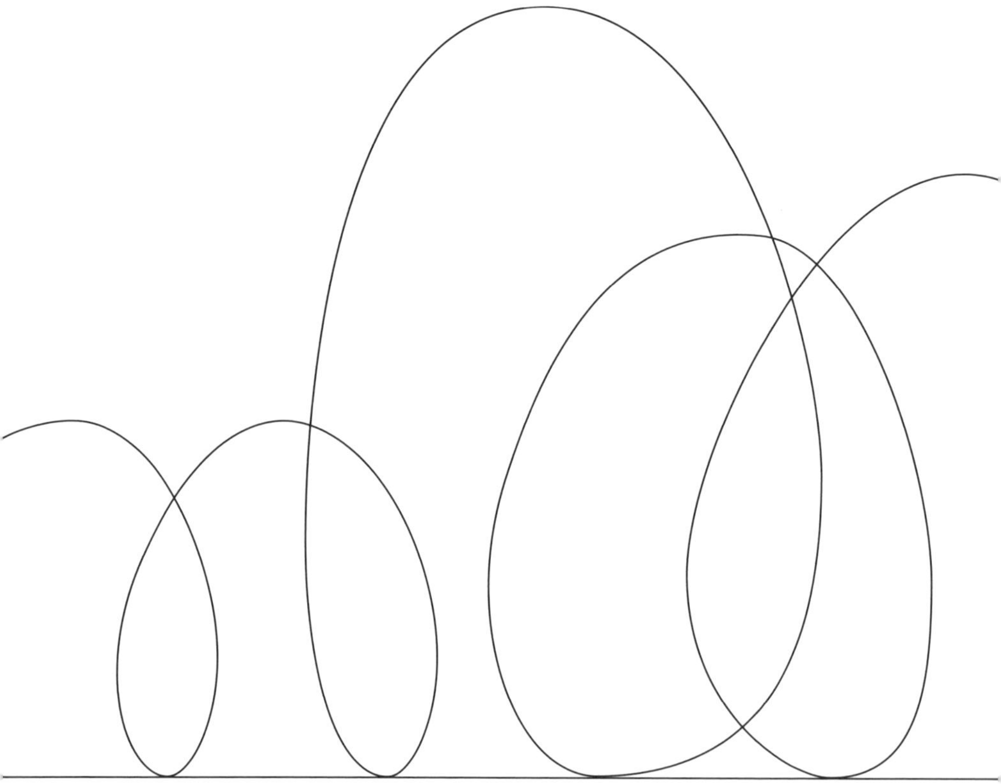

Evolution Spiral: self-learning process of an individual, musical or group organism

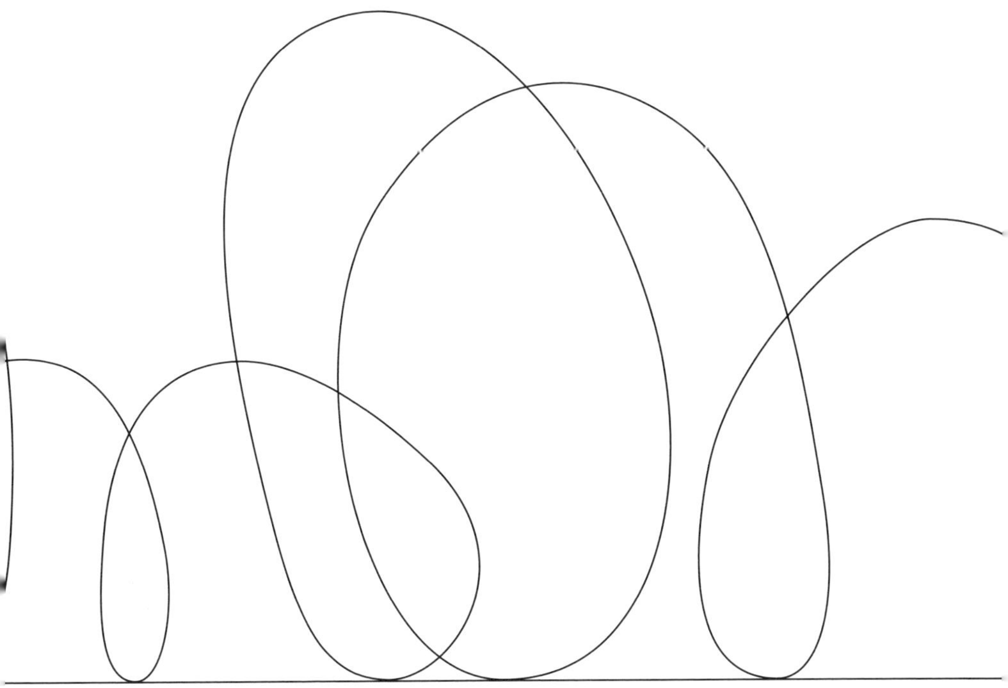

About Current, Constant Collaborators

Kaspar Rast, drums

I have played with Kaspar since we were kids and, even then, he was already a naturally gifted and intuitive drummer. Our musical partnership is a gift from the rhythm universe for me and it continues because we have always found ways of respecting each other in all phases of life, even during the biggest conflicts and hardest disagreements.

Kaspar has a very natural and round way of moving and playing and a highly developed consciousness of sound. When he has studied a new complex beat over a long period of time, it sounds afterwards as if he were already playing it in the third generation – as if it had grown naturally in the tradition of a community: simple and logical. This amazing capacity helps the listener to experience the music more with a natural flow that has already always been here, rather than as "sophisticated art."

This is also why Kaspar doesn't need a drum solo during our concerts. The whole concert is a drum solo without showing it. If you study his ghost note developments, flow variations, pick-up and fill dramaturgies, how he accompanies and how he plays is all designed to serve the song development, so a solo is not needed anymore. It would simply destroy the beauty and focus of his holistic approach.

His need and consciousness of being part of a working band is highly developed. He contributes his own views, ideas and creativity, always with an understanding of the process of playing together and finding the band sound. No technical, individual or artistic view has priority but the understanding of the band as an organism.

His consciousness and taste in choosing the right equipment and tuning for a certain band, song or occasion is super supportive for the band. He also likes to be in a dialogue with the band members about these essential topics for making music.

Kaspar's snare treatment is enormously differentiated and dynamic. Although he has a powerful punch, his snare sound is never aggressive or loudly explosive. The relation of his main notes and ghost notes and of micro and macro phrasing levels on the snare is executed with a strong sense of their meaning and development during a song. Watching and listening to Kaspar's snare playing calms me down and helps me to focus and to be inspired.

It makes me trust in the rhythm of the universe and the beauty of life.

The dynamic treatment of bass drum figures is also one of Kaspar's special qualities; they always breathe and have direction, so that repetitions and grooves do not sound mechanical but have an organic and subtle life and carefully and gradually build with energy during the song.

Kaspar's orchestral treatment in organizing the hi hat, ride cymbal and crash and his taste in deciding when and how to use the toms is a combination of intuition, knowledge and his awareness of context. Kaspar knows that the drum is an orchestra itself, within the band, and he is also an excellent shaker player while drumming.

Kaspar's knowledge of music and record history is huge and not blocked by ideology. His respect for music in general and for his guild and craft is legendary – he knows who played drums on what record without attitude, just because he is so fascinated by the different players and their ways of playing and phrasing.

Playing with Kaspar allows me to play nothing, if required, to hang in or to risk my life while playing. Many of my ideas about beat balances, groove cycles and drum organization and many compositions are directly inspired by Kaspar's playing and often designed to simply show the beauty of drumming.

So in the compositions and in our style, the rhythm often has the function of the melody.

Sha, reeds

As a teenager, Sha was already a very talented reeds player and as a student, he was fascinated by the minimal groove music of his first teacher, reeds player Don Li, and later he studied with jazz hero Nat Su at the Lucerne School of Music.

When we started talking about music in greater depth in 2002, he was interested in taking lessons to learn more about composition. We quickly realized that playing together would make more sense than conversing. Learning from each other means teaching each other. So Sha became a regular member of Ronin and Mobile while also working on his own music and launching his own bands, Sha's Banryu and later Sha's Feckel.

Although he has his own vision and the qualities of a bandleader and composer, he deeply understands and appreciates what it means to play together in a band. As a child, Sha played football in local teams – and was, I must confess, much better than Kaspar and me.
He is still fascinated by team sports.

As a bass clarinet player he has developed and constantly refines an original approach to his instrument, such as a distinctive slapping and ghost note technique, and phrasing. In a public workshop on one of our duo tours, Sha said that he was also a drummer at heart and therefore developed his own percussive technique on the bass clarinet. In addition, his sound culture, minimal motive development and circular breathing are superb, although he never uses them for eclectic playing. When we play in duo, this aspect of cultivating our affinity for drums makes it possible to be a complex mini orchestra, percussive and sonorous.

Sha applies the same aesthetic to the alto sax, on which he rarely plays conventionally. Instead, he tends to move "around the phrase" by leaving out misleading narrative structures. He develops blendings, tremolos and mini motive morphings, interrelating soundscapes and parts of pieces with a great sense of dramaturgy. His sound culture on the sax and also on the bass clarinet reflects

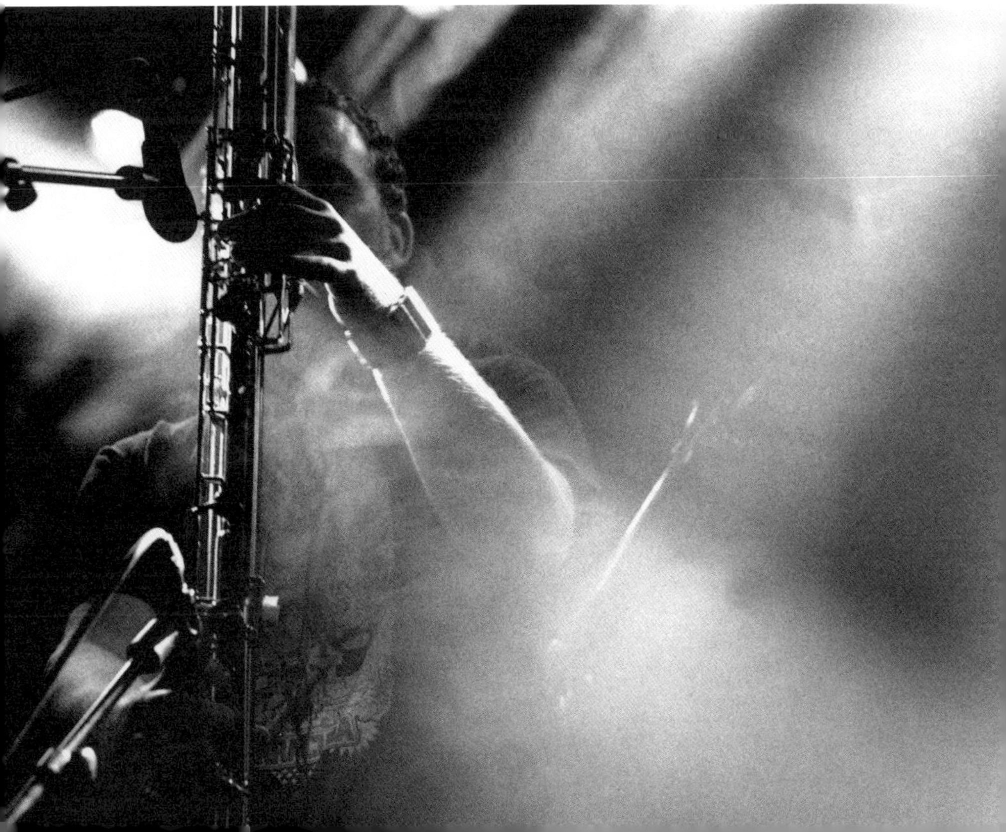

the light and cool sound of Paul Desmond, as well as influences of Romanian reeds playing and Indian flute playing, which he studied in depth with Indian Bansuri player Sujay Bobade.

More can be learned about Sha in Max T. Ciorba's road movie *100 Risings,* filmed during a trip through Moldavia and Romania, where he meets and plays with other musicians from folk music to hip-hop.

Sha also is a powerful solo artist, as demonstrated by *Monbijou,* released in 2021, a futuristic sound trip in the tunnel of the Monbijou bridge in Bern.

Sha's team spirit, his musical and personal commitment to our project is essential to the development of our overall aesthetics. When I play with him, I feel naturally buoyed and free in the phrasing and timing that we share. His own piece "A" on the album *AWASE* is one of the most popular pieces Ronin has recorded. So far, it is the only composition by someone else.

Nicolas Stocker, drums and percussion

In 2013, Mobile's drummer Nicolas Stocker replaced marimba player and percussionist Mats Eser, with whom I had played in projects of new classical music since my late teens. Nicolas had long been interested in our music, often attending our Montags concerts. He has a profound understanding of music and plays a drum set with additional percussion sounds, glockenspiel and gongs. He is a highly intelligent team player with great integrity and skills in both leadership and composition. His creativity in modular improvisation and inventing soundscapes is as developed as his ability to groove and to work with complex meters and rhythms. This is also demonstrated in his solo works and his post-genre Kali trio. Playing with Nicolas is always an adventure. We can take considerable risks in improvising without becoming negligent.

This mutual trust when we make music is of inestimable value in transcending my own inventive limitations.

Jeremias Keller, bass

Bass player Jeremias Keller joined Ronin in 2020, preceded by Ronin founding member Björn Meyer who played with us for ten years, after which Thomy Jordi was our bass player for nine years. The latter two are still occasional guests at the Montags series.

Sha introduced us to Jeremias, and when we played together for the first time in early 2020, it was clear that Jeremias fits in on every level. We are so fortunate and happy to play with him. From the very first note, Kaspar and Jeremias had a natural tightness and sound together and loved playing with each other. It was as if we had always played together. This natural band balance at such an early stage is unusual because it requires self-confidence and the ability to be integrated into the band at the same time. Jeremias is not only a marvelous team player but also a composer, producer and bandleader in his own right. He understands my compositions from deep inside – their harmonic and formal development as well as their architecture and dramaturgy. Jeremias brings a fresh and new bass sound from a younger perspective into Ronin's aesthetics; he has extensive knowledge of musical styles and epochs and vast experience in playing live. May he stay as long as the band exists!

Martin Möll, band photographer

Our friend, photographer and artist Martin Möll took most of the black-and-white band and tour photos, the cover and the abstract photos in this book. Martin also mounted an exhibition with Raum No. in my EXIL studio and published the Ronin band book *Ghost Notes* (Raum No. Press 2012, limited edition).

He died too early in February 2019 at the age of 46. His great talent, modesty, friendliness and integrity are eloquently expressed in a letter of goodbye written at the end of his fight against an incurable disease. It includes the following lines: “Even as a child, the thought occurred to me that I would not grow very old. It is a free, rational thought that never depressed me and was to accompany me my whole life long. This thought is the origin of enjoying every moment of my life and always trying to find my own way among all the many possible ways. I have succeeded pretty well. Because I’m leaving with two twinkles in my eyes.”

Our light and sound engineers

Sound and light are essential in a live show. The communication within the band, its music, presence and aesthetics is co-transmitted by the sound and light engineers. This is why we try to work with the same people as long as we can. Daniel Eaton, light designer and also project co-designer for Mobile, is a musician himself, who plays bass and also composes. Like the sound team with Lars Dölle and Tobias Stritt, he can follow the rhythmic, metric and formal structure of the music and the larger dramaturgy in a live show. Lars and Tobias are both main sound engineers, so that our very experienced Ronin sound engineer Werner Dönni, who, incidentally, also constructs his own PA systems, rarely has to sub them.

Like Sha and Nicolas, Daniel came to the Montags series when still a student and started to help just because he liked the spirit and the idea. He was one of the few people who understood the nature of our working spirit and came almost every time. While still studying physics at the university, he took over the light design of our series, later joining us on tours and ultimately switching from physics to studying the base and sound design. Daniel is a super smart music aficionado and understands how the smallest detail relates to the larger context of an entire tour.

Lars and Tobias belong to a new generation of highly educated sound engineers with a wide musical horizon and skills in studio recording, live recording and mixing and mastering.

All three technicians are constant members of our bands. For Daniel, we have the subs Lena Schmidt and Anto Gujon, who are also thoroughly familiar with our music and background.

My Perfect Day

Buddy Death

The perfect day, I really had one – but it seems so bland when you talk about it. Is it too personal? It's not a public square that everybody can walk around on. It glows inside me. But when you describe it, it sounds like you're bluffing. In contrast, especially imperfect days fill me with narrative delight because you can potentially laugh at yourself and have a good laugh with others – which should, of course, be part of my perfect day, too …

It's remarkable how an unhappy or imperfect day often turns out to be the perfect day for a successful narrative. For example, I remember when I was a naïve kid, barreling through the Peruvian Andes in a car with no windshield. Hitting a hundred for hours on end along a narrow, gravel road strewn with potholes, driver and crew totally drunk, a gaping abyss quietly lurking to the left of us, jagged cliffs racing by to the right. Faced with an imminent car crash, I tried to pray for the first time in my life, but not having been blessed with a religious education, I didn't have any prayers at my disposal to communicate with the Lord, who might have interceded on my behalf. Speeding along in clouds of dust, all I could think of was the philosophically untenable and hopelessly trite inner mantra: "Dear God, if you exist, please don't let me die."

Today, in a situation like that, I would sing the music that I've succeeded in "finding" and developing thanks to countless happy days, weeks and years. In retrospect, that day might not have been one of my happiest but it was undoubtedly one of my most fortunate. Having survived this Andean rally, I went on a crying jag out of tension, fear and happiness. The next morning, high up in the mountains, I looked out over the steaming Amazonian rain forest and saw a magnificent sunrise. I deliberately chose to lumber back to the city in a slow truck, accompanied by (sober) chickens, goats and bags of grain, acutely aware that life is precious and it is a privilege to be alive.

That close call with buddy death has enabled me to recognize and appreciate how many happy days I actually have. Being together, laughing, crying, philosophizing, making love, making music, brushing my teeth: a perfect and happy day is one in which all the activities of daily life seem meaningful and curiously joyous.

Dear Niklaus,

Grandmother was against it. She saw the danger. Grandfather was in favor of it. He saw only the adventure and the love. He gave his grandson Peruvian pesos from the currency exchange for a cup of coffee with a girl. You were 16. Daniel Fueter was in favor, Rico against it and I, your mother, sat at the kitchen table in a dilemma. I know that story. You didn't tell it until a month after you came home from the Andes. I know the narrow, potholed gravel street. I know the quietly lurking abyss, I know the jagged cliffs racing by to the right.

Your struggle with death in the dust and inebriated speeders – I still feel faint at the thought of it. And I still don't feel responsible for the good Lord but if He exists, I think He would have saved your life so that you can make your music and live your life. So that speaks for Him.

And "thank the Lord" there are crying jags, sunsets, sober chickens and toothpaste!

Your loving mother

Thanks to the communicative scope of the Süddeutsche Zeitung, I received your story today, picked up by Rico in Tuscany. A perfect day for me.

Dear Mother

Well, that was my debut as a "publicist." Let me comfort you: I totally exaggerated for the newspaper – à la André Kaminski. I actually did pray but I didn't cry, they didn't drive quite that fast and not all of the windshield was gone, grandfather didn't tell me the money was for a cup of coffee with a girl (I think you made that up although it sounds like him). I think it was "emergency money." Besides, I brilliantly sidestepped the greatest danger of all: AIDS was rampant at the time and in contrast to grandfather's hopes, I didn't get involved. Apparently, I wasn't just lucky, but also reasonable. I still prefer to put my faith in reason than to trust in God.

Thank you for that, it's thanks to you, Rico and my father that I've enjoyed so many perfect days.

Love

Your son

The background of this exchange of letters was the text on the page before, published in a newspaper. It refers to a trip to Peru in 1987, which I did alone to visit a friend, who had stayed in Switzerland as an exchange student before. The interpretation of the adventurous idea to go to Peru alone at that age is a part of our family dynamics. The text and the exchange of letters between my mother and myself show the ambivalence of such adventurism.

Samurai at the Piano

By Peter Rüedi

Everything flows and nobody can step into the same river twice. The river seems to stand still, then it picks up speed, forms eddies, flows backward along the shore. Nik Bärtsch, born in 1971, goes with the flow; he is a supple spirit, a relaxed being. He seems to watch his music, curious to see how it unfolds collectively, how it expands and contracts, accelerates and jams.

This music with its minimal differences also resembles a room that listeners can walk in and out of, a room where they can look around and leave again. The French composer Erik Satie spoke of *musique d'ameublement,* of music that is *blanche et immobile.* How can music, basically a temporal art, be static? Through repetition, through return, through movement in circles, through the hegemony of the cyclical principle, from the tiniest to the largest components. Agitated planes, development that moves forward and, at best, back to the point of departure: that sounds like squaring the circle.

Japan has always loomed large in Nik Bärtsch's life, ever since, as a pacifist fourteen-year-old, he was sucked into the carnage of Akira Kurosawa's film *Ran,* the great Japanese director's last Shakespeare epic. Bärtsch studies Zen. "That is a religion like any other," he says, "but that doesn't affect me. To me Zen is an aesthetic and artistic practice." He has learned that the Japanese embrace paradox: “It energizes them.” The fact that music can simultaneously be dynamic flow and static space is just one of many paradoxes that he himself embraces. Such paradoxes are contradictory only from a Western, Kierkegaardian either/or point of view.

Even the terms that Bärtsch has invented for his art are paradoxical: ritual groove, Zen funk. Another paradox: his music ranging from solo piano to his two groups, Mobile and Ronin, requires extreme concentration and utter relaxation. It is based on the dominance of rhythm. It sets waves of groove in motion, producing layers of great complexity that feed into the dramaturgy so casually that we find ourselves riding on the waves without realizing what is happening to us. Bärtsch wants a maximum of tension, but it is not a tension that seeks release: “We do not play orgiastically.” Nor does it end in exhaustion as in many forms of jazz. The tension has afterlife that lasts long after a piece is finished. That’s what makes the music by Bärtsch and Ronin so eternally refreshing. Utmost urgency and supreme nonchalance.

“When I play I am not the Napoleon of my patterns, I say, okay, what kind of a creature is that, now, let’s see what it can do. I once quoted Stravinsky, who said ‘a composer preludes the way an animal roots.’ On the other hand, a creative process does have to do with decisions, with dramaturgy.”

Ronin, the name of Bärtsch’s group, comes from Kurosawa’s samurai, warriors without a master, who are no longer embedded in a hierarchical structure. A bunch of outlaws, beholden to a higher code of honor. The quintet with Bärtsch on the piano, Sha on saxophone, bass clarinet and contrabass clarinet, bass player Björn Meyer, drummer Kaspar Rast and percussionist Andi Pupato, has so far released two CDs on ECM: *STOA* (2006) and *HOLON* (2008).

Holon, Bärtsch explains, is a word coined by Arthur Koestler, a portmanteau word combining *holos* and *-on,* simultaneously the whole and the single entity, a paradox once again. It refers not only to the tightly interlinked relations within pieces but also to the interrelation between the individual participants, the work as a whole – and the audience. It comes as no surprise that the musicians do not stand out as soloists but instead blend into the collective groove of the overall sound. A sound that has been seasoned and increasingly refined through decades of shared music-making. Bärtsch and his drummer Rast were schoolmates in grade school and already made music together as children.

Every Monday, Ronin play at the club Bazillus, a small venue in Zurich.[1] The musicians have achieved such a high level of mutual anticipation that the music does without expressive eruptions. It is about constant reduction and concentration as a collective. One might put it like this: The group has coalesced into an anti-narcissistic concept of improvisation, a considered restriction to minimal change, interlocking and layering. So tight is the micro-organization of this band that it is hard to tell where a change sets in, where the intensity is revved up a notch. Nothing happens for a long time but intensity never flags and then, suddenly, a burst of activity in a lightning-fast sequence of movements. Bärtsch's fascination with Japanese martial arts is unflagging as well. Opponents may face one another motionless for such a long time that there may not even be a showdown.

How seriously does Bärtsch take himself? Both extremely so and not at all. Without such qualities as persistence, drive and the stage presence of a performer, one can never "make something out of nothing" (Racine in his preface to *Bérénice*). The beginning of all art is the whistling of a child in the woods. Bärtsch wants his to be heard,

1 Editor's note: Since 2009 the Monday concerts have been taking place at the EXIL club in Zurich, co-founded by Nik Bärtsch.

no matter how. Which means that he can occasionally announce an encore as follows: "And now, ladies and gentlemen, in conclusion, listen to 'Module 53' – our famous smash hit." Those are not the words of a prophet. Or at most of one who instantaneously repudiates the epithet.

I live by the conviction that creativity and the urge to create promote a fulfilled life. Role models in the arts help me to overcome weaknesses. One of them is Nik, who pursues his visions and develops his skills with devotion and unremitting concentration. The fact that he is in good hands on various levels, with his partner and wife Andrea, his family and his band, is equally inspiring and exemplary. Drawing on writings by and about Nik and his bands, we have composed this book together on an open-ended journey that explores many of my own and our shared convictions. I am lucky and proud to be Nik's publisher.

Lars Müller

Japanese-Swiss painter Shizuko Yoshikawa's last work *m843*, 2016/2017, shows the cycle of life and death with a reductive strategy.

“Lifere statt lafere.”

“Don’t just talk, do something!”
With a nod to my grandmother, Hanna Anderegg

Acknowledgments

This book is the result of a collaborative spirit. We are thankful for all the encounters and relationships behind it. Our gratitude goes first of all to the reader. The attitude of listening, reading and perceiving is a gift for people who play, talk and perform. At best, this partnership leads to a creative dialogue.

The development of the practical exercises and the systematic presentation of our ideas and work are indebted to the inspiring interest of our students and workshop participants. We have consistently developed our ideas in the ongoing Montags workshops since 2004, in the annual summer workshop since 2009 and in many workshops in different countries and at different schools and institutions. Intense phases with private live-in students at our house from all over the world have also been a very practical and valuable contribution to this process.

No one survives if there is no response, no resonance. To evolve we need interest, feedback, critics and support. I therefore thank all the family members, companions and collaborators who contributed to the development of the ritual groove music:

First of all to my beloved wife and sensei Andrea Pfisterer, who has always been a fair, inspiring, attentive and caring partner through all the beautiful and challenging phases of our lives. Both our families give us ongoing support and interest in what we do: our children, our siblings, our mothers, our fathers and our grandparents.

It is a gift to still be able to work with longtime close companions like Kaspar Rast, Sha, Christoph Kellenberger, Nicolas Stocker, Daniel Eaton and Werner Dönni and to hopefully develop a similar longtime relationship with newer close partners like Jeremias Keller, Lars Dölle, Tobias Stritt, Sophie Clements, Lena Schmidt and Anto Gujon. I am also thankful for the contribution to our music from the members of Mobile Extended and the Ronin Rhythm Clan: Ola Sendecki, Etienne Abelin, David Schnee, Solme Hong, Ambrosius Huber and Adrian Rigopulos; Manuel Troller, Michael Flury, Martial In-Albon and Fabian Capaldi. Special thanks for supporting our book goes to artist Renée Magaña, partner of photographer and longtime companion Martin Möll.

Without a fruitful partnership in management and organization, steady creative output would not be possible. My manager and agent Sven Fobbe is a strong, independent, inspiring and cheering partner and coordinator on all levels. His pragmatic sense of reality and energetic realization of ideas is crucial to the ongoing presence and development of the ritual groove music. Before him the international implementation of our art was co-initiated by my former managers Tatjana Eigus and Ellen Windholz.

Working together with ECM founder and producer Manfred Eicher and his team and network since 2005 has influenced our development on many levels. Their interest in our music and its background, their artistic competence, experience, know-how and enthusiasm for music and art in general enabled us to grow and to learn at a fast clip.

Our gratitude goes to Lars Müller and his whole team, especially Maya Rüegg and graphic designer Michelle Nüssli, to translator and editor Catherine Schelbert and to the proofreader Stephanie Shellabear and to Dan Schmidt for a very attentive reading. We all created the final outcome and aesthetics of this book together. Without the encouragement of Lars, without his experience, artistic competence and free spirit, this book would not have been possible.

I had long been looking for an opportunity to combine my work with the art of Yves Netzhammer. I am very happy that he consented to having us reproduce some of his unique digital drawings in this book.

The photographers represented in this book are Martin Möll, Claude Hofer, Christian Senti, Jonas Holthaus, Reto Camenisch, Mamo Delpero, Caterina Di Perri and Marc Wetli.

I also profited enormously from the mentorship of Christa de Carouge and am happy to have found a new creative companion in her successor DE NIZ and her team. Writer Ilma Rakusa, publicist Martin Meyer and my teacher and mentor Erna Ronca gave me great support when I first started out.

Special thanks to the international promoters and agents who consistently supported us and showed an interest in our development: Rainer Kern and the Enjoy Jazz team, Bill Bragin of the NYU arts center AD, Sander Grande of Mojo Netherlands, Peter Schulze, Hannes Vogel and All Blues, Tom Ohsawa, Bill Royston and Don Lucoff, Ashley Capps, Serious founder John Cumming, the late Pädu Anliker and Ramin Sadighi. Support also comes from our new agents Martine Croce (FR), Katie Van de Velde (BE) and Paolo Caiani (IT).

I thank my local partners and community for their ongoing companionship: Marco Neeser for his support in legal questions, Markus Reuter for his creative friendship and professional help, Urs Bachmann and team for piano maintenance and guidance concerning instruments, Hans Grüninger and WBG for their precise and percussive design, Pia Affolter and Chris Hart for their contribution to logos and art works, Joel Gilardini for his Montags live ambient guitar, Etienne Abelin, Judd Greenstein, Jakob Blumer and Philipp Cron as co-curators of the Apples & Olives Festival, Michi Vollenweider, Dominik Müller, Tosho Yakkatokuo, Stipe Svalina, Pipo Schreiber and Marcel Zuberbühler as partners in the EXIL team, Ramón Oliveras and Nicolas Stocker for their help with the label Ronin Rhythm Records, Marc David Nathmann and Yourstage.live for the enthusiasm and sustainable partnership, Michel Mettler for ongoing support and friendship, Lisa Ramstein for the partnership in several performances and videos, Lukas Bosshard, Andreas Derrer and the OOS team for their support, Jonas Bühler for designing the scores, Silvan Zurbrügg and Monorom for the website design and maintenance, Marco Fumasoli for the ongoing Swiss View project, Eva and Erwin Zehnder from Sato for an ongoing friendship, Jürg Egli for several collaborations for films, Julian Philips for his interest, friendship and film project, all artists of the label Ronin Rhythm Records for their ongoing creativity, Peter Bürli and SRF for their support and interest, David Suivez for his Movement master class productions and Gregor Hilbe from the ZHDK, Bernhard Ley from the Jazzcampus Basel and Joe Townsend from the Trinity Laban Conservatoire London for their interest in my teaching, Ingrid Lukas, Balthasar Zimmermann and Kim Schlichenmaier for a lifelong creative friendship and the Schmidt family for welcoming artists in their house.

My personal development, the Montags series and also the bands are supported by private benefactors, who trust and respect our art production. Without these people the whole community system would not function. I especially thank Alex Rigopulos and Sachi Sato and their family, Francesca and Dieter Pfeffer, Christian Polke, Daniel Niggli, Margrit and Arthur Rüegg, Jacqueline Eichmann, Klaus Geiger, Guido and Irena Stefani, Hubert Meyer, Beatrice von Rechenberg, Milo Huber, Hans Peter Rast, Martina Reineke, Ileana Apostol, and former supporters Christoph Kuenzle, Peter Hauser, Karl Stürzinger and Verena Stähli, Dave Piguet and Ernst Frei.

For ongoing inspiration and teaching in aikido we thank sensei Lewis Bernaldo de Quiros, Hanspeter Dietz, the Kokoro Dojo team, as well as the international aikido community. Important inspiration for the relation of movement and mind were my Feldenkrais teacher Ueli Tank and dancer, Gyrotonic and Gyrokinesis trainer Niki Good.

Silvain and Annemarie Guignard helped us with projects in Japan and taught us more about Japanese culture. The OAG and Daniel Aviolat, former general consul of Switzerland in the Kanzai region supported us during our stay in Japan.

I thank my instrumental and music theory teachers Erna Ronca, Boris Mersson, Hanspeter Reimann, Daniel Mouthon, Martin Christ, Daniel Fueter, Karl Scheuber, Sal Celi, André Desponds, Martin Schlumpf, Felix Baumann, Martina Bovet and Gerald Bennett.

Interest and support over several years has come from the Swiss Arts Council Pro Helvetia, the City of Zurich (Präsidialdepartement, Popkredit), the canton of Zurich (Fachstelle Kultur), the SUISA foundation, the Schweizer Interpretenstiftung and the Swiss Radio and Television SRF, especially Peter Bürli.

The ongoing interest of music journalists has ensured the public presence of our music. Tom Gsteiger followed our music especially in the beginning and his interview about our stay in Japan was transformed into a text in this book. Early in my career, Peter Niklas Wilson gave me the chance to contribute a text on reduction to his book. Constant critical reflection of our music comes in particular from Peter Rüedi, Ueli Bernays, Jim Fusilli, Karl Lippegaus, Markus Schneider, Michael Engelbrecht, Ulrich Stock, Pirmin Bossart, Hanspeter Künzler, Christoph Merki, Alex Rühle, Anil Prasad and Ulrich Steinmetzger.

The contribution and partnership of former companions is also important to me and I thank them here in alphabetical order: Marco Agovino, Hanspeter Ehrsam, Mats Eser, Ueli von Burg, Domenico Ferrari, Michael Gassmann, Thomy Geiger, the members of the Gershwin Piano Quartet: (manager Richard Bächi, and the pianists André Desponds, Marlis Walter and Stefan Wirth), Werner Hasler, Hideto Heshiki, Janine Hirzel, Thomy Jordi, Felix Kauf, Beat Kennel, Patrick Lerjen, Don Li, Ania Losinger, Marko Marffy, Björn Meyer, Scott Woodward Meyers, Daniel Mouthon, Däne Nzekwu, Benjamin Pfäffli, Marijn Pulles, Andi Pupato, Philippe Schaufelberger, Christian Schlumpf, Simone Späni, Imre Thormann, Bernhard Wagner and Wolfgang Zwiauer.

Biographies

Nik Bärtsch, born in Zurich in 1971, is an internationally renowned pianist, composer, producer, founder of the label Ronin Rhythm Records, and co-founder of the Zurich music club EXIL and the indie classical festival Apples & Olives (together with Etienne Abelin and Judd Greenstein). He and drummer Kaspar Rast founded the Montags concert series, with over 850 Monday concerts to date.

Behind Bärtsch's original decision to step away from conventionally interacting ad-hoc ensembles was a wish to explore musical and social energies more deeply with a group based on the idea of community and continuity at multiple levels. This "musically focused community," as Bärtsch calls it, has played concerts of marathon durations – up to thirty-six hours – in which music, lighting and space design, video arts and swordsmanship have been brought together.

Bärtsch's first lessons in piano and percussion at the age of eight culminated in his 1997 graduation from the Zurich Conservatory of Music (today known as the Zurich University of the Arts). There he studied with Sal Celi (drums), Hanspeter Reimann (boogie-woogie and jazz), Boris Mersson (classical music), Daniel Mouthon (new classical music), and at the Zurich University of the Arts with Martin Christ (piano), Daniel Fueter (song accompaniment), André Desponds (classical improvisation) and Erna Ronca (pedagogy and piano).

From 1989–2001 Nik Bärtsch studied philosophy, linguistics and musicology at the University of Zurich. While still studying music, he already played in several international jazz and classical groups and founded his own acoustic music ritual group Mobile in 1997 (later including Mobile Extended) and his Zen funk quartet Ronin in 2001 (including the Rhythm Clan version with three horns and guitar since 2003). He also plays solo piano in his project Hishiryo. In 2003–2004, he spent half a year in Japan with his (then) future wife Andrea Pfisterer, studying aikido, zen meditation and music. Bärtsch has a 3rd dan in aikido.

Since 2005, he has recorded exclusively for ECM records, the internationally renowned German jazz and classical label. He has performed in over fifty countries in clubs, institutions and at festivals. He also composes and performs film music and occasionally collaborates with such artists as Laurie Anderson, DJ Ricardo Villalobos, visual artist Sophie Clements and pianist Hauschka.

www.nikbaertsch.com

Andrea Pfisterer, born in 1970, has been training aikido for twenty-five years and holds a 4th degree black belt. She is a shiatsu therapist and aikido teacher for children and adults, co-founder of Kokoro Dojo Zurich and board member of Traditional Aikido Europe. In the Swiss shiatsu society (SGS) Andrea is responsible for public relations and communication.

Andrea has a PhD in Biology and during her research career studied biodiversity effects in various eco-systems from the fauna of the North Sea to grassland systems in Europe. She was responsible for building up and establishing the Doctoral Program "Science and Policy" with a team at the Zurich-Basel Plant Science Center.

List of Compositions

Nik Bärtsch has written sixty-six modular pieces, so-called Moduls, to date, ranging from one-page pieces to larger modules consisting of several pages, mainly for his own groups Ronin and Mobile and their extended lineups. In addition to these modules, Bärtsch has composed several more for other ensembles, bands, orchestras, collaborations, TV episodes and films. In chronological order:

2021
"Seven Eleven" for percussion quartet, commissioned by Mannheimer Schlagwerk, 12 minutes.

2020
"Bach's Bonsai" for string quartet, commissioned by the Kaleidoscope String Quartet, 5 minutes. Premiered at Fraumünster Church, Zurich.
"Child Galaxy Spin" for soprano voice and piano, based on a poem by Australian poet Jillian Pattinson, commissioned by IGNM Zurich, 3 minutes. Premiered at the Miniaturen concert series.
"Third Coast Culture," commissioned by The Third Coast Percussion Quartet, Chicago, 14 minutes. Premiered in a live stream in.
"Cosmic Appropriation" for percussion quartet, commissioned by the Cosmic Percussion Ensemble Zurich. Premiered at Museum Rietberg, Zurich.
"Shaker Kami" for piano and five percussionists, commissioned by Les Percussions de Strasbourg, 60 minutes. Premiered at the Jazzdor Festival, Strasbourg.
"'352' for 4 pianos," commissioned by the Gershwin Piano Quartet, 15 minutes. Premiered at Tonhalle MAAG, Zurich.

2018
"Camel Brain" for guitar, bass and percussion, commissioned by Temko, Amsterdam.

2017
"9_3_7" for piano, electric guitar, double bass, flute and bass clarinet, commissioned by the Britten Sinfonia, London. Premiered at Wigmore Hall, London.
"For2Pianos," commissioned by Vicky Chow and Saskia Lankhoorn. Premiered at Bimhuis, Amsterdam.

2016
"Three Backbones" for the ensemble Perforator, Amsterdam.
"Arranged Moduls" for Ronin and Big Band, commissioned by the Big Band of the Hessische Rundfunk and the Jazzfest Berlin, 60 minutes.
"Dialogos" for the ballet of the Zurich Opera House with choreographer Felipe Portugal, 30 minutes. Premiered at the Zurich Opera House.

2015
"AIM – Ich gehe" for chamber choir and two pianos, commissioned by the RIAS Kammerchor Berlin, 30 minutes. Premiered at the Chamber Music Hall of the Berliner Philharmoniker.
"MANTA MANTRA – 2 works for 2 pianos and 2 percussionists," commissioned by the New4Art ensemble, 13 minutes. Premiered at the Kunstmuseum Zug.

2014
"Apples & Olives," modular pattern piece for several players, commissioned by the Apples & Olives Festival, Zurich and Bern.
"MODUL 56" for jazz quartet, commissioned by the London Jazz Festival, 8 minutes, premiered at the LJF).

2013
"TWO THREE" for string orchestra, piano, bass clarinet and percussion, for the Zurich Chamber Orchestra, 35 minutes. Premiered at Kaufleuten Klub, Zurich.

2012
"String Quartet No. 1," commissioned by the Brooklyn Rider string quartet, New York.
"ROFU – for two pianos and two percussionists" for the Makrokosmos Quartet, 45 minutes. Premiered at the Morton Feldman Festival, Bern.

2010
"MODUL 26 for Sextet," commissioned by the group Bang on a Can, New York, 20 minutes. Premiered at Merkin Concert Hall, New York.

2008
"ORIT – for three percussionists," 20 minutes. Premiered at Mehrklang Festival, Freiburg.

2005
"Orchestrated Moduls," New Chamber Funk II, for Ronin and the Ensemble für Neue Musik Zürich, 60 minutes. Premiered at MOODS, Zurich.

2004
"Modul Ritual," New Chamber Funk I, for saxophone quartet, piano, Fender Rhodes, drums and percussion, commissioned by the ARTE Quartett, 70 minutes, written in Japan 2003–2004.

2004
"Macbeth" by Shakespeare/Müller, music theater, directed by Nora Somaini. Premiered at Sophiensæle, Berlin.

Multimedia projects with the acoustic music ritual group Mobile:

2016
"The Abu Dhabi Resonance Square," commissioned and co-produced by the NYU Abu Dhabi, 27-hour live performance with exhibition and community space at the NYU Arts Center, Abu Dhabi.

2014 & 2015
"Spiral Space I & II," commissioned by the Enjoy Jazz Festival Mannheim, performed at EMBL Heidelberg, Part I 2014: 6 hours, 9pm – 3am, Part II 2015: from dusk till dawn, 4.54pm – 7.25am.

2008
"Tirol Ritual – museum of rhythms," commissioned by Tiroler Landesmuseum, from dusk till dawn together with the percussion group The Next Step.

2005
"SEE – a live musical sound picture," Mobile together with OOS, performance on the lake stage in Zurich, 4 hours. A co-production with the Zürcher Theater Spektakel, Zurich.
Open-air performance together with the Butoh dancer Imre Thormann and the Gagaku ensemble of the Osaka Gakuin University, Japan, at the Hiyoshi Shrine in Otsu, Japan.
"Perpetual Rhythm – a musical dance ritual," with Butho dancer Imre Thormann & his Bodygarage Tokyo. 8-hour performance in the Rondorama on the Stanserhorn. Co-production with the Stanser Musiktage.

2003
"Water Church Ritual," commissioned by Musikpodium Zurich, in the Wasserkirche, Zurich, with guest Walter Grimmer, cello. 6-hour mirror performance.

2000–2002
BLUE TRILOGY: "AREA BLUE" 2000, "AQUA BLUE" 2001, "MU BLUE" 2002. Three 36-hour multimedia live concerts with light design, video art, architecture and sword art.

Solo multimedia projects in cooperation with other artists:

2019
"When The Clouds Clear – A Light And Sound Poem," commissioned by the Enjoy Jazz Festival, Mannheim and the Barbican Centre, London, together with visual artist Sophie Clements. 70 minutes.

2007
"Stereo," music dance theater together with dancer and choreographer Hideto Heshiki. 60 minutes. Premiered at Theaterhaus Gessnerallee, Zurich.

TV series music for Swiss TV station SRF: *PHOTOsuisse*, *Design Suisse*, *Swissview*

Film music for: *Between Calculus and Random* (2018) by Jürg Egli, *Meisterträume* (2010) by Norbert Wiedmer and Enrique Ros, *Sounds and Silence* (2009) by Norbert Wiedmer and Peter Guyer (features Ronin as one of the ECM label's artists).

Literature

Amdur, Ellis, *Hidden in Plain Sight: Esoteric Power Training Within Japanese Martial Traditions,* Wheaton, IL: Freelance Academy Press, 2018

Barthes, Roland, *Das Reich der Zeichen,* Frankfurt am Main: Edition Suhrkamp, 1981

Craft, Robert, *Stravinsky: Glimpses of a Life,* New York, NY: St Martins Press, 1993

Darwin, Charles, *On the Origin of Species: A Facsimile of the First Edition,* Cambridge, MA: Harvard University Press, 1975

de Carouge, Christa, *Habit Habitat,* Zurich: Lars Müller Publishers, 2000

de Waal, Frans, *The Ape and the Sushi Master: Cultural Reflections of a Primatologist,* New York, NY: Basic Books, 2001

de Waal, Frans, *Our Inner Ape,* New York, NY: Riverhead Books, 2006

de Waal, Frans, *Primates and Philosophers: How Morality Evolved,* Princeton, NJ: Princeton University Press, 2006

de Waal, Frans, *The Age of Empathy: Nature's Lessons for a Kinder Society,* London: Souvenir Press, 2010

de Waal, Frans, *The Bonobo and the Atheist: In Search of Humanism Among the Primates,* New York, NY: W. W. Norton, 2014

de Waal, Frans, *Mama's Last Hug: Animal Emotions and What They Tell Us about Ourselves,* New York, NY: W. W. Norton & Co., 2019

Deleuze, Gilles, *Difference and Repetition (European Perspectives: A Social Thought and Cultural Criticism),* New York, NY: Columbia University Press, 1995

Deleuze, Gilles and Guattari, Felix, *What is Philosophy,* New York, NY: Columbia University Press, 1994

Deshimaru, Taisen, *The Zen Way to Martial Arts: A Japanese Master Reveals the Secrets of the Samurai,* New York, NY: Penguin Books, 1992

Draeger, Donn F., *Classical Budo,* Boston: Weatherhill, 1990

Enwezor, Okwui and Müller, Markus (eds.), Eicher, Manfred, *ECM: A Cultural Archaeology,* Munich: Prestel, 2012

Feldenkrais, Moshé, *Awareness through Movement,* New York, NY: Haper Collins, 1990

Foucault, Michel, *The Order of Things: An Archaeology of Human Sciences,* New York, NY: Vintage, 1994

Gamperl, Ernst, *Dialogue / Zwiesprache,* Esslingen: Edition Cantz, 2020

Holenstein, Rolf, *Stunde Null: Die Neuerfindung der Schweiz 1848. Die Privatprotokolle und Geheimberichte der Erfinder,* Basel: Echtzeit Verlag, 2018

Hustvedt, Siri, *The Delusions of Certainty,* New York, NY: Simon & Schuster, 2017

Hustvedt, Siri, *Living, Thinking, Looking,* London: Sceptre, 2013

Koike, Kazuo and Kojima, Goseki, *Lone Wolf and Cub,* Vol. 1–28, Milwaukie, OR: Dark Horse Comics, 2002

Kriesi, Hanspeter, *Herausforderung Demokratie,* Zurich: Lars Müller Publishers, 2013

Lake, Steve and Griffiths, Paul (eds.), *Horizons Touched: The Music of ECM,* London: Granta Books, 2007

Miller, Rory, *Meditations on Violence: A Comparison of Martial Arts Training and Real World Violence,* Roslindale, MA: YMAA Publication, 2008

Möll, Martin, *Ghost Notes,* Zurich: Raum No Press, 2012

Morris, Ivan, *The Nobility of Failure: Tragic Heroes in the History of Japan,* Austin, TX: Holt, Rinehart and Winston, 1975

Müller, Lars (ed.), *Windfall Light: The Visual Language of ECM,* Zurich: Lars Müller Publishers, 2010

Musashi, Miyamoto, *The Book of Five Rings: A Classic Text on the Japanese Way of the Sword,* Boston, MA: Shambhala, 2005

Palmer, Wendy, *The Intuitive Body: Discovering the Wisdom of Conscious Embodiment and Aikido,* Berkeley, CA: Blue Snake Books, 2008

Peeters, Benoît, *Hergé, Son of Tintin,* Baltimore, MD: Johns Hopkins University Press, 2011

Putnam, Hilary, *Reason, Truth and History,* Cambridge: Cambridge University Press, 2008

Reich, Steve, *Writings on Music, 1965–2000,* Oxford: Oxford University Press, 2004

Ross, Alex, *The Rest is Noise. Listening to the Twentieth Century,* London/New York, NY: Harper Perennial, 2008

Saito, Morihiro, *Traditional Aikido,* Vol. 1–5, Tokyo: Minato, 1976

Sennett, Richard, *Authority,* New York, NY: Alfred A. Knopf, Inc., 1993

Silver, Alain, *The Samurai Film,* New York, NY: The Overlook Press, 2005

Suzuki, Shunryu, *Zen Mind, Beginner's Mind: Informal Talks on Zen Meditation and Practice,* Boston: Weatherhill, 970

Theweleit, Klaus, *Tor zur Welt. Fussball als Realitätsmodell,* Köln: Kiepenheuer & Witsch, 2004

Ueshiba, Morihei, *Budo: Teachings of the Founder of Aikido,* Kodansha International, 2013

Victoria, Brian, *Zen at War,* Boston: Weatherhill, 1997

Weber, Georg, *Christa de Carouge: Schwarz auf Weiss,* Zurich: Römerhof Verlag, 2013

Webern, Anton, *Der Weg zur Neuen Musik / Der Weg zur Komposition in 12 Tönen,* Wien: Universal Editions, 1960

Wilson, Peter Niklas, *Reduktion: Zur Aktualität einer musikalischen Strategie,* Mainz: Schott Musik International, 2003

Wittgenstein, Ludwig, *Philosophical Investigations,* Oxford: Wiley-Blackwell, 2009

Yamamoto, Yohji, *My Dear Bomb,* Antwerp: Ludion, 2010

Text Credits

Quotes

20, 29 Quoted in: Dolin, Aleksander, et al., *Kempo: Die Kunst des Kampfes,* Frechen: Komet, n.d., p. 275. Referring to a quote by Michel Random in his 1977 book published in French: "Martial Arts or the Spirit of Budo," from a traditional martial art school poem on a Makimono.

38 Quoted in: Deshimaru-Roshi, Taisen, *Za-Zen: Die Praxis des Zen,* Heidelberg/Leimen: Kristkeitz, 1978, p. 44.

40 Darwin, Charles, *The Life and Letters of Charles Darwin, Including an Autobiographical Chapter,* London: John Murray, 1887, pp. 101–102.

46 Source unknown

55 Friedrich Dürrenmatt © 2006 Diogenes Verlag AG, Zurich

136 Ueshiba, Morihei, *The Art of Peace,* Boulder: Shambala Publications Inc., 2002, p. 69.

142 Quoted in: Palmer, Wendy, *The Intuitive Body: Discovering the Wisdom of Conscious Embodiment and Aikido,* Berkeley: Blue Snake Books, 2008, p. 28.

182 Deshimaru, Taisen, *The Zen Way to The Martial Arts,* London: Penguin Books, 1991, p. 17.

199 Stravinsky, Igor, *Poetics of Music in the Form of Six Lessons,* Cambridge, MA: Harvard University Press, 1947, p. 55.

208 Quoted in: Sacks, Oliver, *The Man Who Mistook His Wife for a Hat and Other Clinical Tales,* New York: Summit Books, 1985, part 1, chapter 3.

210 Nouvian, Claire, *The Deep: The Extraordinary Creatures of the Abyss,* Chicago: University of Chicago Press, 2007, p. 11.

310, 312 Source unknown

Essays

16 First published in *Traditional Aikido Europe Newsletter, Edition 3,* Spring 2020.

88 Based on an interview with jazz journalist Tom Gsteiger, published in *Passages* no. 39, edited by Swiss Arts Council Pro Helvetia, 2005. Translated from German by John O'Brien.

150 First published in *Magazin des Jazzfest Berlin 2016 / Berliner Festspiele.*

166 First published in *Swiss Peace Supporter,* no. 1, 2019.

178 From: Thomas Preston, *Samurai-Geist. Der Weg eines Kriegers in den japanischen Kampfkünsten,* Leimen/Heidelberg: Kristkeitz, 1999. Translated by Tatjana Eigus.

196 First published in the booklet of *STOA,* 2006, ECM.

200 From: Garrett Laroy Johnson, "Nik Bärtsch's Module: A Musical Holarchy," thesis, 2012.

204 First published in the booklet of *HOLON,* 2008, ECM.

208 First published in the score and booklet of *LLYRÌA,* 2010, ECM.

260 From: Peter Niklas Wilson, *Reduktion. Zur Aktualität einer musikalischen Strategie/NZ 5004,* Mainz: Schott Music GmbH & Co., 2003. Translated from German by Garrett Johnson. Courtesy of SCHOTT MUSIC, Mainz.

314 First published in *Drumhead Magazine,* Issue 81, September/October 2020.

324 First published in *Süddeutsche Zeitung,* June 14, 2005.

328 First published in *Die Zeit,* 18/2008. Courtesy of Peter Rüedi.

Image Credits

Cover, 2–7, 28, 47, 49, 53, 56t, 56b, 59, 63, 68, 70, 71, 75, 76, 78–79, 81, 83, 84, 158–159, 168–169, 176, 177, 180, 188–189, 190, 192, 202, 211, 214–215, 245, 255, 268, 286–287, 309, 314–319 Photos by Martin Möll © Ronin Rhythm Productions GmbH
17 "Gravitatorische Behauptungen," digital drawing, 2020. Copyright by Yves Netzhammer
18 © Aaron Wiecklawskix
20–21 From: Morihiro Saito, *Traditional Aikido: Sword, Stick, Body Arts,* Tokyo, Minato Research & Publishing Company, 1976
23 Copyright unknown
25 © 2021 Les Editions Albert René/Goscinny – Uderzo
31 © Hergé/Moulinsart
34 © 2021 Humanoids, Inc. Los Angeles
37 Ted Benoit, *Le défilé Arumbaya*, 1991, Serigraphy Champaka
39, 103, 311 "Concave Thoughts," 357 digital drawings, diaphanes, 2016. Copyright by diaphanes + Yves Netzhammer
42 Photo by Sasin Tipchai, free commercial use
44 © Weng How Yip, taken in Sipadan Mabul, East Malaysia, 2017
89 www.trigon-film.org
90 Copyrights Kazuo Koike and Goseki Kojima
93 Design by Silvain Guignard © Ronin Rhythm Productions GmbH
94, 153, 164–165, 175, 179, 183, 187, 191, 193, 212, 220, 229–230, 232–237, 246, 276, 283 © Ronin Rhythm Productions GmbH
96 © Ronin Rhythm Productions GmbH and Trix Barmettler
98 Photo by Andrea Pfisterer © Ronin Rhythm Productions GmbH
100 Entomologie/Botanik, ETH Zurich. Photo by Albert Krebs
104–119, 126–127, 132–139, 144–145, 344–351 Photos by Claude Hofer, 2019/2020 © Ronin Rhythm Productions GmbH
140 © Audrey Dussutour, CNRS
148 © G.I. Matsumoto
162, 273, 276 © Nik Bärtsch
178 Design/logo by Pia Affolter © Ronin Rhythm Productions GmbH
184–185 © Mamo Delpero
194–195 © Architekturbild, OOS AG and Ronin Rhythm Productions GmbH
197, 201, 205, 207, 213, 217, 221, 225, 231 Design by Sascha Kleis © ECM Records
198 Photo by Nik Bärtsch © Armin Staudt
218 top © NYU Arts Center Abu Dhabi
218 bottom Photo by Christian Senti © Ronin Rhythm Productions GmbH
219 © Joerg Kallinich
222–223 Photo by Reto Camenisch © Ronin Rhythm Productions GmbH
224 © Sophie Clements and Ronin Rhythm Productions GmbH
226–227 Photo by Caterina Di Perri © ECM Records
243 Photos by Nik Bärtsch © Ernst Gamperl
249 © EXIL GmbH
250 Photo by Lars Müller
251 Design by Jonathan Direwanger, Stipe Svalina, Aina Bärtsch und Nik Bärtsch © EXIL GmbH
252 © Grant Thomas
262 © Weng How Yip, Tioman Island, July 28, 2014
267 © Stefan Minder
271 Photo by Erick Julia
290–291 © Christine Didi Kälin
293 © 2014 ustwo Games Ltd
299 © 1997 Studio Ghibli · ND
331 Photo by Jazzfestival Vilnius 2014
333 © 2021, ProLitteris, Zurich

Listening
Music, Movement, Mind

By Nik Bärtsch in collaboration with Andrea Pfisterer

Translations and copyediting: Catherine Schelbert
Proofreading: Stephanie Shellabear
Editorial coordination: Maya Rüegg
Design: Integral Lars Müller/Lars Müller and Michelle Nüssli
Lithography: prints professional, Berlin, Germany
Printing and binding: Eberl & Kœsel, Altusried-Krugzell, Germany
Paper: Munken Lynx 1.13, 120 gsm

Lars Müller Publishers is supported by the Swiss Federal Office of Culture with a structural contribution for the years 2021–2024.

Lars Müller Publishers
Zurich, Switzerland
www.lars-mueller-publishers.com

Coproduced by Ronin Rhythm Production GmbH

ISBN 978-3-03778-670-3

Distributed in North America by ARTBOOK | D.A.P.
www.artbook.com

Printed in Germany

Listening is made possible thanks to the support of

STANLEY THOMAS JOHNSON FOUNDATION

Kanton Zürich
Fachstelle Kultur

Stadt Zürich
Kultur

ERNST GÖHNER STIFTUNG

CASSINELLI-VOGEL-STIFTUNG

Stiftung Levedo